Navigating Strategic Product Management in the Digital Age

Rajesh Dangi, 2023

It's not the customer's job to know what they want - Steve Jobs

Table of contents

Preface

In the ever-evolving landscape of modern business, the role of product management has taken center stage. It is a dynamic and multifaceted discipline that plays a pivotal role in shaping the success of organizations. As the demands of customers shift, technology advances at an unprecedented pace, and markets become increasingly competitive, the need for effective product management has never been more critical.

This book provides a comprehensive outlook designed to navigate the intricate and exciting world of product management. It explores the essence of product management, from its fundamental definition to its evolving significance in today's rapidly changing environment. It delves deep into the core concepts, skills, and capabilities required to excel in this field, while also examining the convergence of product management and technical product management roles.

The Definition: What is Product Management?

In the initial chapters, we embark on a journey to define what product management truly means. We explore its multifaceted nature and the various dimensions it encompasses. As we dissect its core components, we gain a deeper understanding of the intricate balance between technical prowess, market insights, and customer-centric focus that defines the product management discipline.

Significance in a Changing Landscape

Our exploration then extends to the significance of product management in a landscape characterized by evolving customer expectations, rapid technological advances, and highly competitive market dynamics. We discuss how a customer-centric approach is reshaping product development and how product managers must adapt to meet these new demands.

Product Management or Technical Product Management

A critical examination of the roles of product management and technical product management reveals their distinct characteristics and the areas where they intersect. We outline the key responsibilities, skill sets, and challenges faced by professionals in these roles, setting the stage for a deeper dive into their convergence.

The Balancing Act of Convergence

The New Breed of Product Managers - The convergence of product management and technical product management is a central theme in this book. We explore how these roles are evolving to meet the demands of modern business. Specific examples illustrate the ways in which professionals are bridging the gap between technical expertise and market-driven decision-making.

Opportunities for Hybrid Skill Sets

As the roles of product managers evolve, there is a growing demand for professionals with hybrid skill sets. Those who can effectively bridge the gap between business and technology are increasingly sought after. We discuss the unique opportunities and challenges faced by these individuals and emphasize the importance of multidisciplinary skills and effective collaboration.

Part 1: The Essential Skills & Capabilities

The book is divided into three parts, with the first part focusing on the fundamental skills and capabilities required for success in product management. We delve into technical skills, business acumen, and interpersonal skills, laying the foundation for effective product management.

Part 2: The Product Management Process

The second part explores the intricacies of the product management process. It covers the entire product lifecycle, from ideation to product iterations, providing insights into each stage's significance and the decisions that drive product development and success.

Part 3: Managing Technology Products

The final part addresses the unique challenges of managing technology products. We discuss the technology stack, cross-functional collaboration, managing technical risks, and the importance of staying current with the latest trends in technology.

Conclusion: The Future of Product Management

In the concluding chapters, we peer into the future of product management. We speculate on how this discipline will continue to evolve and adapt to meet the ever-changing demands of the business world.

I invite you to embark on this enriching journey through the world of product management. As the boundaries between technology, business, and customer needs continue to blur, mastering the art and science of product management is the key to driving innovation and creating products that make a meaningful impact. This book can be your milestone on your journey, guiding you toward right path and motivation in the exciting world of product management.

Rajesh Dangi
Bangalore India

Editorials

Shilpa Desai

Shilpa Desai is a seasoned digital marketing expert with a background in engineering and management, making her well-equipped to navigate the ever-changing digital landscape. She's founded Digital by Design Consultancy, having worked with notable companies like HDFC ERGO General Insurance, Fullerton India Credit Company Ltd., IDFC Bank, and ICICI Bank, demonstrating her ability to address the digital marketing challenges across different sectors.

Beyond her consultancy role, Shilpa has shared her knowledge as a visiting faculty at WeSchool and is recognized for her insightful presentations at global conferences. Her expertise has garnered attention in renowned publications such as The Economic Times, Industry forums and Marketing Communities. Beyond her work, she is actively pursuing her PhD from IIT Bombay in the field of Influencer Marketing. Her interest spans several areas, from running marathons, to blogging, to physical fitness and learning music. She is a mother, an entrepreneur, a fitness enthusiast, and a successful marketer.

In her words...

You - The Product & The End Consumer Too! In the vast, ever-evolving landscape of business, where the hustle and bustle of commerce keeps us perpetually on our toes, there is a unique and somewhat baffling dynamic that often goes unnoticed. We are the products, and we are the consumers. We are the hunters and the hunted, the suitor, and the match. This peculiar ecosystem has a profound connection with the field of product management. As we embark on a journey to explore the marketer's perspective on this intriguing relationship, let us dive into the depths of this ecosystem, where products and people seamlessly intertwine.

The Quest for the Perfect Match

The Chief Product Officer's (CPO) revelation was simple yet profound: his website's mission was to help people find their life partners. The lofty goal of playing cupid in the digital age. But beneath the surface, his job entailed a dual challenge: find those who were seeking companionship and, equally crucial, discover individuals who fit the criteria of these seekers. It was, in essence, the task of a matchmaker in the modern world. In many ways, this dual role mirrors the intricacies of marketing and product management. At its core, our role as marketers involves two key aspects: identifying potential customers and creating products or services that meet their needs and desires. The matrimonial website's mission, though unique in its context, underscores the universal essence of our roles. And within this seemingly straightforward task lies an enigmatic twist.

The Interchangeable Identities

The CPO pointed out something intriguing - the prospect, or potential suitor, was not only the end customer of the matrimonial service but also the product, the potential match, for someone else. It is as if roles could be seamlessly swapped, much like the peculiar dance we all perform in the professional world. In this intricate waltz, you become both the brand and the service your brand offers. You, my dear reader, are the hunter and the hunted, the product, and the consumer. It is a dynamic where the lines blur and the roles shift, much like the ever-changing currents of the marketplace. Just as the matrimonial website seeks to pair individuals with their ideal life partners, marketers and product managers aspire to connect consumers with products and services that cater to their unique needs and desires. The interplay between these roles is not a mere coincidence; it reflects the modern business ecosystem, where we, as individuals and professionals, are the very products and consumers we seek to serve.

The Personal Brand and Its Marketability

The notion of personal branding is not new. It is a concept that has been around for decades, evolving with the changing landscape of business and communication. But what the matrimonial website reminds us is that our personal brand is just as important as the services we offer. In a world where we are both the product and the consumer, the spotlight on our personal brand intensifies. It is not just what you do; it is how you present it to the world. Consider this: when someone visits a matrimonial website, they are not just looking for a life partner; they are also evaluating potential matches. In a similar vein, when potential employers, clients, collaborators, or even friends encounter your personal brand, they are not just assessing your skills or offerings. They are also sizing you up as a potential match for their needs and aspirations. In the grand scheme of professional life, you are a product, and your personal brand is the packaging that entices potential consumers, collaborators, and employers.

The Art of Marketing Yourself

This intriguing sport, where the hunter becomes the hunted and the customer is also the product, presents an interesting challenge. The insights highlight the need to master the art of marketing ourselves. Just as he needs to showcase the suitor as the perfect match, we must present ourselves as the ideal solution to the challenges, desires, and needs of our audience. In the world of marketing, the concept of "knowing your audience" is paramount. It is about understanding their pain points, aspirations, and preferences. Applying this principle to personal branding means getting to know your audience - the potential employers, clients, partners, or collaborators - and tailoring your personal brand to address their unique needs. It is not about changing who you are but about highlighting the aspects of your personality, skills, and experiences that align with what they are seeking.

The Marriage of Skill and Personality

In the realm of product management, one of the key elements is the art of creating products that resonate with the consumer. This involves not only meeting their functional needs but also appealing to their emotions and desires. Similarly, in personal branding, it is not just about showcasing your skills; it is about infusing your unique personality and values into your brand. Think of it this way: your skills are the features of the product, while your personality and values are the intangible benefits. Just as a product's design, user experience, and emotional appeal can make or break its success, your personality and values can influence how you are perceived and whether you become the "perfect match" for your audience.

The Humour in the Hunt

Now, let us sprinkle a dash of humour into this dynamic. After all, humour is a universal language, a bridge that connects us all. In this whimsical world of hunting and being hunted, consider the absurdity of our roles. Picture the matrimonial website's CPO, juggling profiles of potential suitors like a seasoned matchmaker. Now, imagine you, the professional, navigating the intricate maze of personal branding and marketing, trying to match your unique qualities with the desires of your target audience. It is a bit like a comedic stage performance, isn't it? A play where you, the protagonist, are both the detective and the mystery to be solved, where the audience, in this case, your potential employers or collaborators, eagerly await the grand reveal. As you stand on this stage, remember that humour can be your greatest ally. It is the universal icebreaker that eases the tension of the professional dance. Embrace the quirks of your dual role, and do not be afraid to inject a touch of humour into your personal brand. It is the seasoning that makes the dish memorable.

The Slice of Life Lessons

In the grand theatre of professional life, we often take ourselves a bit too seriously. We focus on the tasks, the deadlines, and the bottom line. But during this seriousness, there are valuable lessons to be learned from our roles as both product and consumer. Think about it for a moment. The matrimonial website is not just facilitating connections; he is enabling individuals to embark on life-changing journeys. Similarly, when you market yourself, you are not merely pursuing career opportunities; you are opening doors to new adventures and possibilities. Your personal brand is the bridge that connects you with like-minded individuals, sparking collaborations, friendships, and even love stories of a different kind.

The Power of Empathy

Empathy is a core principle of both marketing and product management. Understanding the needs, desires, and pain points of your target audience is the key to success. In your dual role as a product and a consumer, empathy becomes even more significant. It is not just about knowing your audience; it is about being the audience. When you step into the shoes of your potential employers, clients, partners, or collaborators, you gain a deeper understanding of their perspective. You start to see what they truly seek, what problems they wish to solve, and what aspirations they long to fulfil. This newfound empathy is a powerful tool for tailoring your personal brand to align with their needs and desires.

The Art of Adaptation

The matrimonial website recognizes that no two potential suitors are the same. Each person brings a unique set of qualities and desires. Likewise, in the professional world, no two employers, clients, or collaborators are identical. Each one seeks a particular combination of skills, values, and personality traits. Adaptation is the key. Just as the CPO adapts his approach to matching potential suitors, you must adapt your personal brand to meet the diverse needs of your target audience. It is not about being a chameleon, changing your identity with every encounter. Instead, it is about highlighting the aspects of your authentic self that resonate with each unique audience. It is the art of finding the common ground that unites your uniqueness with their needs.

The Journey of Discovery

This unique dance between being the product and the consumer, the hunter and the hunted, the marketer, and the manager, is, at its core, a journey of discovery. It is a journey of self-awareness, of uncovering the facets of your personality, skills, and values that make you the ideal solution for your audience. It is a journey of empathy, of understanding the aspirations and desires of those you seek to connect with. And, above all, it is a journey of adaptation, of finding the perfect blend that bridges the gap between your uniqueness and their needs. As you navigate this journey, remember that it is not just about securing career opportunities or business collaborations. It is about building meaningful connections and creating meaningful relationships. It is about adding value to the lives of others, making a positive impact, and leaving a lasting impression. It is about being the perfect match in the grand theatre of professional life.

The Art of Self-Reflection

In the hustle and bustle of our professional lives, it is easy to get caught up in the day-to-day tasks and challenges. However, the unique role of being both the product and the consumer offers a moment for self-reflection. It is a chance to pause, step back, and ask yourself, "What makes me unique? What value do I bring to the table? How can I better understand and connect with the needs of others?" Self-reflection is a powerful tool for personal and professional growth. It allows you to uncover your strengths, address your weaknesses, and refine your personal brand to better resonate with your target audience. It is a moment of introspection that can lead to meaningful changes and improvements in your professional journey.

The Grand Finale

Embracing Your Unique Role As we conclude our journey through the fascinating intertwining of roles where you are both the product and the consumer, the marketer, and the manager, it is essential to embrace the uniqueness of this dynamic. You stand at the intersection of these roles, and in doing so, you hold the power to create an unforgettable story. In the grand theatre of professional life, you are not just a character but the playwright of your narrative.

The quirks, the humour, and the slice of life lessons enrich the plot and make it unforgettable. Remember, you are not merely pursuing opportunities; you are crafting connections and weaving relationships that extend beyond business.

Your journey is not just about adding value to your professional world; it is about leaving an indelible mark, a legacy that reflects your authentic self. In this final act, be the perfect match, not just for your audience but for your own aspirations. Let the world be captivated by your story, your brand, and your unique essence. In this ever-evolving landscape, where the roles of product and consumer seamlessly intertwine, the power of self-reflection becomes your greatest ally.

Take a moment to pause and ask yourself, "What makes me unique? What value do I bring to the table? How can I better understand and connect with the needs of others?" This introspection is not a mere exercise; it is the key to refining your personal brand and ensuring it resonates with those seeking a perfect match. So, as the curtains end, let your personal brand resonate, not just as a product, but as a reflection of your values, skills, and experiences. Your journey, marked by empathy, adaptation, and self-reflection, is a testament to the infinite potential that lies within the enigmatic theatre where you are the product and the end consumer too.

With humour, insight, and a slice of life, this is your journey as the marketer's perspective on product management. Welcome to the world where you are the product, and the end consumer too.

Kiran Prasad

Kiran Prasad, a seasoned Senior Business Leader with over two decades of expertise in Business Operations, Sales & Marketing, Customer Service and Human Resource Management. With a rich tapestry of experience spanning multiple industries and global terrains, she currently is the Executive in Charge at ILM - Industrial Light & Magic, Mumbai. Her illustrious career has seen remarkable contributions to esteemed entities like Coca-Cola, Bharti Walmart, Himalaya Pharma, Bharti AXA GI, Technicolor, and DNEG. Her forte lies in sculpting, nurturing, and executing annual business strategies that ensure the achievement of project milestones, revenue targets, and a profitable sell-through. Notably, Kiran is celebrated for her agile leadership style, an innate ability to swiftly adapt and thrive in the ever-evolving dynamics of her professional landscape.

In her words...

As a business leader, a marketer, a customer experience leader, and a HR professional, I have engaged with product management professionals on multiple agendas. Whether is a FMCG product, a service product, a pharmaceutical product or a financial product, the relevance of product management cannot be stressed upon enough and has not lost it relevance in the 25 years of my career. As the years have passed by, especially in the Indian context the role has only become more complex and demanding, requiring as in the cricket parlance, an allrounder. Someone who can straddle the multiple roles of strategic thinker, research analyst, financial and technical wizard, and an innovator.

Rajesh Dangi, the author has embarked upon a difficult journey, that of trying to contain the massive world of Product Management into a few hundred pages. Anyone who has dipped their toe into the world of product management understands the enormity of this task. However, the author, Rajesh Dangi has skilfully articulated the panoramic view by setting the context well, providing lucid explanation of the process and skills required to succeed in product management. All this while engaging in a parallel conversation of technical production management.

Emotional & Tangible

The author sets up context for the book, explaining in detail the Definition of Production Management and its relevance in the ever-agile technological landscape. This becomes even more complex in the evolving customer expectations. It touches upon the complexity of customer expectations which is both emotional and tangible. It also emphasises on the need to swiftly adapt to technological advancement and market shifts. My role as Head of Customer Experience had challenged this very aspect. A product, in this case an insurance instrument, by itself had no value if the customer did not understand the final insurance document that was presented. The experience of receiving the final document in a format that made it easy for the customer to understand the product better made a stupendous impact on the acceptance of the product itself. This is an important lesson for a product manager who needs to understand that the product has a life beyond its tangible existence and addressing the intangible effects of the product upfront is equally important.

The author has carefully touched upon the current customer expectations and how to leverage them as a competitive edge. Beginning from a seamless UX to omnichannel engagement requiring a cohesive experience to being all encompassing and yet being unique and specialised to the customer needs are few of the challenges that the author has sought to emphasise upon. The Product managers job is tougher in today's environment with the customer being conscious of inclusivity, sustainability, and ethical aspects of any product.

Innovation and stability

Through the book, the author revisits multiple avenues of challenges and possible solutions. One of the challenges that today's product managers face the need to operate in fast changing environments and keep your product relevant. Innovations could quickly turn a product obsolete and therefore necessitates that the product manager is aligned to emerging tech trends. One of the key success factors lies in how well the product manager can balance innovation with stability for the product. Case in study is the steady growth of Android Operating systems. The flexibility it offers along with the latest innovations keeps it relevant.

Multiple Hats

The books further dwell into the need for the Product manager to be a complete business manager. Product Manager's role has diversified to encompass strategy, business understanding and technical knowledge. All the decisions have further to be backed by solid research.

As a product manager one should begin by ensuring alignment of the product strategy with that of the overall business goals, while keeping an eye on the future environmental changes. A compelling product strategy must be backed with market research and driven with an equally strong marketing strategy. The narratives are quick to change in this social media driven marketing environment. A successful product manager will always keep the product analytics close at hand, using data to guide the future of the product.

An iterative loop

As any business leader would let you know, product management does not end. It is a loop which goes through ideation, research, design, launch review and iterations. Even in products that are well established and successful, the demand of customer is primary and that could change at any point as we witnessed as the world struggled with covid. The new generation wants to operate out of home and that has required the entire Visual effects industry to change how they operate. The industry, which was primarily creative, highly technology dependent and with high security standards had to overnight change it operations from an onsite to home based. This change needed the available products to drastically scale and change the operating model. Not only is the iterative loop a reality but the need for agility has also risen.

The author takes us through this cycle in detail providing critical insights to thrive in a tech-driven ecosystem. From creating a robust product strategy to product evaluation and usability testing and development cycles, the book provides a holistic view of the tools and techniques essential for success.

Of course, the author has focussed on Technology Products in a greater depth in his book however the book is a great study for both who have already been working in product management and any beginners who would like to understand this subject. Rajesh in his characteristic style has simplified the subject, provided insights into possible challenges and strategies that help succeed. This is a book that guides you through complex terrain of product management. As you embark on this journey, prepare to unlock the potential of your products and in doing so redefine the future of your organisation.

Richa Pareekh

Richa Pareekh, the Executive Director of Product at JPMC, is a dynamic Product Manager known for her problem-solving skills, empathetic leadership, and commitment to inclusive practices. Her career has taken her across six countries, fostering a unique and valuable perspective. Richa has an impressive track record of turning products into billion-dollar successes at companies like Yodlee, Google, and Uber. While at Coinbase, she expanded the payments platform to handle transactions worth billions and introduced innovative payment solutions. Beyond her professional achievements, Richa is deeply passionate about experiential education, evident in her non-profit initiative, "Honour Till." She's a strong advocate for inclusive leadership and founded the "Search Ads Coffee Club" at Google, a mentoring program for women in the early to mid-career phase, demonstrating her commitment to equality and growth.

In her words...

In the age of emerging technology, product management has emerged as a linchpin function that bridges the gap between innovation and market success. In a world where new technologies are born every day, the role of a product manager is more critical than ever. They are the stewards of a product's destiny, navigating uncharted territories, and leading the way to success. Product managers are responsible for transforming ideas into tangible solutions. They are the visionaries who define a product's roadmap, align it with business goals, and champion it through its lifecycle. As technology continues to advance at a rapid pace, product managers serve as the compass, ensuring that the product remains on course.

While there are many key traits that are important to the role of a Product Manager, I often focus on the essential pillars that I believe have assisted both me and my teams in navigating the complexities of the numerous products we have developed. Whether it was working on an early Fintech Product at Yodlee, building and scaling products with billions of users at Google, establishing new product verticals in the early days of Uber, or devising ways to make Crypto accessible through Coinbase, these few tenets have consistently proven to be the most valuable.

The Art of Listening and Observing

One of the most important skills a product manager can possess is the ability to listen and observe. The role is not just about making decisions and directing teams; it's about understanding the pain points and needs of the users. A good product manager is a keen listener, attuned to the subtle cues that reveal the true desires of customers. Being a good observer is equally crucial. It's about watching how users interact with your product, identifying patterns, and recognizing areas for improvement. Great product managers are like detectives, uncovering insights that lead to breakthrough innovations.

Transforming the Trajectory of a Product

Strong product managers have the power to transform the trajectory of a product and its ultimate success. They possess the ability to inspire their teams, rally behind a common vision, and drive relentless execution. It's not just about managing a product; it's about shaping its destiny. The impact of a strong product manager goes beyond the product itself. They influence the culture of their organizations, fostering an environment of innovation, collaboration, and continuous improvement. A product manager's leadership can elevate an entire team and drive the organization toward achieving its goals.

The Customer Advocate

Starting with Pain Points Product managers must be the biggest advocates for their customers. It's easy to let personal preferences and biases cloud judgment, but the heart of effective product management always starts with the customer's pain points. Understanding their needs, empathizing with their challenges, and addressing their problems is the cornerstone of successful product development. As product managers, we must be willing to set aside our own opinions and egos in favour of what truly benefits the customer. It's about putting the user at the center of every decision and relentlessly pursuing solutions that make their lives better. The best products are born from a deep understanding of the customer's world.

Simplicity: The Key to Delightful Products

In the world of technology, complexity often abounds. However, the most delightful products are often the simplest. As product managers, we must embrace the principle that simplicity is key. Complexity can lead to confusion, frustration, and ultimately, product failure. Simplifying a product doesn't mean sacrificing features or capabilities. It means designing with clarity, removing unnecessary friction, and making the user experience as smooth as possible. Simplicity is the secret ingredient that turns a good product into a delightful one.

As you dive into the world of product management, remember that it's not just a job; it's a calling. It's a commitment to making the world a better place, one product at a time. It's about connecting the dots, looking backward to see how far you've come, and looking forward to the endless possibilities that lie ahead. Embrace the art of listening, observe with intent, transform trajectories, be a relentless customer advocate, and keep simplicity at the forefront of your product philosophy. By doing so, you will not only succeed as a product manager but also leave a lasting impact on the products you create and the lives you touch. Welcome to the incredible journey of product management. May it be as fulfilling for you as it has been for me.

I am honoured to contribute this editorial for Rajesh Dangi's book. As he emphasizes in the early chapters, Product Management transcends the confines of a mere technical job function; it embodies the art of envisioning and crafting solutions that not only address market needs but also push the boundaries of what is achievable.

Introduction

In an era marked by the rapid advancement of technology and the ever-evolving demands of consumers, the discipline of product management has emerged as a dynamic and intellectually stimulating field. It stands at the crossroads of innovation, business strategy, and human-cantered design, making it a captivating subject of exploration for the intellectually curious.

The Intersection of Innovation and Strategy

Product management is not merely about creating and delivering products; it is a strategic discipline that shapes the very essence of innovation. It entails the art of envisioning and crafting solutions that not only address market needs but also push the boundaries of what is possible. Intellectuals are drawn to this field for its unique blend of creative thinking and strategic planning, where every product is a manifestation of visionary ideas.

The Evolving Customer Landscape

Understanding the intellectual nuances of product management necessitates an appreciation of the changing landscape of customer expectations. Modern consumers are not passive recipients of products; they are active participants in the design process. Intellectuals are intrigued by how product managers navigate this shifting paradigm, orchestrating experiences that engage, delight, and resonate deeply with users.

Technological Frontiers

The spectrum of product management today extends to its intricate relationship with technology. In a world driven by digital transformation, product managers must possess a deep understanding of the technological tapestry that underpins their creations. The intersection of technology and human experience is a fertile ground for intellectual exploration, as it poses questions about ethics, usability, and the future of human-computer interaction.

Convergence of Roles

A captivating facet of contemporary product management is the convergence of roles. Intellectuals are drawn to the evolving dynamics between traditional product managers and their technically inclined counterparts. This convergence sparks discussions about skill sets, the blending of business acumen with technical expertise, and the emergence of a new breed of product managers who bridge the gap between strategy and execution.

Embarking on a Journey

As we delve into the intellectual depths of product management, we embark on a journey that explores the realms of innovation, strategy, technology, and human-centric design. Each chapter of this exploration equips us with knowledge, insights, and perspectives that challenge our intellect and stimulate our curiosity.

Whether you approach this subject as a seasoned intellectual seeking to unravel the intricacies of contemporary business practices or as a curious mind eager to comprehend the world of innovation, product management beckons with its intellectual richness. It is a subject that invites exploration, debate, and the continuous pursuit of excellence in shaping the products that define our digital age.

The Definition

Although There is no one definitive definition of product management, as it is a complex and multifaceted role. However, there are a few key themes that emerge when multiple leaders define product management.

One common theme is that product managers are responsible for the success of a product from its conception to its launch and beyond. This includes defining the product vision, developing the product strategy, and overseeing the product development process. Product managers also need to be able to understand and meet the needs of the market, as well as communicate effectively with cross-functional teams.

Another common theme is that product managers are responsible for driving innovation. They need to be able to identify new opportunities and develop new products and features that meet the needs of the market. Product managers also need to be able to stay up-to-date on the latest trends and technologies, and use this knowledge to their advantage.

Finally, product managers are also responsible for managing the lifecycle of a product. This includes launching the product, measuring its success, and making necessary adjustments along the way. Product managers also need to be able to make tough decisions about when to kill a product or feature. Here are some specific definitions of product management from multiple leaders:

Steve Jobs' philosophy as product manager underscores the importance of a deep understanding of users, a relentless pursuit of excellence, and the courage to innovate and disrupt markets. He emphasized the importance of guiding product development based on a deep understanding of user behaviours, desires, and pain points, rather than solely relying on customer feedback or requests.

Steve believed that product design and simplicity are essential to creating successful products. He inspired a generation of product managers to think big and create products that make a difference in people's lives. His insights into product management are still relevant today and provide valuable lessons for product managers of all levels.

Martin Eriksson, Chief Product Officer at Spotify: "Product management is the art and science of building products that users love and that businesses need."

Sheryl Sandberg, Chief Operating Officer at Meta: "Product management is about creating something that people want to use. It's about understanding the needs of your users, and then designing and building a product that meets those needs."

Jeff Bezos, Founder and CEO of Amazon: "Product management is the process of understanding the customer, what they want and need, and then creating a product that addresses those needs."

Marty Cagan, Silicon Valley product management consultant and author of the book Inspired: "Product management is about translating the user's needs, wants, and pain points into a viable product strategy and roadmap. Product managers work cross-functionally to ensure that the product is developed, launched, and marketed successfully."

What is Product Management

Simply put, Product management is the process of planning, developing, marketing, and continuously improving a company's product or products. It is a critical role in any company that wants to create and sell successful products. Product managers are responsible for ensuring that their products meet the needs of the market and the company's business goals.

In today's rapidly changing world, product management is more important than ever. Customers are more demanding than ever before, and they expect products to be innovative, user-friendly, and affordable. Product managers need to be able to keep up with these changes and deliver products that customers love.

Product management, according to the insights shared by seasoned professionals in the field, is a multifaceted discipline at the intersection of business, technology, and user experience. A prominent product manager emphasizes that its core essence lies in delivering value by solving real problems for people in a manner that aligns with business viability and technological feasibility. This holistic approach underscores the pivotal role product managers play in ensuring a harmonious balance between strategic business goals and the practical application of technology, all while keeping the end-user experience in sharp focus.

Eminent product managers consistently advocate for a customer-centric approach as a fundamental principle of successful product management. They stress the importance of moving beyond the mere construction of features and delving into a deep understanding of customer pain points. The goal is not just to address issues but to exceed expectations, delighting users with innovative solutions that resonate with their needs. This approach positions the customer as a central figure in the product development process, guiding decisions and shaping the overall product strategy.

A recurrent theme in the wisdom shared by these experienced professionals is the iterative and agile nature of product management. They describe it as a continuous cycle involving ideation, implementation, and iteration. Embracing agility and learning from user feedback are highlighted as key components of this cycle. Being ready to pivot when necessary is viewed as an essential characteristic, allowing product teams to adapt to changing requirements and deliver incremental value over time.

Strategic decision-making emerges as a cornerstone of product management, according to the perspectives of distinguished product managers. It involves a nuanced understanding of market trends, evaluation of business goals, and the alignment of the product roadmap with the overarching organizational strategy. This strategic acumen enables product managers to make decisions that not only benefit the immediate product but contribute to the overall success and growth of the business.

Collaboration is emphasized as a central tenet of effective product management. Seasoned product managers liken it to a team sport, where success hinges on seamless collaboration with cross-functional teams. These teams, encompassing diverse skills in areas such as engineering, design, marketing, and sales, collectively contribute to the success of the product. The synergy derived from these varied perspectives fosters an environment where creativity, productivity, and innovation thrive.

Eminent product managers stress the imperative of data-driven decision-making in the contemporary landscape. In an age defined by data, they advocate for leveraging analytics to gain insights into user behaviour, product performance, and market trends. This analytical approach is considered instrumental in guiding product strategies, optimizing features, and enhancing overall performance throughout the product lifecycle.

Finally, the focus on impact emerges as a guiding principle for product managers. They are encouraged to consistently evaluate the significance of their decisions and actions in terms of tangible outcomes for both users and the business. This impact-centric mindset ensures that every effort in product management contributes meaningfully to the success and advancement of the product and, by extension, the company as a whole.

Significance in a Changing Landscape

In the ever-evolving landscape of contemporary business, product management has risen to a position of heightened significance, emerging as a linchpin for companies seeking to thrive across various industries. This elevated importance is underpinned by a combination of compelling factors that highlight the dynamic nature of this discipline. Product managers, in this context, play a pivotal role in shaping the success of companies by adeptly navigating dynamic consumer expectations, staying attuned to technological advances, and effectively responding to competitive pressures. Their multifaceted responsibilities encompass fostering innovation, ensuring user-centricity, and aligning product strategies with broader business objectives.

Today, Product managers must navigate dynamic consumer expectations, technological advances, and competitive pressures, all while fostering innovation, ensuring user-centricity, and aligning with broader business objectives. The significance of this role is underscored by its ability to adapt and excel in a rapidly changing world.

Evolving Customer Expectations

The evolution of customer expectations stands as a transformative force that product managers must deftly navigate. This shift has redefined consumers from passive recipients of products to discerning and well-informed decision-makers. Empowered by the internet and digital platforms, consumers now possess unprecedented access to information, enabling meticulous research and comparison of products. This evolution also entails a growing preference for personalized experiences, where products must adapt to unique user behaviours and preferences, delving far beyond surface-level customizations.

This evolution extends beyond mere functionality; it encompasses the emotional dimension of user experience. While a product's functionality remains pivotal, its competitiveness now hinges on delivering a holistic and enjoyable user journey. This user-centric approach requires a comprehensive design strategy that ensures ease of use, intuitive design, speed, and responsiveness. Products excelling in user experience have the power to evoke positive emotions, fostering brand loyalty and customer advocacy. Achieving this, however, necessitates a holistic approach to design that considers the entire user journey, from initial interaction to post-interaction follow-ups.

Meeting these evolved expectations demands robust data-driven decision-making, where product managers adeptly collect and analyze user data to inform enhancements. The pursuit of seamlessness, a fundamental aspect of modern user experience, calls for cross-platform consistency, unified user profiles, omnichannel engagement, data integration, user-centric design, cross-functional collaboration, technology integration, quality assurance, and a culture of continuous improvement.

Furthermore, the demand for personalization signifies a profound evolution in consumer expectations. Beyond superficial customizations, consumers now seek products that adapt dynamically to their unique behaviours and preferences. This expectation mandates deep customization options while ensuring product coherence. Achieving personalization at scale requires harnessing data and analytics for informed decision-making while respecting user data privacy.

While personalization presents both technical complexities and opportunities for product managers, it is a manifestation of the modern consumer's desire for products aligned seamlessly with their unique identities and preferences. Product managers who master the art of personalization stand poised to create products that not only meet but exceed these elevated expectations, forging potent and enduring connections with their user base. The transformation of consumers into discerning and informed decision-makers represents a profound shift in the business landscape. This shift underscores the importance of product managers being not only responsive to these evolving expectations but also proactive in crafting products that not only meet but exceed the discerning standards of today's empowered consumers.

The quest for personalization is a manifestation of the modern consumer's desire for products that align seamlessly with their unique identities and preferences. Product managers who can master the art of personalization stand to create products that not only meet but also exceed these elevated expectations, fostering strong and lasting connections with their user base.

User Experience as a Competitive Edge

In the ever-evolving landscape of consumer preferences, user experience (UX) has emerged as a decisive factor in shaping purchasing decisions and brand loyalty. It has transcended the conventional parameters of functionality, extending its influence into the realms of emotion and overall satisfaction. This paradigm shift necessitates a nuanced understanding of the critical role that UX plays in contemporary product management. The traditional emphasis solely on functionality is no longer sufficient for a product's success. While efficient performance remains vital, consumers now demand a comprehensive and enjoyable user journey. Factors such as ease of use, intuitive design, speed, and responsiveness contribute to a holistic user experience, driving consumer choices.

Products that excel in UX have the capacity to elicit positive emotions, influencing user perception and behaviour. Whether through the seamless design of a mobile app or the frustration caused by a cumbersome website, these emotional responses significantly impact brand loyalty and customer advocacy. Crafting a superior user experience requires an end-to-end consideration of product design. This holistic approach spans from the initial interaction to the entire user journey and includes post-interaction follow-ups. It involves not only optimizing the product's interface but also ensuring its performance, reliability, support, and environmental impact are aligned with user expectations.

At the core of enhancing user experience lies user-centric design. This approach prioritizes the user throughout the product development process, ensuring that every design choice addresses user needs, preferences, and pain points. Iterative testing and refinement further align the product with evolving user expectations. Superior user experience serves as a potent differentiator in a competitive marketplace. When faced with multiple options offering similar functionality, consumers often opt for products that provide a more pleasant and hassle-free experience.

Product managers focusing on user experience are better positioned to capture and retain market share.

Furthermore, exceptional user experiences cultivate positive word-of-mouth recommendations and user advocacy. Satisfied users become enthusiastic brand promoters, sharing their positive experiences within their social circles and online communities. This organic promotion significantly enhances a product's visibility and reputation. Recognizing that user experience is an ongoing process, product managers must leverage data and user feedback for continuous optimization. Identifying pain points and areas for improvement allows product managers to refine the user experience, ensuring their products remain competitive and user-centric over the long term. In this contemporary landscape of product management, those who acknowledge the transformative power of superior user experience and adopt a holistic design approach are poised to create products that not only meet user needs but also evoke positive emotions, foster loyalty, and outshine the competition.

Seamlessness in Customer Engagement

The contemporary expectation of seamlessness among consumers signifies a profound shift in how individuals interact with products and services. For product managers navigating this landscape, ensuring a smooth and frictionless experience across diverse touchpoints has become an intricate task with multifaceted considerations. In the era of cross-platform interactions, consumers seamlessly transition between various devices and interfaces. Product managers are tasked with guaranteeing not just consistency but also interconnectedness across these platforms. This demands meticulous planning to ensure data synchronization and a seamless user journey.

Unified user profiles have become a cornerstone of seamlessness. Customers expect their preferences and settings to seamlessly traverse from one platform to another. Product managers collaborate with technical teams to establish robust user profile systems that facilitate this unified and seamless experience.

Omnichannel engagement has risen to prominence, requiring a cohesive experience across communication channels. Product managers collaborate closely with marketing and customer support teams to guarantee consistent and timely responses, irrespective of the chosen channel. Seamlessness often hinges on data integration. Product managers play a pivotal role in identifying necessary data sources and technologies, working with data engineers to implement pipelines and integrations that enable real-time access to relevant information.

User-centric design is integral to achieving seamlessness. Understanding user behaviours and preferences at each touchpoint allows product managers to tailor the user experience effectively. User testing and feedback collection become indispensable tools for refining the user journey.

Cross-functional collaboration is imperative in delivering seamlessness. Product managers serve as orchestrators, bringing together teams responsible for design, development, marketing, and customer support. This alignment is essential to ensure a cohesive user journey.

Technology integration is often a crucial component of seamlessness. Product managers must evaluate and select appropriate technologies, APIs, and platforms, staying informed about emerging technologies that enhance the user experience.

Quality assurance is paramount in the pursuit of seamlessness. Collaborating with quality assurance teams, product managers identify potential points of friction or inconsistency, implementing robust testing procedures to maintain seamlessness.

Continuous improvement is inherent in the quest for seamlessness. Product managers embrace a culture of continuous assessment, regularly evaluating user feedback, monitoring performance metrics, and iterating on the user experience. This iterative approach is essential to adapt to changing customer expectations and emerging technologies.

The expectation of seamlessness in today's consumer landscape requires a comprehensive approach spearheaded by product managers. Facilitating cross-functional collaboration, leveraging technology effectively, and adopting a user-centric mindset are essential to create products and services that offer a consistent and hassle-free experience across all touchpoints. Achieving seamlessness is not a one-time task but a dynamic process that demands ongoing attention and adaptation.

Accessibility and Inclusivity

Inclusivity has gained prominence as an integral part of customer expectations. Products are expected to be accessible to individuals of diverse backgrounds, abilities, and needs. This necessitates considerations like accessibility features, diversity in design, and equitable user experiences. In today's ever-evolving business landscape, inclusivity has emerged as a critical component of product management. This transformative shift is driven by several interconnected factors, each emphasizing the importance of creating products that cater to a diverse and discerning user base.

At the heart of this transformation lies the recognition that modern consumers are far from passive recipients of products. They have evolved into discerning and informed individuals who approach the marketplace armed with knowledge and a meticulous eye for detail. The proliferation of digital platforms and the internet has empowered consumers with access to a wealth of information, enabling them to make well-informed choices. Consequently, they seek products that align precisely with their unique needs and preferences.

This discerning consumer behaviour has given rise to a growing demand for personalization. It's no longer sufficient for products to offer surface-level customizations; users expect products to seamlessly adapt to their specific behaviours and preferences. Product managers are challenged to create adaptable, user-centric products that resonate with this desire for personalization.

User experience, once considered secondary to functionality, has now taken center stage as a competitive edge. Consumers no longer judge products solely on their functionality but also on how they feel while using them. This paradigm shift necessitates a holistic approach to product design, where the user experience is thoughtfully crafted from the ground up.

Seamlessness has become an expectation in user interactions across various touchpoints with a product or service. Whether transitioning from a website to a mobile app or engaging with customer support, users anticipate a consistent and hassle-free experience. Product managers play a pivotal role in orchestrating these seamless experiences by aligning cross-functional teams and integrating technologies effectively. Inclusivity extends beyond mere accessibility features; it encompasses creating equitable user experiences. This means ensuring that all users, regardless of their abilities, have an equal opportunity to access and benefit from a product's features and services. Product managers must evaluate user journeys and interfaces to identify potential biases or barriers that may inadvertently exclude certain groups of users.

Furthermore, inclusivity also pertains to cultural sensitivity. In a globalized world, products often cater to a diverse international user base. Product managers need to be mindful of cultural nuances and collaborate with localization experts to ensure that products respect and cater to different cultural backgrounds.

To achieve inclusivity, ongoing engagement with users from diverse backgrounds is imperative. Actively seeking feedback and conducting user testing involving participants with disabilities can unveil usability challenges and ensure that inclusivity is a genuine aspect of product design. Ethical considerations are intertwined with inclusivity, particularly in issues related to bias, discrimination, and privacy. Product managers are responsible for making ethical design and development choices that align with principles of fairness and social responsibility.

Legal compliance is also a significant facet of inclusivity. Many regions have regulations and standards concerning accessibility and inclusivity, such as the Web Content Accessibility Guidelines (WCAG) for digital products. Product managers must be aware of and adhere to these regulations to avoid legal repercussions and safeguard their product's reputation.

Lastly, product managers have a role to play in promoting inclusivity awareness within their organizations and industries. They can advocate for inclusivity-related training and resources, fostering a culture of inclusivity that extends beyond the product development phase.

In conclusion, inclusivity has become an integral component of customer expectations, and product managers are at the forefront of ensuring that products align with this evolving landscape. By embracing inclusivity as a core principle, product managers can create products that resonate with a wide range of users, contribute to a more equitable digital landscape, and adhere to ethical and legal standards.

Real-time Engagement

Customers desire real-time engagement and feedback mechanisms. They expect products to evolve based on their input and preferences. Product managers must establish channels for ongoing communication with users, allowing for iterative improvements and feature enhancements.

In the contemporary landscape of product management, real-time engagement becomes a critical element in meeting customer expectations and ensuring the success of a product. Today's customers, armed with digital tools and platforms, increasingly seek immediate and meaningful interactions with the products they use. This shift in consumer behaviour underscores the importance of real-time engagement for product managers in various ways.

Firstly, customers have come to expect the opportunity for continuous feedback and interaction with the products they purchase and use. They desire the ability to provide input, report issues, and suggest improvements directly to the product teams. Product managers, recognizing the value of this direct feedback loop, must establish channels and mechanisms that facilitate ongoing communication with users. These channels can include in-app feedback forms, customer support chat, social media engagement, and user forums, among others. By enabling real-time engagement, product managers gather valuable insights into user needs, pain points, and preferences.

Secondly, real-time engagement extends beyond mere feedback collection; it encompasses the ability to act on this feedback promptly. Customers expect that their input will lead to tangible improvements in the product. This necessitates product managers to not only listen but also respond effectively to user suggestions and concerns. They must prioritize and implement iterative improvements and feature enhancements based on this feedback, demonstrating a commitment to meeting user expectations and delivering a product that evolves in response to user input.

Overall, real-time engagement has become a pivotal component of product management in the digital age. It empowers product managers to foster a strong connection with their user base, gather real-world insights, and ensure that their products remain relevant and responsive to changing user preferences. By establishing effective channels for communication and actively acting on user feedback, product managers can create products that not only meet but exceed customer expectations, driving user satisfaction and loyalty.

Environmental and Ethical Concerns

In an era marked by heightened environmental and ethical awareness, customers increasingly expect products to align with their values. They seek products that are environmentally sustainable, ethically produced, and socially responsible. With rapidly evolving business landscape today, environmental and ethical considerations have gained substantial prominence, significantly impacting the field of product management.

Customers, now more than ever, place a strong emphasis on the environmental and ethical aspects of the products they choose to support. This shift in consumer behaviours reflects a broader societal awareness of issues such as climate change, fair labour practices, and social responsibility. As a result, product managers are faced with the critical task of addressing these concerns to meet the expectations of a conscientious customer base.

One of the key facets of this transformation is the growing demand for environmentally sustainable products. Customers are increasingly seeking products that have minimal environmental impact, from their production to their disposal. This means product managers must assess the entire product lifecycle, identifying opportunities to reduce carbon footprints, minimize waste, and utilize eco-friendly materials. They may also need to collaborate with suppliers and manufacturers who adhere to sustainable practices, ensuring that the entire supply chain aligns with environmental standards.

Another critical aspect is ethical production. Consumers today are concerned about the conditions under which products are manufactured. They expect products to be made under fair labour conditions, with workers receiving fair wages and safe working environments. Product managers must conduct due diligence when selecting suppliers and manufacturers, ensuring they meet ethical labour standards. This may involve conducting audits, certifications, or partnerships with organizations that promote fair labour practices. Also the products are now increasingly scrutinized for their social responsibility. Customers expect companies and their products to contribute positively to society. Product managers must consider how their products impact communities, diversity, and inclusivity. This may entail incorporating features that enhance accessibility for individuals with disabilities or supporting social causes through product sales or partnerships.

Navigating these environmental and ethical concerns is not only a matter of meeting customer expectations but also of long-term business sustainability. Companies that fail to address these issues risk reputational damage and may struggle to remain competitive in a market where ethical and sustainable practices are increasingly valued.

In an era marked by heightened environmental and ethical awareness, product managers must proactively address these concerns to align their products with the values and expectations of conscientious consumers. This involves evaluating and enhancing the sustainability of the product's lifecycle, ensuring ethical production processes, and considering the broader social impact of their products. Successfully navigating these considerations not only satisfies customer demands but also positions products and companies as responsible and forward-thinking in an ever-evolving business landscape. This transformation in consumer behaviour necessitates a paradigm shift in how products are conceived and delivered, making it imperative for product managers to adopt a customer-centric, adaptable, and innovation-driven approach.

Rapid Technological Advances

The relentless speed at which technology is advancing is an unstoppable force that has not only disrupted traditional industries but has also fundamentally reshaped the core principles of product management. This transformative factor stands as a central pillar in the ever-evolving landscape of product management, and its ramifications are profound and far-reaching.

The rapid technological advances of our era have ushered in a paradigm shift in how products are conceived, developed, and delivered. Product managers now operate in a dynamic environment where the rules of the game are constantly rewritten. Technological advancements have accelerated the pace at which new products are developed, rendering traditional product development lifecycles obsolete. This necessitates a shift towards more agile and adaptive approaches to product management.

Furthermore, these technological leaps have expanded the horizons of what's possible. Innovations such as artificial intelligence, machine learning, and the Internet of Things have opened up new realms of product functionality and user experiences. Product managers are tasked with harnessing these innovations to create products that not only meet market demands but also push the boundaries of what customers can expect.

Moreover, the rapid advancement of technology has democratized product development. Access to cutting-edge tools, platforms, and resources is no longer the exclusive domain of tech giants. Start-ups and small teams now have the ability to compete on a level playing field, provided they can leverage technology effectively. Product managers play a pivotal role in identifying and adopting the right technologies to stay competitive.

In conclusion, the rapid pace of technological advancement is a defining characteristic of the modern business landscape, and its impact on product management is profound. Product managers must be agile, innovative, and technologically savvy to thrive in this environment. Embracing technological change, staying ahead of emerging trends, and leveraging these advances to create exceptional products are imperative for success in the contemporary product management landscape.

Technological Disruption as the New Norm

The phenomenon of technological disruption has transitioned from being an occasional event to the established norm. The relentless emergence of ground-breaking technologies, spanning artificial intelligence, blockchain, the Internet of Things (IoT), and augmented reality, perpetually challenges and reshapes the existing business paradigms. For product managers, navigating this landscape means acknowledging that staying informed and adaptable to these disruptive innovations is not merely a strategic choice but an absolute necessity.

The rapid evolution of technology has fundamentally altered the dynamics of industries, introducing unprecedented possibilities and demanding continuous adaptation. Product managers find themselves operating in an environment where the ability to grasp, assess, and integrate these disruptive technologies is intrinsic to the success of their products and, consequently, the companies they serve. The accelerated pace of technological advancements not only creates new opportunities but also poses the risk of obsolescence for products that fail to align with or harness these innovations.

Moreover, technological disruption extends beyond product features to influence entire business models. Companies that thrive in this environment often leverage disruptive technologies not only to enhance their products but also to revolutionize how they deliver value to customers.

Product managers, therefore, shoulder the responsibility of not only understanding the technical aspects of these innovations but also envisioning how they can be strategically integrated into the overall product and business strategy. The role of product managers now transforms into that of innovation leaders who must proactively scan the technological horizon, assess the relevance of emerging trends, and guide their teams in adapting and capitalizing on these disruptions. The new norm of technological disruption necessitates a culture of continuous learning, agility, and a proactive mindset within product management teams.

In short, technological disruption is no longer an occasional challenge but an enduring characteristic of the contemporary business landscape. Product managers must recognize this reality and embrace a proactive stance, cultivating a deep understanding of emerging technologies, anticipating their impact on products and markets, and steering their teams toward innovative and strategic responses. In doing so, they not only navigate the challenges posed by technological disruption but position their products and companies at the forefront of transformative change.

The Imperative of Agility

Agility is the linchpin of survival in this era of rapid technological advancement. During the era of rapid technological advancements, agility emerges as the linchpin of survival and success. Product managers are at the forefront of this dynamic landscape, and their ability to embrace agility in technology integration is paramount.

Incorporating emerging technologies into products requires a nimble and adaptive approach. Product managers must swiftly assess the relevance and potential impact of these innovations on their product offerings. This entails staying vigilant about technological trends, monitoring industry developments, and evaluating how new technologies align with their product strategy.

Moreover, the integration of emerging technologies should be a seamless process. Product managers must ensure that these innovations enhance the overall user experience and bring tangible value to customers. This involves understanding not only the technical aspects of these technologies but also their practical applications and benefits.

Agility in technology integration also implies a willingness to experiment and iterate. Product managers should be open to piloting new technologies, gathering user feedback, and making adjustments based on real-world usage. This iterative approach allows them to fine-tune their technology integrations, ensuring that they align with evolving customer needs and market dynamics. Thus, fostering a culture of agility within the product team is crucial. This involves encouraging cross-functional collaboration, where technical experts, designers, and marketers work together to explore and implement innovative technologies. Agile methodologies, such as Scrum or Kanban, can also be valuable in facilitating the rapid integration of new technologies.

In essence, agility in technology integration is a core competency for product managers in the face of rapid technological advancement. It enables them to seize opportunities, stay competitive, and deliver products that resonate with customers in an ever-evolving tech landscape.

Moreover, The integration of cutting-edge technology isn't just about staying relevant and agile; it's often the key to gaining a competitive edge. Product managers must realize that technology can be a potent differentiator in crowded markets. Innovations such as machine learning algorithms, predictive analytics, and cloud computing can enhance product functionality, user experience, and overall value proposition to cite few examples.

User Expectations for Tech-Driven Solutions

User expectations for tech-driven solutions have undergone a transformative shift, marking a paradigm where consumers increasingly demand products to leverage technology for their benefit. Product managers play a pivotal and challenging role in navigating this complex terrain of user expectations, particularly in an era dominated by tech-savvy consumers. Modern users are characterized by their active participation in technology, making seamless integration with their tech-driven lifestyles an imperative. Whether it's the integration of smartphones, wearable devices, or smart home assistants, technology has become an integral part of their daily existence.

Convenience has risen to the status of a prerequisite, with users expecting technology to streamline tasks, reduce friction, and enhance efficiency. This includes the growing popularity of voice-activated assistants, smart thermostats optimizing energy consumption, and mobile apps providing instant access to information and services.

Moreover, users now demand real-time insights and data analysis from products. Wearable devices that monitor health metrics and offer personalized recommendations exemplify this trend. Personalization has emerged as a fundamental expectation, with users anticipating products to adapt to their preferences, behaviours, and needs. Whether through content streaming services recommending shows based on viewing history or e-commerce platforms curating personalized product recommendations, personalization is a driving force behind user satisfaction. Interoperability and integration with existing tech ecosystems are also essential user expectations. Products need to seamlessly collaborate with other devices, synchronize across platforms, and allow for effortless data sharing. Transparency and data privacy are paramount considerations, reflecting users' increasing consciousness about how their data is collected and used.

User expectations extend beyond the product's initial release, encompassing the anticipation of continuous improvement over time. This involves regular software updates introducing new features and enhancements to ensure the product remains valuable and competitive. Ethical considerations have gained prominence, with users expecting products to adhere to ethical standards, including fair AI algorithms, responsible data handling, and sustainable practices.

In essence, product managers must align with these evolving expectations, leveraging technology strategically to meet the multifaceted demands of modern users. The challenge lies not only in meeting these expectations at the product's inception but also in ensuring continuous adaptation and improvement in alignment with the dynamic landscape of technology and user preferences.

Alignment with Emerging Tech Trends

In the digital age, remaining in sync with emerging tech trends is a linchpin of effective product management. It entails not just recognizing these trends but also comprehending their potential implications across various dimensions such as the market, user behaviour, and the competitive landscape. Product managers, in this context, are akin to visionaries, charting the course for products that are not only contemporary but also future-proof. Let's delve into the intricacies:

The Dynamic Nature of Technology Trends

Technology trends are inherently dynamic, continually evolving as innovation accelerates. Whether it's the advent of 5G networks, the rise of blockchain applications, or the integration of artificial intelligence into everyday products, these trends have the potential to disrupt industries, redefine user expectations, and alter competitive dynamics.

Market Relevance and Competitive Edge

Understanding emerging tech trends is instrumental in ensuring the market relevance of products. Products that harness the latest technological advancements often gain a competitive edge. For instance, a mobile app incorporating augmented reality can provide users with immersive experiences, setting it apart from competitors.

Anticipating User Behaviour

Tech trends significantly influence user behaviour. As users adopt new technologies and platforms, their preferences and expectations change.

Product managers must anticipate these shifts to tailor products that align with evolving user behaviour. For instance, the surge in remote work has led to increased demand for collaboration tools, reshaping the landscape of workplace software.

Navigating the Competitive Landscape

An intimate knowledge of tech trends is indispensable for navigating the competitive landscape. It allows product managers to assess the strengths and weaknesses of competitors' offerings and identify unexplored niches. For example, the emergence of electric vehicles has prompted established automotive companies and newcomers to innovate in this space, leading to a competitive race for market share.

Mitigating Obsolescence

Staying attuned to emerging tech trends is a strategy to mitigate the risk of product obsolescence. Products that fail to adapt to changing technological paradigms can quickly become outdated. Product managers must proactively steer products towards tech trends that are likely to endure.

Enabling Future-Ready Products

Product managers are the architects of future-ready products. By aligning with tech trends, they enable products to seamlessly incorporate new features and functionalities as technology evolves. This flexibility allows products to remain relevant and adaptable over time.

Assessing Risks and Opportunities

Tech trends also carry risks, including security vulnerabilities, regulatory challenges, and market saturation. Product managers must assess these risks while capitalizing on the opportunities presented by emerging tech. A deep understanding of trends allows for informed decision-making in this regard.

Collaborative Ecosystems

Many tech trends involve collaboration within ecosystems. For instance, the Internet of Things often requires partnerships with various device manufacturers. Product managers must excel at fostering these collaborations to harness the full potential of tech trends.

The alignment with emerging tech trends is akin to looking through a crystal ball for product managers. It enables them to foresee potential disruptions, capitalize on opportunities, and create products that not only address current market needs but also position themselves favourably in an ever-changing technological landscape. It's a dynamic and forward-thinking approach that underlines the importance of being not just a product manager but a product visionary.

Balancing Innovation and Stability

The challenge for product managers lies in striking a delicate balance between innovation and stability. While adopting new technologies is crucial, stability and reliability are equally vital. Overly aggressive adoption of unproven technologies can lead to product instability and customer dissatisfaction.

The delicate equilibrium between innovation and stability is a central challenge for product managers, requiring astute decision-making and strategic foresight. This dynamic interplay is crucial for the sustained success of products.

The Dual Imperatives

Product managers operate within the dual imperatives of fostering innovation and ensuring stability. Innovation is essential for staying competitive, meeting evolving user expectations, and carving out a niche in the market. On the other hand, stability is paramount for building trust with users, maintaining product reliability, and avoiding disruptions that can lead to customer dissatisfaction.

Assessing the Risk-Reward Ratio

The adoption of new technologies inherently carries risks. Product managers must carefully assess the risk-reward ratio of incorporating innovations. While a ground-breaking technology might offer a competitive edge, its unproven nature may introduce uncertainties that can compromise stability. Effective risk management involves a nuanced understanding of the potential impact on user experience and overall product performance.

Incremental vs. Disruptive Innovation

The balancing act involves distinguishing between incremental and disruptive innovation. Incremental innovation involves gradual enhancements to existing features, minimizing the risk of destabilizing the product. Disruptive innovation, on the other hand, introduces radical changes that can significantly alter the product's dynamics. Striking the right balance involves judiciously incorporating both forms of innovation based on the product's lifecycle and market demands.

User-Centric Innovation

Innovation should align with user needs and expectations. User-centric innovation ensures that new features or technologies resonate with the target audience. Product managers must gather user feedback, conduct usability studies, and employ data-driven insights to guide innovation in directions that enhance user satisfaction without compromising stability.

Piloting and Prototyping

To mitigate the risks associated with adopting new technologies, product managers can use piloting and prototyping. Piloting involves implementing innovations on a smaller scale before full-scale deployment, allowing for real-world testing and refinement. Prototyping enables the creation of experimental models to assess the feasibility and impact of innovations.

Technical Debt Management

Technical debt, accrued through shortcuts or quick solutions, can accumulate and impede stability. Product managers need to manage technical debt effectively by prioritizing the resolution of accumulated issues and ensuring that new features are built on a solid technical foundation.

Continuous Monitoring and Iteration

The balancing act is not a one-time endeavour; it requires continuous monitoring and iteration. Product managers should closely monitor the impact of innovations on product stability through metrics, user feedback, and performance indicators. Based on these insights, iterative adjustments can be made to strike the optimal balance.

Transparent Communication

Transparent communication is vital in managing user expectations. If a product is undergoing significant changes, product managers should communicate these developments transparently, outlining the benefits while acknowledging potential temporary disruptions. Clear communication helps build trust and understanding among users.

In conclusion, the challenge of balancing innovation and stability is an inherent part of product management. Striking the right equilibrium involves a nuanced understanding of the product, user needs, and the broader market context. Successful product managers navigate this challenge by making informed decisions, prioritizing user satisfaction, and maintaining a strategic vision for the product's long-term success.

Technological Ecosystems

The concept of technological ecosystems has become central to modern product management, reflecting the intricate interplay of products, services, and platforms within the digital landscape. Navigating these ecosystems is both an art and a science, requiring product managers to orchestrate seamless interactions while harnessing the capabilities they offer.

Technological ecosystems encompass a multifaceted landscape where products, services, and technologies interact and coexist. These ecosystems are characterized by interconnectedness, with each component influencing and enhancing the capabilities of the others. This interconnectedness can span various domains, including software, hardware, cloud services, and data.

Third-Party Integrations

Modern products often rely on integration with third-party platforms, services, and APIs (Application Programming Interfaces) to augment their functionalities. For instance, a mobile app may integrate with social media platforms for sharing content, or an e-commerce website may use payment gateways to process transactions. Product managers are responsible for identifying and integrating these external components to enhance the user experience.

Partnerships and Collaborations

Strategic partnerships and collaborations are common features of technological ecosystems. These partnerships can involve technology providers, complementary products, or service providers. Product managers play a crucial role in negotiating and managing these partnerships, ensuring that they align with the product's objectives and contribute to its overall value proposition.

Modern products rarely exist in isolation; they are part of complex ecosystems. Strategic partnerships allow product managers to expand and enrich these ecosystems. Whether integrating with third-party platforms, leveraging APIs, or forming alliances with tech providers, these collaborations enhance a product's capabilities and utility.

While partnerships offer numerous benefits, they also introduce risks. Product managers must identify potential risks, such as dependency on a single partner or conflicts of interest, and implement risk mitigation strategies to safeguard the product's interests.

Interoperability and Compatibility

Interoperability and compatibility are fundamental considerations within technological ecosystems. Products must seamlessly work together and share data when necessary. Product managers must ensure that their product adheres to industry standards and protocols to enable smooth interactions with other components in the ecosystem.

Data Exchange and Security

As products interact within ecosystems, data exchange becomes a critical facet. Product managers must address data security, privacy, and compliance to protect user information and adhere to regulatory requirements. This includes implementing encryption, access controls, and data-sharing agreements.

Ecosystem Growth and Evolution

Technological ecosystems are not static; they evolve over time. Product managers must monitor ecosystem changes, including the introduction of new technologies, updates to APIs, and shifts in partner strategies. They must adapt their product strategies to align with these changes to remain competitive and relevant.

User Experience and Seamless Flow

The user experience is paramount within technological ecosystems. Product managers must ensure that interactions between their product and other ecosystem components are seamless and intuitive for users. A disjointed or cumbersome user experience can lead to frustration and abandonment.

Value Proposition Enhancement

Technological ecosystems offer opportunities for product managers to enhance their product's value proposition. By strategically integrating with complementary components or services, they can provide users with a more comprehensive and valuable experience.

Risk Management

Navigating technological ecosystems comes with inherent risks, including potential dependencies on external providers, security vulnerabilities, and changes in partner strategies. Product managers must conduct risk assessments and develop contingency plans to mitigate these risks.

The technological ecosystems represent the intricate web of interactions that define the modern digital landscape. Product managers are tasked with orchestrating these interactions, ensuring interoperability, and leveraging partnerships to enhance their product's capabilities and user experience.

Successful navigation of technological ecosystems requires a deep understanding of the product's place within the ecosystem, a proactive approach to changes and innovations, and a commitment to delivering value within this interconnected digital realm.

Product managers are tasked with not only this understanding of emerging technologies but also with orchestrating their seamless incorporation into products managing and or mitigating risks. They must be forward-thinking visionaries who leverage technology to meet evolving user expectations, gain a competitive edge, and navigate the complex landscapes of innovation.

Innovation as a Competitive Edge

In today's competitive business landscape, where markets are saturated with a multitude of products and services, innovation emerges as a key differentiator. Product managers play a pivotal role in driving innovation to ensure that their products not only stand out but also meet the evolving needs and expectations of users.

Distinguishing in a Crowded Market

In crowded markets where similar products vie for attention, the ability to innovate becomes a critical factor in distinguishing one product from another. Innovation allows a product to offer unique features, functionalities, or experiences that resonate with consumers and set it apart from competitors.

Markets are dynamic, with ever-changing consumer preferences, technological advancements, and external factors. Product managers leverage innovation as a strategic response to these dynamics, ensuring that their products remain relevant and adaptive to emerging trends.

Creating Value Propositions

Innovation is integral to crafting compelling value propositions. By introducing novel features, addressing pain points, or introducing disruptive technologies, products can offer unique value that attracts and retains customers. This value proposition is crucial in capturing market share and building brand loyalty.

User-Centric Innovation

Successful innovation aligns closely with user needs and preferences. Product managers champion a user-centric approach, actively seeking insights into user behaviour, conducting usability studies, and gathering feedback. This user-centric innovation ensures that products not only meet functional requirements but also deliver positive and enjoyable user experiences.

Enhancing User Engagement

Innovative features or design elements have the power to enhance user engagement. Whether it's a new functionality that simplifies a task or a design innovation that makes the product more aesthetically pleasing, these elements contribute to a positive user experience, fostering user satisfaction and loyalty.

Competitive Resilience

Innovation contributes to the resilience of a product in the face of competition. Products that continually evolve and introduce new elements are better positioned to withstand challenges and maintain their competitiveness over time. This resilience is a key characteristic of products that consistently leverage innovation.

Adapting to Technological Advancements

Innovation often involves harnessing the latest technologies to improve products. Product managers ensure that their teams stay abreast of technological advancements and strategically incorporate them into the product development process. This not only keeps the product technologically current but also aligns it with industry trends.

Balancing Risk and Reward

Innovation inherently involves a degree of risk. Product managers must navigate the balance between pushing boundaries to bring about meaningful innovations and managing the potential risks, such as market acceptance and technical feasibility. This requires strategic planning, market research, and a willingness to experiment.

Sustainable Growth

Innovation is a catalyst for sustainable growth. Products that continually innovate are more likely to experience prolonged success and growth. Product managers, therefore, focus on creating a culture of innovation within their teams, fostering an environment where new ideas are encouraged and rewarded.

Establishing Market Leadership

Products that consistently leverage innovation can establish themselves as market leaders. They not only respond to market demands but also anticipate and shape industry trends. Market leadership brings not only revenue advantages but also a strong brand presence.

In essence, innovation is not merely a feature; it's a strategic imperative for product managers. By driving innovation, product managers ensure that their products not only meet current market demands but also lead the way in shaping the future of their respective industries. This emphasis on innovation is a dynamic force that propels products to the forefront of competition and sustains their relevance in ever-evolving markets.

Product Management or Technical Product Management

In recent times, the roles of Technical Product Management and Product Management have emerged as highly complementary functions within organizations. These roles collaborate closely, each contributing a distinct perspective and skill set to the product development process. While Product Managers maintain a broad view of the product, aligning it with market demand, customer needs, and overarching business strategy, Technical Product Managers specialize in delving deep into the technical intricacies of a product to ensure its technical feasibility and viability. The effective synergy between these roles is pivotal in the creation of successful products that are not only technically robust but also precisely aligned with market requirements.

Product Management, often referred to as the "big picture" role, involves defining the strategic vision for a product. Product Managers are responsible for identifying market opportunities, conducting extensive market research, understanding customer pain points, and determining how the product can address these needs while aligning with the broader business strategy. They focus on creating a roadmap for the product, setting strategic objectives, and prioritizing features to maximize value for both customers and the company. Product Managers act as the bridge between various stakeholders, including customers, marketing, sales, and engineering teams, ensuring that the product meets both market and business needs.

Conversely, Technical Product Managers are the technical experts within the product management realm. They bring in-depth technical knowledge to the table, often stemming from backgrounds in engineering or related fields. These professionals concentrate on the nitty-gritty technical details of a product's development. They assess the feasibility of proposed features, evaluate the scalability and architecture of the product, and collaborate closely with engineering teams to ensure that the product can be built effectively. Technical Product Managers also play a crucial role in troubleshooting technical challenges that may arise during development, ensuring that the final product is not only aligned with the strategic vision but also technically sound.

The collaboration between these two roles is imperative for product success. Product Managers provide the strategic direction and market insights necessary to guide product development in the right direction. They prioritize features and functionalities based on market demand and customer feedback. Technical Product Managers, on the other hand, ensure that these features are technically feasible, scalable, and sustainable. They work to find solutions to technical challenges and make sure that the final product not only meets customer needs but also maintains a high level of technical integrity.

In essence, the synergy between Product Management and Technical Product Management is akin to the perfect marriage of vision and execution. While Product Managers dream up the product's future and understand its market fit, Technical Product Managers ensure that these dreams can be transformed into a technically viable and robust reality. This collaboration, when executed effectively, leads to the development of products that not only align with market demands but also possess the technical prowess to deliver value to both customers and the organization. Let us dive little deeper in these two aspects..

Overview of Product Management

Product management is a dynamic and well-rounded approach that empowers product managers to make informed decisions, create products that resonate with customers, and contribute meaningfully to their organization's growth and success. It involves collaborating across functions, allocating resources wisely, and staying closely connected to the market and customer preferences to drive product excellence.

Holistic Product Strategy

A holistic product strategy is at the core of effective product management. It encompasses a market-centric approach, strategic decision-making, and the alignment of the product with the company's overarching business goals. At the epicentre of effective product management lies a holistic product strategy, a comprehensive framework that integrates a market-centric approach, strategic decision-making, and alignment with the broader business goals of the company. This strategic compass empowers product managers to navigate the complex terrain of product development with precision and purpose.

Market-Centric Focus: Unlocking Customer Insights

A foundational pillar of a holistic product strategy is the cultivation of a deep understanding of the market. Product managers delve into extensive market research, meticulously identifying trends, probing customer needs, uncovering pain points, and spotting emerging opportunities. This customer-centric approach forms the bedrock upon which proactive product development is built. By intimately grasping the evolving needs and preferences of customers, product managers can strategically position their products to resonate profoundly with the target audience.

Mitigate Market Risks: Proactive Risk Management

In the realm of holistic product strategy, market research is not just an investigative tool but a shield against potential risks. Through rigorous analysis of market dynamics, product managers identify lurking risks and craft strategic plans to mitigate them. This proactive stance is akin to fortifying the product against potential market failures, ensuring resilience and adaptability in the face of ever-changing market conditions.

Tailor Products - Precision in Product Development

Empowered by the wealth of market insights, product managers wield the ability to tailor products with precision. Armed with a nuanced understanding of market segments, they craft products that are not generic solutions but finely tuned to address specific needs. This bespoke approach ensures that the product is not merely relevant but becomes a valuable and indispensable solution for its intended audience.

A holistic product strategy is the guiding star for product managers. It propels them to engage in market-centric exploration, equips them with proactive risk management tools, and empowers them to tailor products with finesse. As a dynamic framework, it allows for adaptability in a constantly evolving market landscape, ensuring that products not only meet but exceed customer expectations and contribute significantly to the overarching success of the company.

Strategic Decision-Making

Effective product managers are strategic decision-makers. They consider a range of factors when making decisions to ensure that they align with the product's long-term vision and objectives. Effective product managers are akin to skilled navigators, steering their products through the ever-changing currents of the market. Strategic decision-making is the compass that guides these managers, ensuring alignment with the product's long-term vision and objectives.

Market Demand - Anticipating Needs and Gaps

At the heart of strategic decision-making is a vigilant assessment of market demand. Product managers engage in a comprehensive analysis of both current and anticipated market needs. They pose critical questions such as, "Is there a genuine need for this product?" and "Does our product fill a gap in the market?" This insightful examination ensures that the product isn't just a creation but a solution that addresses real and pressing market demands.

Competitive Landscape - Analyzing for Differentiation

Understanding the competitive landscape is a strategic imperative. Product managers meticulously analyze competitors' offerings, strengths, weaknesses, and market positioning. This in-depth analysis is not just about awareness but about uncovering opportunities for differentiation. By discerning what makes their product stand out in a crowded market, product managers can craft strategies that give their product a competitive edge.

Long-Term Viability - Beyond Short-Term Gains

Strategic decision-making extends far beyond the lure of short-term gains. Product managers, in their role as stewards of long-term success, evaluate the sustained viability of the product. Factors such as scalability, adaptability to changing market conditions, and sustainability become paramount considerations. This forward-thinking approach ensures that decisions made today contribute not only to immediate success but also to the enduring relevance and resilience of the product over time.

In essence, strategic decision-making in product management is a forward-looking and multifaceted process. It involves anticipating market needs, strategically positioning against competitors, and ensuring the enduring viability of the product. As product managers navigate the complex waters of the market, these strategic decisions become the rudder that propels their products towards long-term success and sustained relevance.

Alignment with Business Goals

A holistic product strategy ensures that the product aligns with the broader business goals of the organization In the intricate tapestry of product management, alignment with broader business goals serves as the guiding star, ensuring that every decision and action taken by product managers contributes cohesively to the organization's success.

Revenue Objectives - Balancing Growth and Profitability

One of the pivotal considerations in aligning with business goals is understanding how the product contributes to revenue generation. Product managers don multiple hats as they delve into the intricacies of revenue. They develop pricing strategies that strike a delicate balance between growth and profitability. Exploring monetization options becomes a strategic endeavour, seeking to optimize revenue streams while enhancing the product's value proposition. Continual tracking of the product's financial performance ensures that revenue objectives remain on course, with adjustments made when necessary to steer towards success.

Strategic Alignment - Weaving the Threads of Purpose

Products, in their essence, must weave seamlessly into the fabric of the company's overall strategic objectives. Product managers are the storytellers, articulating how their product supports the organization's mission and vision. They don't merely create products in isolation but meticulously craft them as integral components in a larger narrative. Each feature and functionality is designed with purpose, aligning with the strategic direction set forth by the company. This alignment ensures that the product not only meets the immediate needs of the market but also advances the organization towards its long-term goals.

Resource Allocation - Maximizing Impact with Prudence

Resource allocation, a responsibility donned by product managers, is where strategy meets pragmatism. It involves assessing resource requirements, acknowledging budget constraints, and determining resource availability. The goal is to ensure that the product can be developed, launched, and maintained efficiently within the company's means. It's an exercise in maximizing impact while exercising prudence. Resource allocation becomes the art of orchestrating the symphony of product development, ensuring that each note resonates harmoniously with the company's financial capabilities.

The alignment with business goals is the cornerstone of effective product management. It encompasses understanding revenue dynamics, weaving products into the company's strategic narrative, and judiciously managing resources. Like a seasoned navigator, product managers chart a course that ensures every product they shepherd is not just a creation but a strategic vessel, sailing towards the horizon of success envisioned by the organization.

In summary, The holistic product strategy in product management is a dynamic and well-rounded approach that encompasses market-centricity, strategic thinking, and alignment with broader business goals. It empowers product managers to make informed decisions, create products that resonate with customers, and contribute meaningfully to the organization's growth and success.

Cross-Functional Collaboration

Product managers work with cross-functional teams that include designers, engineers, marketers, and salespeople to bring the product to market successfully. They champion user-centric design principles to create products that not only function well but also provide an excellent user experience. In the world of product management, cross-functional collaboration emerges as a symphony where different instruments come together to create a harmonious composition. Product managers, much like conductors, play a crucial role in ensuring that every note resonates perfectly.

Championing User-Centric Design

Product managers are the torchbearers of user-centric design principles. They understand that a product's success doesn't hinge solely on its functionality but on the experience it delivers. To achieve this, they work closely with designers, engineers, marketers, and salespeople, fostering a culture where user experience is paramount. They orchestrate the seamless integration of design, technology, and marketing, ensuring that products not only function well but also provide an excellent user experience. It's about creating products that not only meet needs but also evoke emotions, leaving a lasting imprint on users.

Resource Allocation

Effective resource allocation is where strategy meets pragmatism. Product managers don multiple hats as they allocate resources, balancing various factors like market demand, business strategy, available resources, and competitive positioning. They are not just stewards of product development; they are also entrusted with the responsibility of managing budgets related to product development, marketing, and sales. This entails making informed decisions about where to invest and when, optimizing the allocation of resources for maximum impact. It's a judicious art, ensuring that resources are used efficiently to achieve both short-term and long-term goals. Moreover, influencing without formal authority is a key skill they employ, persuading stakeholders to align with their vision.

Market and Customer Focus

At the heart of every successful product is an unwavering focus on the market and customers. Product managers understand that their compass must always point in the direction of the market, guiding every decision. Market research becomes a core part of their role, allowing them to gain deep insights into market dynamics, customer needs, pain points, and emerging trends. They prioritize the delivery of products that not only address customer pain points but also create substantial value for the target audience. It's not just about meeting expectations; it's about exceeding them by crafting products that truly resonate with users.

In essence, cross-functional collaboration, resource allocation, market and customer focus, and the art of influencing without formal authority form the pillars of effective product management.

Product managers are the maestros, orchestrating collaboration among diverse teams, allocating resources with precision, navigating the intricate landscape of the market and customer preferences, and persuading stakeholders to embrace their vision. Like skilled conductors, they ensure that every element of product development aligns perfectly, creating a symphony that resonates with both users and the organization's overarching goals.

Technical Product Management

Technical project management is a discipline focused on planning, executing, and overseeing projects with a strong technical or technological component. Technical project management is a multifaceted discipline that revolves around the planning, execution, and supervision of projects with significant technical or technological aspects. it's about orchestrating the successful completion of projects that involve complex technical components, such as software development, hardware integration, or engineering endeavours.

Technical Focus

Technical product managers are pivotal in ensuring that a product's technical elements are both robust and in harmony with industry standards. They primarily concentrate on understanding and overseeing various technical dimensions of the product. For example, This includes in-depth involvement in software development, where they work hand-in-hand with development teams to articulate precise technical requirements and make informed choices about the technology stack for optimal scalability and compatibility. Moreover, they take charge of quality assurance, guaranteeing the software's compliance with quality benchmarks while striving to eliminate critical defects.

Beyond software, technical product managers are also responsible for the hardware aspects of a product when applicable. This entails the meticulous selection of hardware components, accounting for factors such as processing capabilities, memory capacity, and connectivity. Their oversight extends to the integration of these hardware components into the overall product architecture and thorough testing and validation to ensure performance and reliability standards are met.

Furthermore, they address infrastructure requirements, facilitating efficient product operation within the chosen infrastructure, whether it involves cloud services, scalability planning, or robust security measures. At the core of their role lies a profound technical expertise that enables effective communication with engineering teams, adept problem-solving, and the ability to stay attuned to the latest technological trends, ensuring the product remains competitive and adheres to industry best practices.

Collaboration with Technical Teams

Collaboration with technical teams is a cornerstone of success for technical product managers. Their role demands close coordination with engineers, developers, and various technical experts to ensure that the product not only aligns with the company's vision but also excels from a technical perspective. Here's a detailed exploration of their collaboration with technical teams:

Ensuring Technical Feasibility

Technical product managers work in tandem with engineering teams to ascertain the technical feasibility of proposed product features and functionalities. This entails comprehensive discussions to evaluate the technical challenges, resource requirements, and potential roadblocks. By engaging early in the process, they contribute to the refinement of product concepts, ensuring that they are not only desirable from a market perspective but also achievable from a technical standpoint.

Creating Detailed Technical Specifications

One of the core responsibilities of technical product managers is the creation of detailed technical specifications. These specifications serve as a comprehensive blueprint that guides the entire product development process. They outline the intricacies of how the product should be built, including software architecture, data models, integration points, and technical constraints. This documentation is invaluable for engineers and developers as it provides clarity on the technical intricacies of the project.

Facilitating Effective Communication

Technical product managers act as intermediaries between non-technical stakeholders and technical teams. They excel in bridging the communication gap by translating business requirements and market insights into technical terms that engineers can readily understand and implement. This skill is essential for ensuring that the product's technical execution aligns seamlessly with its strategic objectives.

Iterative Collaboration

Collaboration with technical teams is not a one-time event but rather an iterative process throughout the product's development lifecycle. Technical product managers engage in ongoing discussions, addressing questions, providing clarifications, and adapting to changing technical requirements or challenges that may arise during the development journey.

Technical Oversight

Beyond the initial planning stages, technical product managers maintain a vigilant eye on the product's technical progress. They monitor the development process, conduct regular reviews, and address technical issues as they surface. This proactive approach helps ensure that the final product aligns with both technical and business expectations.

In short, collaboration with technical teams is a fundamental aspect of technical product management. Technical product managers actively engage with engineers and developers to validate technical feasibility, create comprehensive technical specifications, facilitate effective communication, and provide ongoing technical oversight. This synergy between technical expertise and product vision is instrumental in delivering products that are not only innovative but also technically robust.

Alignment with Business Goals

Technical product managers serve as a crucial bridge between the technical intricacies of product development and the overarching business objectives of their organization. Their role extends beyond the realm of technology, requiring them to ensure that every technical decision made aligns seamlessly with the broader business goals and strategies.

Strategic Decision-Making

Technical product managers are responsible for making decisions that transcend the purely technical realm. These decisions encompass evaluating market demand, understanding the competitive landscape, and assessing the long-term viability of the product. By considering these factors, they contribute to shaping the product's strategy in a manner that aligns with the company's business goals. This strategic decision-making process involves selecting which technical features to prioritize based on their potential to drive business value and differentiate the product in the market.

Resource Optimization

Effective technical product managers are adept at resource allocation, ensuring that available technical resources are directed towards initiatives that have a direct impact on achieving business objectives. This involves making informed choices about where to allocate engineering efforts, development time, and financial resources to maximize the product's alignment with the broader business strategy. Their decisions weigh technical feasibility against potential business impact to ensure resource optimization.

Market-Centric Approach

Technical product managers adopt a market-centric approach that emphasizes understanding customer needs and market dynamics. They actively gather insights into user behaviour and preferences, which they translate into technical requirements that enhance the product's appeal and competitiveness. By maintaining this customer-centric focus, they ensure that the technical decisions they champion are rooted in delivering real value to users, thus contributing to the attainment of business objectives.

Measuring Business Impact

In addition to technical metrics, technical product managers are deeply involved in assessing the business impact of their decisions. They monitor key performance indicators (KPIs) that gauge the product's success in achieving specific business objectives, whether it's revenue growth, customer retention, or market share expansion. This ongoing evaluation allows them to refine their technical strategies to better align with evolving business priorities.

Effective Communication

Communication forms the bedrock of alignment with business goals. Technical product managers excel at articulating the rationale behind technical decisions in a language that non-technical stakeholders can comprehend. This effective communication ensures that everyone within the organization, from executives to marketing teams, grasps the link between technical initiatives and the broader business strategy.

In summary, alignment with business goals is an integral facet of the role of technical product managers. While they possess a strong technical focus, they also bear the responsibility of guiding technical decisions that align seamlessly with the overarching business objectives and strategies. This multifaceted role requires them to employ strategic decision-making, optimize resource allocation, adopt a market-centric approach, measure business impact, and communicate effectively. By maintaining this alignment, technical product managers play a pivotal role in the successful fusion of technology and business objectives, resulting in products that not only function exceptionally but also contribute significantly to the organization's growth and success.

The Balancing Act of Convergence: The New Breed of Product Managers

Today, Product management and technical product management roles are seen converging in a number of ways. First, the increasing complexity of technology products is requiring product managers to have a deeper understanding of the technology behind their products. Thus Product managers are increasingly involved in the technical aspects of product development. They are working with engineers to define technical requirements, design products, and test new features.

In order to effectively manage the development and launch of complex technology products, product managers need to be able to communicate effectively with engineers and other technical professionals. They also need to be able to understand the technical challenges involved in building and delivering their products. Thus Technical product managers are taking on more responsibility for product strategy and marketing. They are working with cross-functional teams to develop and launch products that meet the needs of the market.

Both product managers and technical product managers are using data to make informed decisions about product development, marketing, and sales. They are using data to understand customer needs, identify market trends, and measure the success of their products. For sake of our understanding we will mentioned this convergent role as "Product Manager" henceforth.

This convergence of product management and technical product manager roles is creating new opportunities for product managers who have both technical and business skills. Product managers who are able to bridge the gap between business and technology are in high demand.

Second, the rise of agile development practices is leading to more cross-functional collaboration between product managers and technical teams. In an agile environment, product managers work closely with engineers and other technical professionals on a daily basis to plan and develop products. This requires product managers to have a good understanding of the agile development process and the tools and technologies that are used in agile development.

Finally, the growing importance of data in product development is leading to a convergence of product management and technical product management roles. Product managers are now expected to use data to make informed decisions about product development, marketing, and sales. This requires product managers to have a good understanding of data analysis tools and techniques.

Navigating the Convergence

Product managers are increasingly involved in the technical aspects of product development. They collaborate closely with engineers to define technical requirements, provide input on product design, and participate in the testing of new features. This hands-on involvement helps bridge the gap between technical feasibility and customer needs.

Technical product managers are taking on more significant roles in product strategy and marketing. They collaborate with cross-functional teams to shape product strategies that align with market demands. They also contribute to the development and launch of products that meet both technical and business objectives.

Both product managers and technical product managers leverage data to make informed decisions. They use data analytics tools to gain insights into customer behaviour, preferences, and market trends. This data informs critical decisions related to product development, marketing strategies, and measuring product success.

In the dynamic landscape of product development, a significant shift is unfolding as traditional boundaries between product managers and technical product managers blur. This convergence introduces a new paradigm where both roles are intricately woven into the fabric of product creation, each contributing distinct expertise to bridge the gap between business strategy and technical implementation.

Product Managers - A Closer Embrace of Technical Realities

In the landscape of product development, product managers find themselves immersed in the intricate realm of technology, marking a departure from traditional roles. This shift involves a more profound collaboration with engineers, transcending high-level planning. Product managers are now active contributors throughout the entire product development lifecycle.

This involvement goes beyond conceptualization; product managers play a pivotal role in defining the technical requirements that underpin the development process. Their insights become instrumental in shaping product design, ensuring that the final output aligns not only with the vision of the business but also with the expectations of end-users. This nuanced involvement in design is a strategic move, as it allows product managers to infuse the product with a user-centric approach, addressing specific needs and preferences.

Beyond design, product managers actively participate in the rigorous testing phases of new features. This hands-on engagement serves a dual purpose: validating the technical aspects of the product and gaining first-hand insights into how users interact with and respond to the new features. By being deeply involved in testing, product managers contribute to the refinement of the product, making adjustments based on real-world usage and feedback. This closer embrace of technical realities positions product managers as a bridge between the conceptualization of a product and its practical implementation. They act as conduits, translating the business strategy into technical requirements while ensuring that the final product resonates with the intricacies of customer needs. This hands-on engagement not only enhances the technical feasibility of the product but also fosters a deeper understanding of the user experience, ultimately contributing to the creation of more robust and user-friendly products.

Technical Product Managers - Strategic Players in Product Development

On the other side of the spectrum, technical product managers are assuming more prominent roles in shaping product strategy and marketing. They have emerged as key players in the realm of product strategy and marketing. Their contributions within cross-functional teams have become instrumental in crafting product strategies that not only align with but also leverage market demands effectively. These professionals are now assuming more prominent roles that span the entire product development lifecycle, from initial conception to successful market launch.

One of the significant shifts in the responsibilities of technical product managers is their involvement in shaping product strategy. Their deep understanding of the technical aspects of a product allows them to provide valuable insights into how the product can address market needs and capitalize on emerging opportunities. By collaborating closely with cross-functional teams, they help formulate strategies that not only ensure technical feasibility but also resonate with customer expectations and market trends. This comprehensive approach positions technical product managers as strategic thinkers who can bridge the gap between technology and market demands.

Furthermore, technical product managers are integral to the product development process from start to finish. They participate actively in the conception and planning phases, where their technical expertise informs crucial decisions about product design and features. Throughout the development cycle, they ensure that the product aligns seamlessly with technical specifications while remaining in tune with overarching business objectives. This holistic involvement guarantees that the final product is not only technically robust but also strategically positioned in the market.

In short, Technical product managers have evolved into multifaceted professionals who bring together technical acumen and strategic thinking. Their role extends beyond the confines of pure technical execution; they are now instrumental in shaping the overall product vision, strategy, and execution. This convergence of technical and strategic roles highlights the importance of bridging the gap between technology and business to create products that excel in both realms.

A Common Ground – The Data

Product managers and technical product managers share a common and powerful tool in navigating the intricate landscape of product development, the data. Armed with data analytics tools, both roles delve deep into understanding customer behaviours, preferences, and market trends. This analytical prowess becomes a guiding force in making critical decisions that span the entire product development spectrum.

The utilization of data is particularly evident in the process of feature prioritization. By analyzing data related to customer interactions, feedback, and usage patterns, product managers and technical product managers can identify which features are most crucial to users. This data-driven approach ensures that the development team focuses on building functionalities that align with customer needs and preferences, ultimately enhancing the product's value proposition.

In the realm of marketing strategies, leveraging data is equally essential. Both types of managers use data insights to tailor marketing campaigns effectively. Understanding customer behaviours allows for the creation of targeted and compelling messages that resonate with the intended audience. This data-driven marketing approach maximizes the impact of promotional efforts and increases the likelihood of capturing the attention of potential users.

Moreover, data plays a pivotal role in the ongoing measurement of product success. Through various key performance indicators (KPIs) and metrics, product managers and technical product managers continuously assess how well the product is performing in the market. Metrics such as user engagement, retention rates, and customer satisfaction are closely monitored to gauge the impact of product changes or updates. This iterative process allows for informed decision-making, as adjustments can be made based on real-time data to enhance the product's overall success.

The reliance on data as a common tool underscores the data-driven nature of modern product management. Both product managers and technical product managers recognize the invaluable insights that data analytics provide, using them to guide decisions, refine strategies, and ensure that products not only meet but exceed customer expectations in a dynamic and competitive market landscape.

Hybrid Skill Sets - The Demand for Versatility

The convergence of product management and technical product management signifies a significant shift in the professional landscape, ushering in a demand for individuals who possess hybrid skill sets. These individuals have the remarkable ability to fluidly navigate and bridge the seemingly disparate realms of business strategy and technical intricacies. This newfound proficiency is swiftly becoming a prized asset in today's competitive job market.

Professionals equipped with this versatility find themselves in a unique and advantageous position. They are the architects of innovation, serving as vital conduits between the conceptualization of a product and its practical technical implementation. Their role extends beyond ensuring technical feasibility; they are instrumental in orchestrating the alignment of products with the ever-evolving expectations of customers in a landscape marked by rapid and relentless change.

These versatile professionals possess a multifaceted skill set. They can deftly switch hats between understanding market dynamics, customer needs, and overarching business objectives, and delving into the intricate technical details of product development. This duality of expertise allows them to not only conceive ground-breaking product ideas but also shepherd them through the complex journey of development, testing, and successful market launch.

Their ability to seamlessly traverse these realms brings several benefits to organizations. Firstly, it streamlines communication between traditionally distinct teams, fostering collaboration between business and technical units. This enhanced collaboration leads to more informed decision-making, reduced misunderstandings, and improved efficiency in product development.

Secondly, these professionals are well-equipped to identify innovative opportunities that others might overlook. By combining their understanding of market trends and customer needs with technical feasibility assessments, they can propose and champion product ideas that are not only visionary but also viable.

Lastly, in a landscape where customer expectations are in a state of constant flux, professionals with hybrid skill sets are agile in responding to these shifts. They can adapt products swiftly to align with changing customer preferences, ensuring that the organization remains competitive and customer-centric.

The convergence of product management and technical product management has given rise to a new breed of professionals who are the architects of innovation and adaptability. Their unique ability to traverse the multifaceted landscape of modern business places them at the forefront of driving successful product development in an era where meeting customer expectations is paramount. As such, their role is not just a response to change but a proactive force in shaping the future of product management.

Mastering the Triad - Market, Business Goals, and Technology

Mastering the triad of understanding the market, aligning with business goals, and comprehending technology constitutes the crux of successful product management. This multifaceted approach requires a delicate balance between various domains to ensure that products are not only relevant but also innovative in a swiftly evolving tech landscape.

At the core of this triad is a profound understanding of the market. Product managers delve into comprehensive market research to discern customers' evolving needs, identify emerging trends, and understand the intricacies of the competitive landscape. This customer-centric approach is fundamental, allowing for the proactive development of products that resonate with the target audience.

Aligning with business goals is another critical dimension. Product managers must ensure that their products are strategically positioned to contribute meaningfully to the overarching objectives of the company. This involves a keen focus on revenue objectives, where considerations such as pricing strategies, monetization options, and financial performance tracking become integral aspects of decision-making.

Simultaneously, effective communication with technical teams is imperative. Product managers need to bridge the gap between the conceptualization of a product and its technical implementation. This involves articulating the business requirements in a manner that technical teams can comprehend and ensuring that the final product aligns with the company's technological capabilities. Staying closely connected to technological trends is vital, as it allows product managers to anticipate shifts and incorporate innovations seamlessly.

The synergy of these three elements ensures a holistic product management approach. A deep understanding of customers and market trends informs strategic decisions, and this, in turn, aligns the product with broader business goals. Effective communication with technical teams and a continuous awareness of technological advancements guarantee that the product not only meets current standards but also anticipates and adapts to future changes.

This triad mastery is not a static achievement but an ongoing process. As markets, businesses, and technologies evolve, successful product managers need to perpetually refine their understanding of the market, realign with shifting business objectives, and adapt to emerging technological landscapes. In doing so, they position themselves as dynamic leaders in the field, capable of navigating the complex interplay of market dynamics, business strategy, and technological innovation.

In essence, the convergence of product management roles necessitates a dynamic skill set that can navigate the intricacies of both business and technology. Those who can adeptly balance these spheres are poised to create products that resonate with customers, contribute to the company's bottom line, and remain at the forefront of technological innovation.

Three Rings of Product Management – Jock Busuttil

To drive this point of convergence I remember a good reference point to highlight, while going through the fundamentals of product management, is the Jock Busuttil's book "The Practitioner's Guide to Product Management" that emphasizes the importance of balancing these three rings to create successful products. Product managers need to find the right balance between these three rings to ensure that the product meets the needs of the customers, is profitable, and uses reliable and scalable technology.

Product: This ring focuses on the product itself, including its design, features, and functionality. Product managers need to ensure that the product meets the needs of the customers and is competitive in the market.

Business: This ring focuses on the business aspects of the product, including market research, pricing, and revenue. Product managers need to ensure that the product is profitable and aligns with the company's overall strategy.

Technology: This ring focuses on the technology used to create the product, including the software, hardware, and infrastructure. Product managers need to ensure that the technology is reliable, scalable, and secure.

In addition to the three rings of product management as described by Jock Busuttil, Product managers also need to be able to manage people and work with cross-functional teams, including designers, engineers, marketers, and salespeople building relationships, motivating people, and resolving conflict and learn to Influence without authority.

Part 1: The Essential Skills & Capabilities

The role of a product manager demands a diverse skill set and a wide range of capabilities. From technical proficiency to business acumen, effective communication to strategic thinking, a product manager must wear many hats. They need to understand the technology behind their products, align them with the company's business objectives, and work collaboratively with cross-functional teams. Market research and analytics skills help them make data-driven decisions, while their ability to think creatively fuels innovation.

In this dynamic landscape, product managers must continuously evolve, staying attuned to the latest technological trends and emerging market opportunities. This section explores these essential skills and capabilities, providing a comprehensive guide for aspiring and seasoned product managers alike.

Fundamental Skills

Drawing from three decades of my professional experience. I want to share few key skills that are irrespective of their role everyone must possess since each of these fundamental skills has played a pivotal role in shaping my career, and I believe they hold timeless significance for professionals across various fields.

Communication

Over the years, I've come to realize that communication is not merely about words; it's about the art of conveying ideas, emotions, and intentions effectively.

Communication, far beyond the realm of mere words, unveils itself as the artistry of conveying thoughts, emotions, and intentions with utmost precision and empathy. Through the passage of years, I've uncovered its profound significance — it's the keystone that has unlocked numerous opportunities. Be it the crafting of persuasive emails, the delivery of compelling presentations, or the immersion in meaningful dialogues, this skill has served as the key to countless doors.

The finesse of effective communication extends far beyond everyday interactions; it's the conduit through which cultural divides are bridged, complex deals are negotiated, and enduring relationships are forged. The ability to articulate thoughts with precision and infuse empathy into discussions has been transformative. It has empowered me to navigate diverse cultural landscapes, fostering understanding and collaboration where differences once stood.

In the intricate tapestry of professional life, this skill has been the linchpin of success. It's not merely about transmitting information but about crafting narratives that resonate, compelling stories that captivate, and messages that evoke desired responses. Precision in communication has been the bedrock of my achievements, allowing me to navigate intricate negotiations with finesse and clarity.

Moreover, the empathy woven into effective communication has been the cornerstone of lasting relationships. Understanding others' perspectives, acknowledging their emotions, and aligning intentions through dialogue has established bonds that transcend the superficial. It has been the enabler of trust, forming connections that endure and flourish beyond the boundaries of professional encounters.

Problem-Solving

In my journey, I've encountered a multitude of challenges, some seemingly insurmountable. Amidst the intricate tapestry of trials and tribulations, one steadfast companion has consistently accompanied me is the art of problem-solving. This invaluable skill has proven to be more than a mere tool; it has been a guiding force, allowing me to unravel complex issues, unearth root causes, and craft innovative solutions.

The journey of problem-solving is a profound exploration, akin to navigating a maze where every obstacle presents an opportunity for growth. Encountering challenges, instead of viewing them as impassable roadblocks, I've come to perceive them as crucial stepping stones in the path to personal and professional development. It's within the crucible of adversity that this skill truly shines, transforming challenges into fertile ground for innovation and evolution.

In essence, problem-solving is more than a strategic approach; it's a mindset, a lens through which challenges are reframed as opportunities. It has been the compass guiding me through crises, uncertainties, and uncharted territories. When faced with seemingly insurmountable hurdles, this skill has not only provided a roadmap for resolution but has instilled a resilience that turns setbacks into catalysts for advancement.

The transformative power of problem-solving extends beyond the immediate solution; it cultivates a mindset that perceives challenges as integral to the journey, not detours from it. Through the prism of this skill, every obstacle becomes a gateway to enhanced understanding, creative thinking, and ultimately, personal and professional growth. It is, indeed, the alchemy that turns adversity into opportunity on the path to mastery.

Problem-solving has remained my trusted companion, enabling me to dissect complex issues, identify root causes, and devise innovative solutions, the skill that has transformed adversity into opportunity, guiding me through crises and uncertainties.

Collaboration

Collaboration, as I've experienced it, is akin to conducting a symphony. It's about harmonizing diverse talents, perspectives, and strengths to create something greater than the sum of its parts. The orchestration of collaboration, as I've intimately experienced it, transcends the individual notes to create a melody that is far more profound than the sum of its parts. Collaborative efforts involve the delicate art of harmonizing diverse talents, perspectives, and strengths, weaving them together into a tapestry of collective brilliance.

In my journey, I've donned both the mantle of a team leader and a collaborative team member, each role providing unique insights into the transformative power of collaboration. Witnessing its effectiveness, I've come to recognize it as a dynamic skill capable of propelling creativity, productivity, and innovation to unparalleled heights. Collaboration, in its truest form, has been the catalyst for not just generating ideas but transforming them into tangible realities.

This skill has served as my guide in leading teams, emphasizing the orchestration of collective genius. Effective collaboration is more than a process; it's a culture that fosters an environment where ideas not only take root but flourish into visionary outcomes. Through collaborative endeavours, I've witnessed the magic that unfolds when individuals synergize their talents, creating a space where innovation thrives and organizational visions materialize.

Collaboration, therefore, is not a mere task to be accomplished; it's a skill that demands the nurturing of an ecosystem where diverse voices are not just heard but embraced. It's the conductor's wand that directs the symphony of talents toward a shared goal, creating a masterpiece that resonates far beyond the individual contributions. In the grand narrative of innovation, collaboration emerges as the transformative force that turns collective potential into extraordinary achievements.

Adaptability

Throughout my journey, I've borne witness to seismic transformations in technology, industry dynamics, and the very fabric of work environments. Adaptability, akin to a well-honed compass, has proven instrumental in not only weathering these transformative storms but also charting a course towards relevance and prosperity.

The art of adapting gracefully has been my compass, guiding me through the intricate maze of evolving landscapes. It's a skill that extends beyond a mere survival mechanism; it's the catalyst for thriving amidst constant change. The capacity to pivot when circumstances demand it has not only allowed me to navigate the ebb and flow of industry trends but has also empowered me to proactively embrace new technologies that define the forefront of progress.

Adaptability is the force that propels me to traverse the ever-shifting sands of organizational change with poise and confidence. As structures evolve and paradigms shift, the skill to adapt becomes the linchpin for maintaining not just relevance but a leadership stance amid the flux. It's not merely about weathering storms but about leveraging the winds of change to sail toward new horizons and seize emergent opportunities that define the cutting edge.

In essence, adaptability is the transformative skill that turns the uncertainties of change into opportunities for growth and advancement. It's a dynamic force that empowers individuals not only to survive but to thrive in a world where the only constant is change. Embracing this skill has been my compass, pointing the way forward in a world where evolution is the norm, and those who can adapt stand resilient, ready for whatever the future may unfold.

Time Management and Organizing

Amidst the chaotic symphony of modern life, time management and organizational prowess emerge as the virtuoso conductors orchestrating the harmonious rhythm of productivity. In the ever-accelerating pace of our endeavours, these skills serve as the guiding baton, ensuring that tasks are not merely completed but executed with precision and purpose. They are the architects of structure, the silent architects that transform chaos into a symmetrical arrangement.

The art of time management is not merely about ticking off tasks from a to-do list; it's a strategic dance with the clock. Over the years, I've refined this dance, learning to choreograph my work in a way that not only meets deadlines but ensures each movement contributes to the grand performance of my goals. It's about prioritizing with finesse, recognizing the crescendos of importance, and orchestrating a seamless progression through the various movements of my professional symphony.

Organizing, on the other hand, is the art of crafting a meticulously composed score. It's about creating a structure that resonates with efficiency and clarity. The skill to organize has been my instrument in sculpting a workspace where every note finds its place, every resource is readily available, and every project progresses in a harmonious cadence. This orchestration is not merely about order; it's about ensuring that every instrument in the ensemble contributes to the overall masterpiece.

The honing of these skills has bestowed upon me the invaluable gift of time – a currency more precious than gold. In a world where every second counts, the ability to navigate the cacophony of demands with grace has not only reduced stress but has allowed me to dwell in the rarefied space where productivity and fulfilment intersect. Time management and organizing are not just skills; they are the guardians of a delicate balance, fostering both professional achievement and personal well-being. They are the orchestrators that transform the tumult of tasks into a symphony of success.

Leadership

Leadership, in my view, is not defined by titles or authority but by influence and impact. My journey, adorned with experiences leading teams both modest and sprawling, has been a testament to the philosophy that effective leadership transcends titles and is deeply rooted in authenticity, vision, and the transformative power to inspire.

Authenticity forms the cornerstone of impactful leadership. It's the unwavering commitment to one's true self, resonating with sincerity and transparency. As a leader, I've discovered that authenticity is the magnetic force that forges genuine connections, earning the trust and respect of those I have the privilege to lead. In the realm of influence, authenticity serves as a beacon, illuminating the path for others to follow with confidence.

Vision, a compass that directs collective efforts toward a shared purpose, is the keystone of effective leadership. A leader's ability to articulate a compelling vision acts as a north star, guiding the team through uncharted territories. I've learned that a well-defined vision not only propels individual aspirations but also unites diverse talents under a common umbrella, fostering a sense of purpose that transcends individual roles.

Inspiration, the ethereal elixir of leadership, breathes life into visions and catalyzes collective efforts. The skill of inspiring others is a nuanced dance, where words, actions, and unwavering belief converge. In my leadership journey, I've witnessed the transformative impact of inspiration, turning challenges into triumphs, and hurdles into stepping stones. It's the ability to kindle the flame of enthusiasm, even in the face of adversity, that distinguishes a leader.

Empowerment, a guiding principle in my leadership philosophy, entails nurturing an environment where every team member feels not only heard but also valued. It's about fostering a culture of innovation where diverse perspectives are not only welcomed but celebrated. Effective leadership, as I've experienced it, is the art of providing the fertile ground for ideas to flourish, talents to blossom, and collective goals to be achieved.

In the mosaic of leadership styles, I've found a resonance with situational and natural leadership. At times, the situational demands of a dynamic environment call for adaptability and flexibility in leadership approaches. Natural leadership, an innate ability to guide and influence, has been a forte that emerges organically, grounded in a deep understanding of the team's dynamics and the nuances of the task at hand.

Leadership, therefore, is not a static role but a dynamic force that adapts to the rhythm of changing landscapes. It's the art of navigating uncertainties, inspiring confidence, and sculpting a collective journey toward shared aspirations. As I reflect on my leadership voyage, I recognize that titles may fade, but the impact of genuine influence endures, resonating as an indelible melody in the hearts and minds of those I've had the privilege to lead.

Technical Proficiency

In our digital age, technical proficiency has transcended its niche and become a universal language. Understanding the basics of technology has been a transformative force, enabling me to navigate the intricate nuances of our digital realm. Even in roles traditionally deemed non-technical, this proficiency has served as a bridge, fostering effective communication with colleagues and stakeholders. It's akin to speaking a shared language, transcending barriers and ensuring clarity in conveying ideas, strategies, and collaborative efforts.

The empowerment that comes with technical proficiency extends beyond the realm of communication. It forms the bedrock upon which informed decision-making rests. In a landscape where data-driven insights steer the course of actions, having a grasp of technological fundamentals equips me to interpret, analyze, and leverage information to make strategic decisions that align with organizational objectives.

Adaptability to digital transformations, a hallmark of our age, hinges on a foundational understanding of technology. I've observed that technical proficiency provides a compass to navigate the ever-shifting terrain of technological advancements. It's not merely about keeping pace with the latest trends but about embracing them with a discerning eye, understanding their implications, and strategically incorporating them into the professional toolkit.

Moreover, technical proficiency serves as a catalyst for innovation. In non-technical roles, it sparks a creative synergy where ideas are not hindered by technological constraints but fuelled by a nuanced understanding of what technology can enable. It's this intersection of creativity and technical know-how that breeds innovative solutions, fostering a culture of continuous improvement and progress.

As I reflect on the significance of technical proficiency in my professional journey, I see it not as an isolated skill but as a dynamic force that amplifies effectiveness, enhances collaboration, and fortifies decision-making. In the digital age, where every sector is touched by the transformative hand of technology, this proficiency emerges as a universal currency, enriching professional endeavours and contributing to the collective evolution of industries.

Emotional Intelligence

Amidst the myriad challenges, the most impactful and intricate ones often emanate from the realm of human interactions. In this landscape where emotions shape perceptions and relationships, I've discovered the paramount role of emotional intelligence as an invaluable compass.

Emotional intelligence, the nuanced ability to comprehend and navigate the intricacies of emotions, has emerged as a guiding light in the complex mosaic of workplace dynamics. It extends beyond a mere recognition of emotions; it involves a deep understanding and management of these emotional currents that course through professional relationships. This skill has proven instrumental in transforming workplace challenges into opportunities for growth and collaboration.

Navigating the ebbs and flows of workplace dynamics requires more than technical prowess or strategic acumen; it demands an acute awareness of the emotional currents shaping interactions. Emotional intelligence serves as a beacon, allowing me to decipher unspoken cues, understand varying perspectives, and respond with empathy and tact. It's the difference between merely addressing conflicts and forging resolutions that strengthen relationships and foster a positive work environment.

One of the hallmarks of emotional intelligence is its transformative impact on conflict resolution. In the crucible of differing opinions and competing interests, this skill has empowered me to navigate through conflicts with finesse. Instead of escalating tensions, emotional intelligence enables me to seek common ground, fostering a culture where diverse viewpoints coalesce into innovative solutions.

Effective negotiation, a cornerstone of professional success, is elevated by the finesse of emotional intelligence. Understanding the motivations, concerns, and aspirations of colleagues and collaborators allows for negotiations that transcend the transactional and venture into the realm of mutual benefit. It's a skill that transforms negotiations from zero-sum games into collaborative endeavours, creating win-win outcomes.

Beyond its immediate applications, emotional intelligence permeates the very fabric of leadership, enabling me to create a positive work environment. By recognizing and responding to the emotional needs of my team, I've cultivated a culture of trust, open communication, and collaboration. It's this emotional resonance that engenders a sense of belonging and motivates individuals to contribute their best.

As I reflect on the profound impact of emotional intelligence on my journey, I recognize it not only as a skill but as a transformative force. It's the glue that binds teams, the compass that navigates interpersonal challenges, and the catalyst that propels professional growth. In the intricate dance of human interactions, emotional intelligence emerges as a silent yet powerful orchestrator, harmonizing the collective efforts of individuals and fostering an environment where everyone can thrive.

Analytical Skills

In an era defined by data, analytical skills have become indispensable. They've allowed me to transform vast amounts of information into actionable insights. At the heart of analytical prowess lies the ability to decipher patterns, trends, and correlations within the vast sea of data. This skill transcends the mere comprehension of numbers; it involves the art of distilling meaningful narratives from the raw data canvas. Whether immersed in the analysis of market trends, evaluating project performance, or steering strategic decisions, analytical skills empower me to navigate the intricate landscape of business with clarity and precision.

Market trends, in their dynamic and ever-changing nature, are a crucible for analytical acumen. The ability to scrutinize and interpret market data allows for not only a comprehensive understanding of current dynamics but also the foresight to anticipate future shifts. Analytical skills enable me to identify emerging opportunities, assess competitive landscapes, and align strategies with the evolving market, thus positioning businesses for success in a competitive environment.

Assessing project performance demands more than a retrospective glance; it requires the keen eye of analytical scrutiny. By dissecting project data, I can glean insights into efficiency, identify areas for improvement, and optimize future endeavours. Analytical skills serve as a diagnostic tool, allowing me to measure success, learn from setbacks, and continuously enhance project outcomes.

Strategic decision-making, the cornerstone of effective leadership, is greatly fortified by the analytical lens. Whether formulating business strategies, allocating resources, or navigating uncertainties, analytical skills provide a structured framework for decision-makers. The ability to interpret complex data sets fosters informed decision-making, mitigates risks, and maximizes the likelihood of success.

In essence, analytical skills are not just about interpreting data; they represent a transformative capacity to convert information into actionable intelligence. This skill has been my ally in deciphering the language of data, unveiling insights that shape informed decisions and drive tangible outcomes. As industries continue to evolve in the era of big data, the mastery of analytical skills remains a beacon illuminating the path toward success in a landscape where data is not just information but a strategic asset.

Customer Focus

Regardless of the industry, understanding and prioritizing customer needs has been paramount. It's a skill that has guided my product development efforts, marketing strategies, and overall business approach. Placing the customer at the center has not only driven innovation but also fostered loyalty and growth.

Placing the customer at the epicenter of product development transforms the process into a symphony of innovation. It demands an intimate comprehension of customer desires, pain points, and aspirations, allowing businesses to craft solutions that not only meet but exceed expectations. This customer-centric ethos ensures that every facet of a product resonates with end users, creating a profound sense of value and relevance.

In the realm of marketing, customer focus goes beyond promotional endeavours; it involves crafting narratives that deeply resonate with the target audience. By comprehending customer motivations, preferences, and communication channels, businesses tailor their messaging to address unique needs. This approach transforms marketing into a powerful tool for building connections and fostering brand loyalty, as it speaks directly to the hearts and minds of consumers.

The impact of customer focus extends beyond isolated facets of business, permeating the overall approach. Businesses that prioritize the customer experience in every interaction cultivate an environment of trust and satisfaction. This holistic approach involves aligning organizational processes, policies, and values with the aim of delivering exceptional value to customers. By doing so, businesses not only retain existing customers but also attract new ones through positive word-of-mouth and reputation building. In essence, customer focus becomes a guiding philosophy that transforms the operational fabric of organizations, fostering enduring success in a competitive landscape.

Ethical Judgment and Integrity

Throughout the trajectory of my career, I have encountered a myriad of ethical dilemmas, each presenting a unique challenge to the principles I hold dear. In the face of these complex scenarios, the commitment to upholding ethical judgment and integrity has been non-negotiable, forming the very essence of my professional identity.

The compass of ethical judgment has been my unwavering guide in navigating the intricate landscape of decision-making. Even in the midst of challenging choices, I have adhered to a set of principled values that transcend the immediate gains or losses. This commitment ensures that each decision is grounded in a moral framework, contributing to the cultivation of a workplace culture steeped in trust and reliability.

Integrity, as the bedrock of my professional reputation, has been the cornerstone upon which lasting relationships are built. It goes beyond the superficial gloss of transactions; it is a commitment to honesty, transparency, and accountability. Colleagues, partners, and stakeholders alike have come to trust not only in the quality of the work delivered but also in the ethical underpinnings that define every professional interaction.

The enduring impact of ethical judgment and integrity extends beyond individual decisions to influence the broader organizational ethos. By consistently embodying these values, a culture of ethical responsibility is fostered, permeating through teams and shaping collective behaviour. In an era where trust is a precious commodity, the adherence to ethical principles stands as a testament to the enduring nature of professional relationships built on integrity.

Resilience – Survival of the fittest

Resilience, akin to the age-old adage of "survival of the fittest," has proven to be the unwavering spirit that propels me through the most formidable challenges in both professional and personal spheres. In the face of adversity, this indispensable skill has been my constant companion, shaping not only my ability to endure but also my capacity for growth.

Ambiguity, setbacks, and challenges, viewed through the lens of resilience, are transient phases that mark points of transformation and opportunity. The understanding that these are not insurmountable roadblocks but rather stepping stones toward personal and professional development has been a guiding principle. Resilience, as a mindset, prompts me to approach difficulties not as insurmountable barriers but as gateways to new possibilities.

The true test of resilience lies in its capacity to facilitate a rebound from failures and the assimilation of lessons from mistakes. It is not merely about weathering storms but emerging from them stronger, wiser, and more equipped for the journey ahead. Each setback becomes a fertile ground for learning, and mistakes serve as blueprints for improvement.

Beyond individual growth, resilience has been instrumental in shaping me into a natural leader. The ability to navigate challenges with composure, inspire perseverance in others, and foster a culture that embraces resilience as a shared value has become a hallmark of my leadership style. In the ever-evolving landscape of professional life, resilience stands as a beacon, guiding not just survival but the thriving evolution of both self and the teams I lead.

In essence, these skills have not only defined my professional journey but have also become the compass by which I navigate my personal life in the ever-changing landscape of the modern world. They are the threads that have woven together my career and wellbeing, and I have every confidence that they will continue to guide me, and others, toward success in the decades to come.

Technical Skills

Coming back to our topic pf product management, In the modern time, technical skills have emerged as an indispensable asset, serving as the linchpin that binds together the intricate threads of technology, strategy, and user experience for the product manager. While the role of a product manager may not entail hands-on coding, a foundational understanding of the technology driving their products is not merely advantageous; it is a fundamental necessity.

In the contemporary landscape of product management, technical skills have become an indispensable cornerstone, serving as the linchpin that interconnects the intricate threads of technology, strategy, and user experience for the product manager. While the product manager's role may not necessitate hands-on coding, a foundational understanding of the technology steering their products is not merely advantageous; it is a fundamental necessity.

Enabling Effective Collaboration

A primary advantage of technical proficiency for product managers lies in their ability to engage in substantive discussions with engineers and technical experts. Speaking the language of technology, they establish effective collaboration and bridge the often-wide communication gap between technical and non-technical teams. This fluency empowers them not only to convey their product vision effectively but also to understand and appreciate the intricacies and challenges that the engineering team encounters throughout the product development process.

Comprehensive Decision-Makin

Moreover, possessing a foundational understanding of the technology stack provides product managers with a comprehensive view of the product's capabilities and limitations. This knowledge proves invaluable when making critical decisions about feature prioritization, resource allocation, and crafting long-term product roadmaps. It ensures that the product manager's vision aligns seamlessly with what is technically feasible, significantly enhancing the product's prospects for success.

While product managers may not be directly responsible for writing lines of code, their technical proficiency equips them to orchestrate the intricate interplay of technology, strategy, and user experience. This orchestration is vital to ensuring that their products are not only visionary in concept but also technically robust, capable of addressing the challenges and seizing the opportunities presented by the ever-evolving technological landscape. The benefits of technical proficiency for product managers are manifold.

One of the primary advantages of technical proficiency for product managers lies in their ability to engage in substantive discussions with engineers and technical experts. Speaking the language of technology, they establish effective collaboration and bridge the often-wide communication gap between technical and non-technical teams. This fluency empowers them not only to convey their product vision effectively but also to understand and appreciate the intricacies and challenges that the engineering team encounters throughout the product development process.

Moreover, possessing a foundational understanding of the technology stack provides product managers with a comprehensive view of the product's capabilities and limitations. This knowledge proves invaluable when making critical decisions about feature prioritization, resource allocation, and crafting long-term product roadmaps. It ensures that the product manager's vision aligns seamlessly with what is technically feasible, significantly enhancing the product's prospects for success.

Adaptability and Strategic Prowess

In essence, their technical acumen serves as the linchpin for ensuring that products are not just well-conceived but also well-executed, effectively meeting the expectations of both customers and the rapidly advancing tech industry. This adaptability and strategic prowess are crucial in a world where technology is in a constant state of flux.

The convergence of business and technology in the realm of product management heralds a new era where professionals with hybrid skill sets are in high demand. Those who can seamlessly traverse between the realms of business strategy and technical intricacies find themselves uniquely positioned to drive innovation, ensuring not only technical feasibility but also meeting the ever-evolving expectations of customers in a rapidly changing landscape.

Future Landscape

In conclusion, the narrative of technical proficiency in product management is not just about understanding code; it's about grasping the essence of technology as a strategic enabler. It empowers product managers to navigate complexities, foster collaboration, and make informed decisions that lead to the creation of products that are not just technologically sound but also visionary and aligned with the demands of the market. As the landscape of technology continues to evolve, the role of technical proficiency in product management will only become more pronounced, underlining its status as an essential competency for those driving product success in the digital age.

The convergence of business and technology in the realm of product management heralds a new era where professionals with hybrid skill sets are in high demand. Those who can seamlessly traverse between the realms of business strategy and technical intricacies find themselves uniquely positioned to drive innovation, ensuring not only technical feasibility but also meeting the ever-evolving expectations of customers in a rapidly changing landscape.

In conclusion, the narrative of technical proficiency in product management is not just about understanding code; it's about grasping the essence of technology as a strategic enabler. It empowers product managers to navigate complexities, foster collaboration, and make informed decisions that lead to the creation of products that are not just technologically sound but also visionary and aligned with the demands of the market. As the landscape of technology continues to evolve, the role of technical proficiency in product management will only become more pronounced, underlining its status as an essential competency for those driving product success in the digital age.

Business Skills

In the multifaceted role of a product manager, possessing robust business skills is akin to having a compass that guides decision-making and strategy. Beyond understanding the technical intricacies of their products, product managers must also comprehend the broader business context in which their products operate.

In the multifaceted role of a product manager, possessing robust business skills is akin to having a compass that guides decision-making and strategy. Beyond understanding the technical intricacies of their products, product managers must also comprehend the broader business context in which their products operate.

Alignment with Business Goals

First and foremost, this demands a deep understanding of the company's overarching business goals. Product managers need to align their product strategies with these goals, ensuring that every product decision contributes to the company's success. Whether it's driving revenue growth, expanding market share, or enhancing customer satisfaction, a product manager's actions must align with the broader organizational objectives.

Financial Management Proficiency

Additionally, proficiency in financial management is essential. Product managers are often tasked with developing and managing budgets for their products. This involves allocating resources effectively, making trade-offs between competing priorities, and ensuring that the product remains financially viable throughout its lifecycle. Tracking product performance against key financial metrics allows them to make data-driven decisions and adjust strategies as needed to maximize ROI.

Driving Tangible Business Value

Ultimately, strong business skills empower product managers to make informed decisions that not only meet customer needs but also drive tangible business value. By navigating the intersection of technology and business, they ensure that their products not only resonate with users but also contribute significantly to the company's bottom line.

The role of a product manager is multifaceted, demanding a comprehensive skill set that spans technology, user experience, and business acumen. This holistic approach ensures that products are not only technically sound but also strategically aligned with the company's vision and financial objectives. As the bridge between technology and business, product managers are well-equipped to steer their products toward success.

Additionally, proficiency in financial management is essential. Product managers are often tasked with developing and managing budgets for their products. This involves allocating resources effectively, making trade-offs between competing priorities, and ensuring that the product remains financially viable throughout its lifecycle. Tracking product performance against key financial metrics allows them to make data-driven decisions and adjust strategies as needed to maximize ROI.

Ultimately, strong business skills empower product managers to make informed decisions that not only meet customer needs but also drive tangible business value. By navigating the intersection of technology and business, they ensure that their products not only resonate with users but also contribute significantly to the company's bottom line.

People Skills

Product managers need to be able to work effectively with people from different backgrounds and disciplines where diverse teams collaborate to bring a vision to life, people skills emerge as the glue that binds ideas, expertise, and efforts into a cohesive whole. Product managers are not solitary figures; they are orchestrators of cross-functional harmony, requiring a unique set of interpersonal capabilities.

Product managers must articulate their vision, strategy, and goals clearly and persuasively to teams comprised of individuals from various backgrounds and disciplines. Few of such skills allows them to foster a shared understanding and a unified sense of purpose, ensuring that everyone is aligned towards a common objective. Let's elaborate on the significance of people skills in the role of a product manager:

Working Effectively Across Diverse Teams

In the dynamic world of product management, diverse teams come together to bring a product vision to life. These teams comprise individuals with varying backgrounds, expertise, and disciplines. People skills become the linchpin that binds these diverse elements into a cohesive whole. Product managers are not solitary figures but orchestrators of cross-functional harmony, demanding a unique set of interpersonal capabilities.

Effective Communication

At the core of people skills lies effective communication. Product managers must excel at articulating their vision, strategy, and goals clearly and persuasively to teams composed of individuals from different backgrounds and disciplines. This skill enables them to foster a shared understanding and a unified sense of purpose, ensuring that everyone is aligned towards a common objective. Importantly, communication is a two-way street. In addition to articulating their vision, product managers must be active listeners, receptive to feedback and input from their team members. This open dialogue fosters a culture of trust and collaboration, where everyone feels valued and respected.

Building and Nurturing Relationships

Building relationships is not just a soft skill but a strategic asset. Product managers must cultivate strong relationships with engineers, designers, marketers, and other stakeholders. These relationships are the lifeblood of effective collaboration, encouraging knowledge sharing and creating an environment of trust and cooperation. Moreover, relationship building is an ongoing process. It is not enough to build relationships with stakeholders at the start of a project; product managers must nurture these relationships throughout the development process. This involves regular communication, transparent decision-making, and a commitment to supporting the success of their team members.

Motivation and Empathy

Motivation is another vital aspect of people skills. Product managers must inspire their teams, igniting passion and commitment towards the product's success. This ability to motivate is rooted in empathy — understanding what drives each team member, recognizing their contributions, and providing the support and resources needed for their growth and success. Motivation is more than just giving pep talks; it involves creating a supportive and inspiring work environment where team members feel valued for their contributions and have the opportunity to learn and grow. This involves setting clear goals, providing regular feedback, and celebrating successes.

In essence, people skills are not merely a complement to the technical and business aspects of product management; they are the conduits through which ideas are transformed into reality. Product managers who excel in these skills become effective collaborators, leaders, and motivators, capable of steering cross-functional teams towards the realization of their product vision. People skills are essential for product managers in all aspects of their role, from gathering user feedback to negotiating with stakeholders. By developing their people skills, product managers can become more effective leaders, collaborators, and communicators, ultimately leading to greater success for their products and organizations.

Product managers who excel in these skills become effective collaborators, leaders, and motivators, capable of steering cross-functional teams towards the realization of their product vision.

Capabilities that shape the Role

While skills provide the foundation, it is a product manager's capabilities that drive the engine of product success. These capabilities encompass a range of strategic and tactical proficiencies that enable them to navigate the complex landscape of product development, from ideation to post-launch analysis.

Being a Product Strategist

Product strategy is the compass that guides a product manager through the intricate landscape of product development, ensuring every step aligns with a meticulously defined vision. In my three decades of experience, I've witnessed the transformative power of a well-crafted product strategy. It serves as the linchpin, connecting a company's overarching business goals with the dynamic demands of the market. Thus it is an indispensable tool in a product manager's arsenal. It's the guiding force that empowers product managers to create products that not only meet market needs but also drive business success. By meticulously considering market dynamics, customer needs, and overarching business goals, product managers can craft and execute a product strategy that leads to success in the dynamic world of modern business.

Consider Product strategy as the harmonious interplay of visionary thinking and pragmatic planning, a fusion of inspiration and execution, weaving the narrative of a product's journey, from the moment of conception to its profound impact on the market. By crafting clear objectives and translating them into a well-defined roadmap, product managers ensure that this journey is not a meandering path but a purposeful odyssey toward success.

At its core, product strategy is about envisioning the product's journey, from its inception to its ultimate impact on the market. It calls for product managers to embody the roles of both visionaries and tacticians, charting a clear path forward. This journey commences with the establishment of clear and actionable objectives, a roadmap that sets the direction of the product's evolution.

The Visionary and The Tactician

Product managers are not just custodians of a product; they are its architects and storytellers. They must envision the product's destiny, foresee its role in customers' lives, and imagine the transformation it can bring. This visionary aspect of is the spark that ignites the entire journey.

But vision without a roadmap is merely a dream. This is where the tactician emerges. Product managers must translate their vision into concrete, actionable objectives. These objectives aren't vague aspirations but tangible, measurable milestones that illuminate the path ahead.

The Art of Setting Clear Objectives

Clear objectives serve as the guiding stars of product strategy. They define what the product aims to achieve, painting a vivid picture of its purpose and impact. Whether it's increasing user engagement, expanding market reach, or enhancing profitability, these objectives are the north on the product's compass.

The roadmap: Navigating the Journey

Setting objectives is akin to plotting the destination on a map, but the journey requires a roadmap. The product roadmap is the tactical plan, the turn-by-turn directions that outline the critical features, milestones, and strategies needed to reach those objectives. It's the granular detail that transforms the vision into a step-by-step plan.

Imagine, for instance, that your objective is to enhance user engagement by introducing a new feature. The roadmap outlines the phases of development, testing, and deployment. It details how the feature will align with user needs and market trends, ensuring that every step of the journey advances the product's evolution.

Alignment with Business Goals

A critical facet of product strategy is alignment. Ensuring that the product's vision and objectives are in perfect harmony with the company's broader business goals is paramount. It is not a mere checkbox on the product manager's to-do list; it's the very essence of effective product strategy. It's the commitment to sail in the same direction as the organization, knowing that this synchronized journey is the path to mutual success. This alignment serves as the lighthouse, guiding every effort and resource invested in the product toward meaningful contributions to the organization's overarching success, it is nothing short of a compass, directing every move, every decision, and every resource allocation towards the ultimate success of the organization.

The Crucial Facet of Alignment

Imagine a symphony orchestra playing a masterpiece. Each instrument contributes its unique sound, but it's the conductor who ensures that every note harmonizes seamlessly. In the realm of product management, alignment with business goals is akin to that conductor, orchestrating a harmonious performance.

A Symphony of Purpose

At the heart of this alignment lies the idea that a product should not operate in isolation. Instead, it should be a strategic instrument that resonates with the overarching objectives of the organization. It's not just about building something; it's about building something that contributes meaningfully to the company's prosperity.

Harmony in Action

Alignment with business goals ensures that every effort poured into a product is purposeful. It means that the features developed, the resources allocated, and the strategies employed are all in sync with what the organization aims to achieve. It's a deliberate choice to move forward in a way that advances not only the product but the entire company.

The Lighthouse in the Storm

Picture a ship navigating through treacherous waters. In the darkest of nights, a lighthouse serves as a beacon, guiding the ship safely to harbour. Similarly, alignment with business goals acts as a luminous guide, especially in the turbulent seas of the business world. It ensures that product managers and their teams stay on course, even when faced with challenges and uncertainties.

Thus when product strategy and business goals are aligned, every note played, every feature developed, and every resource allocated becomes a meaningful and purposeful contribution to the symphony of success.

Strategic Resource Allocation

Strategic resource allocation is another pivotal element of product strategy. Product managers must possess the acumen to assess and allocate resources effectively, whether it's budget, talent, or time. This allocation must be agile, capable of adapting to the ever-evolving market dynamics and business landscape.

The Pivotal Role of Strategic Resource Allocation

Imagine a general strategizing for a crucial battle. Every soldier, every piece of equipment, and every minute of time must be allocated with precision. Similarly, in the realm of product management, strategic resource allocation is about ensuring that every resource is a force multiplier, contributing significantly to the product's triumph.

Budget, Talent, and Time: The Trifecta of Resources

At the core of strategic resource allocation lie three critical components: budget, talent, and time. These are the currencies of product development, and their judicious allocation determines the project's trajectory. Effective budgeting ensures financial sustainability; tapping into the right talent pool fosters innovation, and time management guarantees timely market entry.

Agility in Allocation

The business landscape is not a static painting; it's a dynamic, ever-changing masterpiece. Hence, strategic resource allocation must be agile. It's about adapting swiftly to evolving market dynamics, adjusting sails when the winds of consumer preferences shift, and realigning resources when new opportunities or challenges emerge.

Akin to Chess, Not Checkers

Strategic resource allocation in product strategy is akin to playing chess, not checkers. It involves thinking several moves ahead, anticipating needs, and positioning resources strategically. It's not just about the present; it's about setting the stage for future triumphs.

The Symphony of Success

Imagine an orchestra where each instrument is given just the right amount of focus and time to shine. Similarly, strategic resource allocation orchestrates the elements of product development, ensuring that each component receives the attention it deserves. This symphony of allocation is what transforms a product from mere concept to a market triumph.

Thus in the larger canvas of product strategy, strategic resource allocation is the thread that weaves success. It's about making conscious choices, aligning resources with objectives, and ensuring that every investment propels the product towards its goals. When executed with finesse, strategic resource allocation becomes a key differentiator, setting the stage for a product's ascendancy in a competitive market. It's not just about managing resources; it's about orchestrating a symphony of success.

The Blueprint for Success

In essence, the product strategy is the blueprint that informs a product manager's decisions and actions. It provides the product's trajectory, ensuring that it not only addresses market needs but also propels the company toward its strategic objectives. By adeptly crafting and executing a product strategy, product managers ascend to the role of architects, not just of products but of market success. It's the paradigm that informs every decision, every action, and every resource allocation, ensuring that a product not only caters to market needs but also propels the entire company toward its strategic zenith. this blueprint is the product strategy. It's the guiding star that informs every decision, every action, and every resource allocation, ensuring that a product not only caters to market needs but also propels the entire company toward its strategic zenith.

At its core, product strategy embodies a product manager's dual role as both visionary and tactician. It's about envisioning the entire journey of a product, from its inception as a concept to its final impact on the market. This journey commences with the establishment of clear and actionable objectives, akin to the cornerstones upon which a skyscraper rises.

Imagine the intricate dance of cogs in a well-oiled machine. That's what strategic alignment within product strategy accomplishes. It ensures that the product's vision and objectives are perfectly synchronized with the broader business goals. It's the North Star, guiding every endeavour and resource invested in the product toward meaningful contributions to the organization's overarching success.

Resource allocation within the product strategy is akin to orchestrating a symphony. Budgets, talent, and time are the instruments, each playing a vital role in the product's crescendo. It's about ensuring that these resources are deployed strategically, fostering innovation and progress.

Further, In a world of ever-evolving market dynamics, agility is paramount. The product strategy must be capable of adapting swiftly, akin to a skilled navigator adjusting the sails to changing winds. It anticipates market shifts, seizes new opportunities, and navigates challenges with finesse.

The product strategy is the architect's blueprint for success. It's the art of crafting a vision into reality, translating ideas into products, and concepts into market triumphs. It is not merely a document; it's a dynamic, living framework that guides every facet of product management. By adeptly crafting and executing a product strategy, product managers ascend to the role of architects, not just of products but of market success. They are the visionaries who breathe life into ideas, the leaders who navigate complexities, and the strategists who drive both product and organizational triumph.

Benefits of a Well-Defined Product Strategy

A well-defined product strategy offers a plethora of benefits, serving as a guiding light for both product teams and organizations. It fosters focus, alignment, clarity, efficiency, and agility. These advantages collectively contribute to the creation of products that resonate with customers and drive organizational growth.

A well-defined product strategy serves as a guiding light for both product teams and organizations, offering a plethora of benefits. One key advantage is the fostering of focus. By clearly outlining specific goals and objectives, a product strategy directs the efforts of the product team toward the most important tasks, ensuring that everyone is working cohesively towards shared objectives. This focus is instrumental in avoiding wasted time and resources, allowing the team to concentrate on what truly matters for the success of the product.

Another significant benefit is alignment. A robust product strategy ensures that the efforts put into product development align seamlessly with the broader business goals of the organization. This alignment is crucial for a synchronized and harmonious operation where every product-related endeavour contributes meaningfully to the overarching success of the company. It acts as a unifying force, guiding teams to work collaboratively towards common objectives and enhancing the overall efficiency of the organization.

Clarity is also a hallmark benefit of a well-defined product strategy. It provides clear direction not only to the product team but also to stakeholders and customers. With a shared understanding of the product's vision and objectives, everyone involved is on the same page, reducing confusion and enhancing communication. This clarity is invaluable for making informed decisions, as it ensures that everyone is working towards a common goal, fostering a sense of purpose and unity within the organization. In essence, a well-crafted product strategy acts as a multifaceted tool, driving focus, alignment, and clarity for both product teams and the broader organization.

To conclude, Product strategy is an indispensable tool in a product manager's arsenal. It's the guiding force that empowers product managers to create products that not only meet market needs but also drive business success. By meticulously considering market dynamics, customer needs, and overarching business goals, product managers can craft and execute a product strategy that leads to success in the dynamic world of modern business.

At its core, product strategy is about envisioning the product's journey – from its inception to its ultimate impact on the market. It requires product managers to act as both visionaries and tacticians, charting a clear path forward. This begins with setting clear objectives that outline what the product aims to achieve. These objectives are not just a wish list; they are actionable and measurable goals that provide a sense of direction.

Alignment is another critical facet of product strategy. Product managers must ensure that the product's vision and objectives are in perfect sync with the company's broader business goals. This alignment ensures that every effort and resource invested in the product contributes meaningfully to the organization's success.

Strategic resource allocation is also a vital to assess and allocate resources, whether it's budget, talent, or time – to support the product's journey. This allocation must be agile, adapting to evolving market needs and business dynamics.

The product strategy is the blueprint that guides a product manager's decisions and actions. It provides a clear trajectory for the product, ensuring that it fulfils market needs while advancing the company's strategic objectives. By adeptly crafting and executing a product strategy, product managers become architects of not just products, but also of market success.

Market Research

A deep understanding of market dynamics is imperative. Product managers are tasked with conducting comprehensive market research to gain insights into customer behaviours, preferences, and pain points. This knowledge forms the foundation upon which informed product decisions are made, ensuring that the product resonates with the target audience.

Market research stands as the cornerstone upon which successful product strategies are built. It is the process through which product managers gain deep insights into the intricate web of market dynamics, customer behaviours, desires, and pain points. This knowledge, meticulously acquired and analyzed, forms the bedrock upon which informed product decisions rest. Market research is not merely a step in the product development process; it is an ongoing journey of discovery. It begins with identifying the target audience – understanding who the customers are, what motivates them, and what challenges they face. This demographic and psychographic understanding paves the way for product managers to tailor their offerings to precisely meet these needs.

Moreover, market research extends beyond customer personas. It delves into the competitive landscape, exploring the strengths, weaknesses, opportunities, and threats that surround the product. This comprehensive view allows product managers to position their offerings strategically, differentiating them in the crowded marketplace.

Market research is a multifaceted process that equips product managers with crucial insights to make informed decisions throughout the product development lifecycle. Here, we'll delve into the strategies, references, and approaches that product managers can employ for effective market research

Customer Personas

Developing customer personas is a fundamental approach to comprehending your target audience deeply. It requires product managers to create rich and detailed profiles of their ideal customers. These personas are not just based on assumptions; rather, they are grounded in real data and insights gathered through a variety of methods.

The approach typically begins with surveys and interviews. Product managers reach out to existing customers or potential users to understand their needs, preferences, and pain points. These conversations are invaluable in uncovering the motivations that drive customers' decisions. For instance, a company offering financial services might discover that its customers are motivated by a desire for financial security and retirement planning.

To build these personas, references are primarily drawn from internal data sources. This includes mining customer databases, analyzing past purchase history, scrutinizing customer support interactions, and carefully considering customer feedback. By examining this data, product managers can identify recurring patterns, preferences, and pain points that are shared among their customer base.

Elaborating on the process, customer personas go beyond demographic information. They delve into the psyche of the customer. For example, a software company might create personas like "Marketing Manager Mary" or "IT Director David." These personas encompass details such as their job roles, goals (e.g., increasing website traffic), challenges (e.g., budget constraints), and preferred communication channels (e.g., email or social media).

By creating these detailed profiles, product managers gain a humanized understanding of their audience. This allows them to tailor products, marketing efforts, and customer experiences accordingly. Customer personas, when meticulously constructed, serve as compasses that guide product development, ensuring that every decision aligns with the real needs and desires of the target audience.

Competitor Analysis

Competitor analysis is a strategic approach that involves the systematic examination of your competitors' strategies, products, and market positioning. It's akin to studying the moves of chess opponents to anticipate their next play. Product managers employ various methodologies, including SWOT analysis (Strengths, Weaknesses, Opportunities, Threats), to identify areas where their product can differentiate itself effectively.

The approach begins with a thorough investigation of competitors' websites and product offerings. Product managers scrutinize every aspect, from features and pricing to user experience and messaging. They assess what competitors excel at and where they fall short. For instance, a company offering cloud storage solutions might find that a competitor offers superior file-sharing features but lacks a mobile app.

The primary reference for competitor analysis is external data. Product managers pore over customer feedback and reviews related to competitor products. They monitor industry publications for news and updates about competitors, seeking to identify shifts in strategy or new product launches. Additionally, social media and online communities can offer insights into customer sentiments and discussions about competing products.

Competitor analysis is about more than just keeping tabs on your rivals; it's about understanding their strengths and weaknesses. By conducting SWOT analyses, product managers can pinpoint opportunities to outperform competitors. For example, if a competitor's product receives praise for its features but criticism for its customer support, a product manager might prioritize improving customer support as a unique selling proposition. It's this meticulous evaluation of the competitive landscape that equips product managers with the intelligence to craft strategies that lead to market success.

Surveys and Questionnaires

Surveys and questionnaires represent a quantitative approach to gathering specific information from a larger sample of respondents. It's akin to taking a scientific survey to understand public opinions, but in this case, the focus is on your target audience. Product managers create structured sets of questions designed to elicit precise insights, and they collect data from participants, which can then be statistically analyzed to draw meaningful conclusions.

The approach typically involves a clear and systematic process. Product managers begin by defining their research objectives, which could range from assessing customer satisfaction to identifying pain points in a user journey. These objectives serve as the foundation upon which the survey questions are constructed.

References for surveys and questionnaires are both internal and external. Internally, product managers can leverage their existing customer databases and email lists to reach out to current customers. Externally, they might engage professional survey firms with expertise in research methodologies, or they can utilize online survey platforms like SurveyMonkey, Google Forms, or specialized market research tools.

Elaborating on the process, surveys allow product managers to gather data on customer preferences, pain points, satisfaction levels, and more. For instance, an e-commerce company might conduct a survey to understand why customers abandon their shopping carts. The results could reveal common issues such as unexpected shipping costs or a confusing checkout process.

Armed with this data, product managers can make data-driven decisions to improve the customer experience. They might prioritize initiatives to streamline the checkout process or offer more transparent pricing. Surveys and questionnaires, when executed effectively, offer a quantitative perspective on customer needs, allowing product managers to address pain points, fine-tune their products, and ultimately enhance customer satisfaction.

These three market research strategies. i.e. customer personas, competitor analysis, and surveys/questionnaires that represent essential tools in a product manager's arsenal. Each approach offers unique insights that, when carefully integrated, provide a comprehensive understanding of the market, customer preferences, and competitive landscape. By using these strategies strategically, product managers are equipped to make informed decisions, craft effective strategies, and drive their products toward market success.

The insights garnered from market research empower product managers to make informed decisions at every juncture of product development. From ideation to feature prioritization, from pricing strategies to marketing campaigns, market research serves as the guiding light, ensuring that the product not only resonates with the target audience but also thrives in a competitive ecosystem. In essence, it is the art of listening to the market's heartbeat and responding with precision and empathy.

Product Development & Build

Collaboration reigns supreme in product development, and product managers serve as the linchpin. In the intricate symphony of product development, collaboration takes center stage, and product managers assume the role of the orchestra conductor. This capability demands finesse in navigating the complex ecosystem of cross-functional teams, seamlessly uniting engineers, designers, marketers, and more. By fostering a harmonious collaboration, product managers ensure that the product not only meets the ever-evolving needs of the market but also remains in sync with the company's strategic objectives.

Collaboration is not merely a buzzword in product development; it is the lifeblood of innovation. Product managers must adeptly orchestrate this collaborative effort, aligning diverse skill sets and perspectives toward a common goal towards creation of a successful product. Effective collaboration begins with a shared vision. Product managers must ensure that every member of the team comprehends the overarching product vision, its strategic significance, and the role they play in bringing it to life. This alignment of purpose fosters a sense of ownership and commitment among team members.

Moreover, the product manager serves as a bridge between technical and non-technical teams, translating technical jargon into comprehensible language and vice versa. This bridging capability ensures that everyone speaks the same language, promoting effective communication and preventing misunderstandings that can derail the project. This capability to navigate and orchestrate cross-functional collaboration is the key to successful product development. It ensures that the product not only emerges as a solution to market needs but also advances the company's strategic goals. It transforms a diverse group of professionals into a united force, working harmoniously to transform a vision into a tangible, market-ready product.

Product Marketing

Launching and marketing a product effectively requires a distinct set of skills. Product managers need the capability to craft compelling product narratives, devise go-to-market strategies, and communicate the product's value proposition to customers. Launching and marketing a product is akin to orchestrating a grand symphony, and product managers are the conductors of this complex composition. It's a role that demands a distinct set of skills, a keen sense of strategy, and the ability to communicate the product's value proposition effectively. This capability is the cornerstone of a successful product introduction and establishing a resounding presence in the market.

At the heart of product marketing lies the art of storytelling. Product managers must possess the skill to craft compelling narratives that not only explain what the product does but also resonate with the aspirations and desires of the target audience. This narrative weaves together the product's features, benefits, and unique selling points into a captivating story that captures the imagination of potential customers. But storytelling alone is not enough; it must be complemented by a well-devised go-to-market strategy. Product managers must meticulously plan how the product will be introduced to the market, considering factors like timing, channels, and competitive positioning. This strategy is the roadmap that guides the product's journey from the development phase to the eager hands of customers.

Crafting Compelling Product Narratives

At the core of product marketing is the art of storytelling. It's about more than just listing the features and functionalities of a product; it's about creating a narrative that captivates the audience. Product managers need to possess the skill of weaving a compelling story around the product—one that not only explains what the product does but also taps into the aspirations, desires, and pain points of the target audience.

This narrative serves as the thread that connects the product's features, benefits, and unique selling points into a coherent and engaging story. It's akin to painting a vivid picture in the minds of potential customers, helping them visualize how the product fits into their lives and addresses their specific needs.

Consider, for instance, the launch of a new smartphone. It's not merely a device with advanced technology; it's a gateway to staying connected, capturing memories, and achieving productivity. The narrative crafted around it should evoke emotions, showcase how it enhances everyday experiences, and make potential customers eager to become a part of this story.

Devising Go-To-Market Strategies

Beyond storytelling, effective product marketing hinges on meticulous planning and strategy. Product managers are tasked with devising comprehensive go-to-market strategies that outline how the product will be introduced to the market. This involves a strategic roadmap that considers crucial factors such as timing, distribution channels, and competitive positioning.

A well-crafted go-to-market strategy is like a detailed orchestration plan for a symphony. It ensures that all elements of the product launch are harmoniously aligned. For instance, the timing of the launch should coincide with market trends or events that create a buzz. The choice of distribution channels should be in sync with where the target audience is most active.

Moreover, competitive positioning is pivotal. Product managers must assess the competitive landscape, identifying unique selling propositions and potential areas for differentiation. This strategic positioning helps the product stand out amidst the noise of the market.

Imagine launching a new software solution for businesses. The go-to-market strategy might involve a phased approach, initially targeting early adopters in a specific industry segment. The timing could align with a major industry conference where the product can be showcased, and partnerships with industry influencers can be leveraged for endorsements.

Communicating the Value Proposition

Crucially, product managers must also be adept at communicating the product's value proposition. This goes beyond listing features; it's about conveying how the product can solve specific problems or enhance the lives of customers. It involves empathizing with the customer's pain points and articulating how the product provides a solution.

This process entails deep empathy with the customer's pain points. Product managers need to understand the challenges the target audience faces and translate how the product provides a solution. It's about communicating the transformational impact the product can have on their lives.

For instance, consider a health and fitness app. It's not just about tracking steps and calories; it's a tool that empowers users to take control of their health, achieve fitness goals, and lead a healthier, more fulfilling life. Product managers must convey this value proposition, showcasing how the app can be a game-changer in users' fitness journeys.

In essence, product marketing is the art of making the product's presence felt in the market. It's about creating anticipation, excitement, and a deep understanding of why the product matters. With these capabilities— crafting compelling narratives, devising go-to-market strategies, and communicating the value proposition—product managers ensure that their products not only launch successfully but also continue to resonate with the audience, creating enduring value in the market.

Product marketing is the art of making the product's presence felt in the market. It's about creating anticipation, excitement, and a deep understanding of why the product matters. With this capability, product managers ensure that their products not only launch successfully but also continue to resonate with the audience, creating enduring value in the market.

Product Analytics

In the contemporary landscape of product management, the ability to harness the power of analytics stands as an indispensable skillset. Product managers are no longer mere custodians of products; they are data virtuosos, orchestrating a symphony of information to guide their decision-making processes. Proficiency in product analytics has become the compass that navigates them through the complex seas of user behaviours, performance optimization, and product innovation.

At its essence, product analytics is the art of translating raw data into actionable insights. Product managers are entrusted with the responsibility of not only collecting data but also diving deep into its analysis. It's about deciphering the story concealed within the numbers— a narrative that reveals how users interact with the product. Questions such as which features engage users the most, where they encounter friction, and how their behaviour evolves over time find their answers in the realm of product analytics.

Data Transformation into Actionable Insights

In the ever-evolving landscape of product management, data serves as the bedrock upon which informed decisions are built. Product managers are akin to explorers in this vast sea of data, tasked with navigating through a labyrinth of user interactions, behaviours, and performance metrics. While the raw data itself is a valuable resource, its true potential is unlocked when it is transformed into actionable insights.

Imagine a product manager at the helm of an e-commerce platform. Their mission is to enhance the user experience and, subsequently, boost conversions. To embark on this quest, they turn to data analytics. In their data trove, they unearth a significant trend: a substantial number of users abandon their shopping carts during the payment process. This revelation, in isolation, is informative but lacks the actionable essence.

The transformation into actionable insight commences with a deeper dive into the data. The product manager scrutinizes the user journey during the payment process, meticulously examining each step. As they immerse themselves in this digital voyage, patterns begin to emerge. They uncover that users frequently encounter complications with payment options, and excessive loading times exacerbate the frustration. These specific pain points, illuminated by data-driven exploration, become the linchpin of actionable insight.

Now armed with a profound understanding of the hurdles users face, the product manager takes on the role of a conductor, orchestrating a harmonious collaboration with the development team. Together, they craft a solution to streamline the payment process, eliminate complexities, and optimize loading times. This data-driven decision is not a shot in the dark; it's a targeted intervention aimed at addressing the root causes of cart abandonment.

As the changes are implemented and the data is monitored, the impact becomes evident. Cart abandonment rates begin to decline, and the user experience during the payment process improves. This transformation from raw data to actionable insight has not only stemmed the tide of lost customers but has also sculpted a more user-centric and conversion-friendly e-commerce platform.

In essence, data transformation into actionable insights is the alchemy of product management. It's the process of turning data into gold, where informed decisions are the currency that drives product enhancement and, ultimately, customer satisfaction. It's a skill that empowers product managers to navigate the labyrinth of data, extracting treasures of understanding that illuminate the path toward product improvement and market success.

Mastery of Key Metrics

A fundamental aspect of product analytics is the mastery of key metrics. Product managers must identify and monitor the metrics that have the most significant impact on their product's success. These metrics serve as guiding stars, illuminating the path toward growth, improvement, and overall product success. The mastery of key metrics stands as a fundamental pillar of success for product managers those are akin to captains of ships navigating through the vast ocean of data, and these metrics serve as their North Star, guiding them toward safe harbour of growth, improvement, and overall product triumph.

Consider a scenario where a product manager is at the helm of a mobile app. Within this bustling world of digital interactions, a plethora of metrics beckon for attention. However, the skill lies in discerning which metrics are the compass points that truly matter, which ones have the power to steer the ship in the right direction.

In this scenario, our product manager identifies user retention as one of these cardinal metrics. User retention serves as a litmus test for the app's success, reflecting its ability to not only attract but also retain users over time. As the product manager closely monitors retention rates, a nuanced story begins to emerge.

They notice a decline in user engagement following a recent app update. Instead of dismissing this as a mere statistical blip, they delve deeper. With an unwavering focus on mastering this key metric, they unearth valuable insights hidden within the data.

This relentless pursuit leads to a crucial revelation: a specific app feature introduced in the recent update has triggered user frustration. Armed with this knowledge, the product manager takes swift and decisive action. They collaborate with the development team to address the issue, rectifying the feature's shortcomings and optimizing the user experience.

The impact is palpable. User retention rates start to climb once more, and the user base becomes more satisfied and engaged. This is the result of mastery over a key metric, where the product manager's ability to identify, monitor, and act upon the most critical data point has steered the product toward success.

The mastery of key metrics is the art of choosing the right stars to navigate by in the vast expanse of data. It's about understanding that not all metrics are equal, and some hold the key to unlocking the full potential of a product. With this skill, product managers not only measure success but actively shape it, ensuring that the product remains on course for growth and continuous improvement.

Envisioning the Product's Future

The power of data analytics extends far beyond the realm of understanding the present. It serves as a potent tool for peering into the crystal ball of the product's future. This forward-looking facet of analytics involves a kind of data-driven clairvoyance, where trends and patterns from existing data are the building blocks for anticipating future user behaviour and the ever-evolving dynamics of the market.

Imagine a product manager steering the ship of a streaming service through the vast and ever-shifting seas of content consumption. In their arsenal is the treasure trove of user data, a rich tapestry woven with insights into how users interact with the service.

As they embark on their analytical journey, they notice a consistent surge in the consumption of a particular genre of content — let's say, documentaries. This isn't just a fleeting blip on the data radar; it's a persistent and upward trajectory. Rather than merely registering this observation and moving on, the product manager recognizes the potential within this trend.

It's akin to glimpsing a ripple on the surface of the water and realizing it might herald a tidal wave. In this case, the documentary genre is the ripple, and it signifies a growing and perhaps underserved demand among users.

With this insight, the product manager dons the mantle of a strategic visionary. They foresee the burgeoning appetite for documentaries and the potential to not only meet but exceed this demand. Armed with data-backed foresight, they craft a proposal — the creation of more documentary content and the design of tailored marketing campaigns to capitalize on this emerging trend.

This proactive approach isn't about chasing trends; it's about setting sail for them before they even appear on the horizon. By leveraging the power of data analytics to anticipate user preferences, this product manager positions the streaming service ahead of the curve. They are ready to meet user demands before they become mainstream, ensuring that the product remains not just relevant but pioneering in a landscape of ever-evolving content consumption.

In essence, product analytics isn't just a rear-view mirror; it's a crystal ball that empowers product managers to navigate toward a future where user needs are not just met but anticipated and fulfilled to the core.

Keeping Abreast of Technological Trends

In the rapidly evolving landscape of technology, product managers must stay informed about emerging trends and innovations. enhance their products, play a crucial role as navigators, charting a course through uncharted waters of emerging technologies. To do this effectively, they must stay vigilant, keeping their finger on the pulse of emerging trends and innovations. This foresight isn't just a luxury; it's a strategic imperative that empowers them to harness new technologies to enhance their products and stay ahead in the ever-competitive market.

Imagine a product manager at the helm of a popular fitness app, responsible for steering its trajectory in the digital fitness realm. They are well aware that the tech landscape is akin to a tempestuous sea, with new innovations emerging like surging waves.

One day, as they scan the technological horizon, they notice a significant and recurring trend of proliferation of wearable fitness trackers and health monitoring devices. This isn't a mere blip on their radar; it's a seismic shift in consumer behaviour, a paradigmatic change that's transforming how people approach their health and fitness.

Rather than dismissing this trend as a passing fad, the astute product manager recognizes it as an opportunity; a golden ticket to enhance their app's value proposition and align it with the broader movement of health-conscious consumers adopting wearable technology.

They envision a future where their fitness app seamlessly integrates with these wearables, offering users a holistic and data-rich fitness experience. Heart rate monitors, step counters, sleep trackers – all seamlessly woven into the app's fabric. This strategic move not only enhances the app's functionality but also positions it as a forward-thinking player in the fitness tech arena.

With this foresight, the product manager steers their ship toward this new technological frontier. They collaborate with developers, designers, and external common interest groups or communities to ensure a smooth integration of these newer elements into their product ecosystem. The result is a product that not only keeps pace with emerging trends but actively shapes them.

In essence, the ability to keep abreast of technological trends is not just a skill; it's a superpower that empowers product managers to ride the crest of innovation. By strategically leveraging new technologies, they ensure that their products remain not just relevant but pioneering in a world where tech evolution is the only constant. It's the difference between sailing through calm waters and conquering turbulent seas, and it's a testament to the foresight and adaptability of effective product managers.

Consider a product manager responsible for a fitness app. With the rise of wearable fitness trackers and health monitoring devices, they recognize an opportunity to integrate these technologies into their app. By doing so, they not only enhance the app's value proposition but also align it with the broader trend of health-conscious consumers adopting wearable tech. This move, albeit strategic keeps the product relevant and competitive in a tech-savvy market.

Technology is in a perpetual state of flux, and product managers must be vigilant in understanding how emerging technologies can strategically and creatively improve their products. They are tasked with seeing the bigger picture as to how their products fit into the broader company strategy and how these innovations can be leveraged to ensure continued relevance and competitiveness in the market.

In summary, proficiency in product analytics empowers product managers to decipher complex data, identify key performance indicators, envision the product's future, and strategically leverage emerging technologies. It's a multifaceted skill set that drives informed decision-making, optimization, and innovation in the ever-evolving landscape of product management. It empowers product managers to look into the future. By discerning patterns and trends within the data, they can spot opportunities for enhancement and innovation. It's a continuous journey of refinement, where each data-driven decision shapes the product's evolution and its alignment with ever-evolving user expectations.

In conclusion, product analytics is not just a skill; it's a transformative capability. It equips product managers with the tools to make informed decisions, optimize product performance, and uncover the treasures concealed within user behaviour. It empowers them to navigate the intricate intersection of data and product management, ensuring that their products evolve strategically, resonate with users, and remain at the forefront of technological advancement. It all boils down to product manager's capabilities to transform their skills into actionable strategies and tangible results. These competencies empower them to orchestrate the entire product lifecycle effectively, from inception and development to launch and optimization, ensuring that their products not only meet customer needs but also drive business success. Product managers have the opportunity to create products that make a real difference in people's lives. They also have the opportunity to work on cutting-edge technologies and learn from some of the brightest minds in the business.

Part 2: The Product Management Process

Product Management Process is a dynamic and cyclical journey. It's not a one-way street but a continuous loop of ideation, research, strategy, design, validation, launch, evaluation, and refinement. At its core, this process is about bringing innovative and valuable products to the market while adapting and evolving in response to the ever-changing landscape of customer needs and market dynamics. This part of the book provides a comprehensive overview of the product management process. Peeling off each layer of the process in phases..

Ideation Cycle

This is where the journey begins. Product managers are tasked with generating and evaluating new product ideas. This phase places a strong emphasis on creativity and innovation. It's about brainstorming, thinking outside the box, and exploring novel concepts. In this stage, the goal is to identify opportunities that align with the company's goals and market demands.

Market Research / Business Case

Once ideas are on the table, the product manager moves on to conducting comprehensive market research. This step is crucial for understanding customer needs and the dynamics of the market. It involves collecting and analyzing data to gain insights that will inform the product's development. In parallel, the product manager also builds a compelling business case to support the idea, showcasing its potential value and feasibility.

Product Strategy

With a deep understanding of customer needs and market dynamics, the product manager formulates a product strategy. This strategy is the roadmap that guides the product's development. It ensures that the product aligns with both the demands of the market and the overarching goals of the company. It's about setting clear objectives and a direction for the product's evolution.

Product Design

In the design phase, product managers dive into the specifics of product development. This includes User Experience (UX) design, which focuses on creating a user-friendly and engaging interface, and prototyping to visualize how the product will function. This stage bridges the gap between the abstract concept and a tangible product.

Product Validation

Once the product is designed, it's time to validate its concepts and designs with the target users. This step involves gathering feedback and conducting tests to ensure that the product genuinely meets user needs and expectations. User validation is a critical checkpoint before moving forward.

Product Launch

With a validated product in hand, the product manager embarks on the journey of launching it. This phase covers all the critical steps involved in making the product available to the market. It includes defining marketing strategies, deciding on distribution channels, and ensuring that the product reaches its intended audience effectively.

Product Evaluation

Post-launch, the work is far from over. The product manager now focuses on assessing the product's performance. This involves collecting data, feedback from customers and stakeholders, and evaluating whether the product is meeting its objectives and making the desired impact.

Product Iterations

Based on the insights gathered during evaluation, the product manager initiates a process of continuous improvement. Data-driven insights and customer feedback are used to make refinements and enhancements to the product. This iterative approach ensures that the product remains relevant and competitive.

Ideation Cycle

The Ideation Cycle is the inception of the product management process, where the spark of innovation is ignited. Product managers are entrusted with the essential task of generating and assessing new product ideas. This initial phase places a significant emphasis on fostering creativity and embracing innovation.

In the Ideation Cycle, product managers delve into the realm of brainstorming and idea generation. It's a period of unbridled creativity where they and their teams think beyond the conventional, seeking to break boundaries and explore uncharted territories. The goal is not to limit themselves but to push the boundaries of imagination.

One of the core objectives of this phase is to identify opportunities that not only resonate with the company's overarching objectives but also address the ever-evolving needs and demands of the market. It's about aligning the innovative concepts with the company's strategic goals and understanding the market dynamics.

The Ideation Cycle embodies a fundamental principle in product management: the recognition that innovation often springs from the unconventional. It's not about adhering strictly to existing paradigms but, rather, about daring to think outside the box. This is where product managers embark on a quest to discover ground breaking ideas that could potentially become the next big thing in their product portfolio.

Moreover, the Ideation Cycle is not limited to the product manager alone; it often involves collaborative efforts with cross-functional teams, fostering a culture of innovation within the organization. This team-oriented approach can generate a broader spectrum of ideas and ensure that the concepts generated are both feasible and aligned with the company's capabilities.

The Ideation Cycle - Fostering Innovation

In the realm of product management, the Ideation Cycle marks the inception of the entire product creation process. During this pivotal phase, product managers are tasked with the critical mission of generating and evaluating novel product ideas. A cornerstone of this initial step is the nurturing of creativity and the embracement of innovation.

Unleashing Creativity through Brainstorming

The Ideation Cycle, often called the idea generation phase, is where the seeds of innovation are sown. It's a dynamic and creative period where product managers, along with their teams, delve into the realm of brainstorming. This phase encourages a state of unbridled creativity, allowing teams to push the boundaries of conventional thinking. Here, the objective isn't to restrict ideas but to boldly venture beyond the limits of imagination.

Breaking the Mold of Convention

In this creative quest, product managers aim to break free from the shackles of convention. The status quo is not the guiding light; it's an exploratory journey into the uncharted territories of possibility. The ideation phase often fosters an environment where unconventional and even seemingly outrageous ideas are encouraged.

Aligning Innovation with Objectives

However, this phase isn't a free-for-all exercise in creativity. It's purposeful innovation. It's about aligning innovative concepts with the overarching objectives of the company and understanding the evolving needs and demands of the market. The creative sparks that emerge during the Ideation Cycle are not isolated; they're intended to be potential solutions to real-world problems or opportunities.

Team-Centric Ideation

Crucially, the Ideation Cycle is not an isolated mission for the product manager alone. It often involves cross-functional teams and encourages a collaborative approach to fostering innovation. This broader team-oriented perspective generates a broader spectrum of ideas and ensures that the concepts generated are both feasible and aligned with the company's capabilities.

The Creative Birthplace of Breakthroughs

In essence, the Ideation Cycle serves as the cradle of innovation in the product management process. It's where creativity takes its first breath, and innovation finds its initial sparks. These innovative ideas, once nurtured and developed, hold the potential to evolve into products that not only meet market demands but also drive a company's success. This initial phase sets the stage for the entire product management journey, and its value extends far beyond the drawing board.

Unleashing Creative Thinking

Within the Ideation Cycle, the emphasis is placed on cultivating a spirit of creativity and imaginative thinking. This phase is characterized by brainstorming sessions and idea generation where product managers and their teams are encouraged to break free from traditional constraints and explore uncharted territories. The primary objective is to transcend boundaries and delve into the realm of unconventional ideas.

In the Ideation Cycle, creativity takes center stage. It's a phase that celebrates imaginative thinking and encourages teams to break away from the constraints of convention. This is where brainstorming sessions come into play, becoming the birthplace of novel product ideas. Product managers, together with their teams, are urged to think beyond the ordinary, push the limits of their imagination, and venture into uncharted territories of possibility.

Breaking Free from Tradition

The Ideation Cycle is not a time for conformity or adhering to existing paradigms. Instead, it's a period of exploration, where the objective is to break free from the traditional molds of thought. It's a journey into the unknown, where the status quo is left behind, and teams are empowered to challenge the expected, question the usual, and embrace the unusual.

Venturing into the Unconventional

In essence, this phase dares product managers and their teams to think beyond the confines of convention. It's a platform for exploring bold, unconventional, and sometimes even seemingly outrageous ideas. Rather than inhibiting creativity with restrictions, the Ideation Cycle encourages the emergence of ground breaking concepts.

The Quest for Unconventional Ideas

The Ideation Cycle is where the quest for unconventional ideas begins. While not all these ideas will necessarily make it to the next stages of product development, they represent the foundation of innovation. It's about fostering an environment where wild ideas are celebrated, where no notion is too far-fetched to be considered, and where creativity is allowed to roam freely.

In summary, the Ideation Cycle is the phase of the product management process where creativity is unleashed. It's a time for imaginative thinking, brainstorming, and the exploration of unconventional ideas. It sets the stage for the entire product creation journey, nurturing the innovative spirit that drives product managers and their teams to break new ground and challenge existing boundaries.

Aligning Innovation with Strategic Goals

The Ideation Cycle isn't just about wild creativity; it's a structured process where innovative concepts are sought to align with the overarching goals of the company. The challenge is to fuse these ground breaking ideas with the company's strategic objectives while having a comprehensive understanding of the dynamics of the market.

The Ideation Cycle is more than just a free-for-all creative exercise; it's a structured process that demands creativity to be harnessed and aligned with the company's strategic objectives. It's the delicate act of merging ground breaking ideas with the overarching goals of the organization.

Innovative Concepts and Strategic Alignment

In this phase, the challenge for product managers is to unearth innovative concepts that are not only innovative but also seamlessly fit within the framework of the company's strategic objectives. It's about finding that sweet spot where creativity meets practicality.

Market Dynamics and Informed Creativity

Amidst this creative journey, it's imperative for product managers to keep their fingers on the pulse of market dynamics. While fostering innovation, they must be well-versed in the ever-evolving landscape of customer demands, industry trends, and competitive forces. This knowledge allows them to fine-tune their creative process, ensuring that their ideas are not detached from the real-world market conditions.

Comprehensive Understanding of Market Dynamics

A critical aspect of this process is gaining a comprehensive understanding of market dynamics. Product managers need to comprehend the complex interplay of customer needs, industry trends, and competitive forces. With this insight, they can fine-tune their creative process, ensuring that their innovative ideas resonate with market realities.

Innovative Alignment

The Ideation Cycle represents a balancing act. It's about achieving alignment between innovation, strategy, and market dynamics. It's here that product managers fuse imaginative thinking with the organization's strategic objectives while being fully aware of the ever-changing market landscape.

In summary, the Ideation Cycle is a phase where creativity meets structure. It involves the strategic process of aligning innovative concepts with the company's overarching goals. Product managers must navigate the complex interplay of market dynamics and strategy, seeking that delicate balance where ground breaking ideas become a driving force for achieving the company's objectives.

Collaborative Innovation

Moreover, the Ideation Cycle often involves collaborative efforts with cross-functional teams. This teamwork fosters a culture of innovation within the organization and promotes the generation of a more extensive array of ideas. It's also a mechanism to ensure that the concepts generated are not only innovative but also practically feasible and compatible with the company's existing capabilities.

Teamwork is the engine of innovation

In the Ideation Cycle, collaboration takes center stage. It's a phase that thrives on the collective efforts of cross-functional teams. This collaborative approach serves as a catalyst for fostering a culture of innovation within the organization. It's about creating a dynamic environment where a multitude of perspectives converge, giving birth to a broader spectrum of ideas.

Cross-Functional Synergy

Within this collaborative ecosystem, cross-functional teams work together, each member contributing their unique expertise and insights. This synergy often results in a fusion of ideas from various disciplines, enriching the ideation process.

From Ideas to Reality

One of the key benefits of this collaboration is that it not only generates innovative concepts but also factors in practicality. The diversity of skills and knowledge within the team ensures that the generated ideas are not detached from the company's existing capabilities.

Ensuring Feasibility

The collaborative approach is a built-in mechanism to ensure that innovation goes hand in hand with practicality. Ideas are not only innovative but also rooted in the company's capabilities and resources, making them feasible for implementation.

A Culture of Innovation

Beyond generating ideas, this collaborative effort nurtures a culture of innovation within the organization. It sends a message that creativity is valued, and it's not confined to a specific department but is a company-wide mindset. The Ideation Cycle is not just about brainstorming innovative ideas; it's a catalyst for fostering a culture of innovation within the organization. This transformative phase transcends the mere generation of concepts and leaves a lasting legacy of innovative thinking that permeates all aspects of the company.

At its core, this cultural shift is marked by the recognition and celebration of creativity. It sends a resounding message that innovation and creative thinking are not confined to specific departments or roles but are universally cherished throughout the organization. Every team member is encouraged to think outside the box, challenge the status quo, and contribute to the abundant pool of innovative ideas. This democratization of innovation dismantles traditional hierarchies, welcoming inspiration from every corner of the organization, regardless of one's role or title.

In this cultural transformation, the silos that might have isolated departments and teams are dismantled, fostering the cross-pollination of ideas. It encourages collaboration among diverse teams, where professionals from various domains work together to generate innovative solutions. The Ideation Cycle's cultural impact extends far beyond a single phase of product development. It shapes a legacy of innovation where creativity is deeply valued, and innovative thinking is a shared mindset propelling the organization to new heights. In essence, the Ideation Cycle is not only the cradle of inventive ideas; it's the cornerstone of a culture of innovation that celebrates creative thinking and inspires a continuous quest for innovative solutions.

The Birthplace of the Next Big Thing

The Ideation Cycle is undeniably a critical phase in the product management process, serving as the bedrock upon which all future steps are built. It's the spring of creativity, the source of innovative ideas that, when nurtured and developed, have the potential to evolve into ground breaking products. It essentially represents the genesis of the next major product breakthrough, reminding us that innovation knows no bounds.

At the core of the product management process, the Ideation Cycle emerges as a dynamic catalyst for innovation. During this pivotal phase, product managers bear the significant responsibility of generating and evaluating a fresh wave of product ideas. It is within this initial step that a profound emphasis is placed on fostering creativity and championing the spirit of innovation. This foundational phase serves as the very genesis of the product creation journey, igniting the spark that propels the process forward.

Fostering Creative Thinking: The Innovation Breeding Ground

Embedded within the Ideation Cycle is an unyielding commitment to cultivating a spirit of creativity and imaginative thinking. This phase is characterized by spirited brainstorming sessions and an unabashed exploration of ideas that transcend traditional boundaries. Product managers and their teams embark on a creative journey that encourages them to break free from conventional constraints, exploring uncharted territories where innovation knows no limits. It's an incubation period for novel and unorthodox concepts, where the primary objective is not to restrict creative thinking but to transcend the confines of conventional ideas.

Aligning Innovation with Strategic Goals: The Balanced Approach

The Ideation Cycle is not a free-for-all creative exercise. Instead, it's a structured process that strikes a delicate balance between stimulating innovation and anchoring ideas in the organization's strategic goals. It's a challenge that calls for innovative concepts to merge seamlessly with the company's overarching objectives while maintaining a comprehensive understanding of the ever-evolving market dynamics. This critical phase serves as a bridge between creative thinking and practicality, ensuring that the concepts generated are not just imaginative but also inherently aligned with the company's capabilities.

Collaborative Innovation: A Team Effort

The Ideation Cycle is rarely a solitary journey for a product manager. It frequently involves collaborative efforts with cross-functional teams, a testament to fostering a culture of innovation within the organization. This teamwork provides a fertile ground for the generation of a more extensive array of ideas, driven by diverse perspectives. More significantly, it ensures that the innovative concepts that emerge are not only visionary but also practically feasible, harmonizing with the company's existing capabilities.

A Culture of Innovation: The Enduring Legacy

In the fast-paced world of modern organizations, the ability to innovate is the lifeblood that propels them forward. Yet, innovation is often regarded as an elusive quality, confined to the realm of a select few. It was within this backdrop that the Ideation Cycle emerged as a transformative force within our organization.

The Ideation Cycle, while officially a phase in the product management process, was, in fact, the spark that ignited a culture of innovation. It was a profound metamorphosis, far beyond the generation of creative ideas; it was the birth of a new era.

In our journey, it became evident that the Ideation Cycle was not merely a phase to be completed and moved on from. It was the crucible of creativity, the birthplace of innovation, and the wellspring of ideas that had the potential to reshape our entire organization.

As product managers, we didn't only generate ideas; we became advocates of creativity. The realization struck us that innovative thinking wasn't limited to specific departments or roles. It was a trait that should be universally celebrated. Our collective creativity wasn't confined by traditional silos. It broke free, transcending departmental boundaries.

The impact of this transformation was profound. It wasn't merely about having more innovative ideas; it was about changing how we thought as an organization. The Ideation Cycle's cultural influence became enduring, a legacy that outlasted any product it helped create.

Creativity was no longer the prerogative of a select few. It was a shared mindset that touched every facet of our organization. Every team member, from marketing to development, was encouraged to think beyond the ordinary, to challenge the status quo, and to be a part of our innovation story.

Democratizing innovation had profound implications. It opened the floodgates for ideas to emerge from the most unexpected corners of our organization. It recognized that inspiration knows no boundaries – it can strike anyone, regardless of their role or title.

The Ideation Cycle, once a defined phase, became a way of life. It was a lasting legacy of the transformative power of innovation. It left a trail of creative thinking and a shared mindset that shaped our future. It propelled our organization to new heights, serving as a reminder that innovation knows no bounds. In the end, the Ideation Cycle had not just given birth to innovative ideas; it had sowed the seeds of a lasting culture of innovation.

In short, the Ideation Cycle is a critical phase in the product management process, as it lays the foundation for what comes next. It's the gateway to creativity, and it's where the seeds of innovation are sown. These innovative ideas, once nurtured and developed, have the potential to transform into products that meet market demands and drive a company's success. It is, in many ways, the birthplace of the next big product breakthrough.

Market research / Business Case

The Market Research and Business Case phase marks a pivotal transition in the product management process. Once a plethora of innovative ideas has been generated, the product manager now embarks on the journey of conducting comprehensive market research. This step is nothing short of foundational, serving as the compass that guides subsequent product development activities.

In this phase, the primary objective is to gain a profound understanding of the market dynamics and customer needs. It's about peering into the market landscape, analyzing consumer behaviour, and delving into the intricacies of what makes a product resonate with its intended audience. Market research becomes the key to unlocking valuable insights that will shape the product's development journey.

To conduct effective market research, product managers must gather, process, and interpret data from various sources. They may explore user demographics, preferences, and pain points, as well as scrutinize market trends and the activities of competitors. This data-driven approach not only helps product managers understand their potential customer base but also allows them to assess the competitive landscape.

Understanding the Market Landscape

The Market Research and Business Case phase represent a pivotal juncture in the product management process, marking the transition from creative ideation to practical market readiness. Within this phase, product managers delve deeply into market research, setting the stage for well-informed product development. The primary objective is to gain a profound understanding of market dynamics and customer needs. By exploring consumer behaviour, analyzing market trends, and scrutinizing competitor activities, this phase unlocks valuable insights that guide the product's evolution

Understanding the Market Landscape phase is a crucial milestone in the product management journey, signifying the shift from imaginative brainstorming to the pragmatic preparation for market entry. During this phase, product managers embark on an in-depth exploration of market research, laying the groundwork for a product development process grounded in substantial insights. The primary aim is to cultivate a profound understanding of both market dynamics and customer needs.

Consumer-Centric Exploration

Central to this phase is a meticulous examination of consumer behaviour. Product managers delve into the intricacies of consumer actions, preferences, and pain points. This consumer-centric exploration is essential for crafting a product that not only aligns with market demands but also resonates with the target audience. By understanding the behavioural patterns of potential users, product managers can tailor their offerings to meet specific needs and preferences.

Decoding Market Trends

In addition to understanding consumer behaviour, product managers analyze prevailing market trends. This involves scrutinizing shifts in consumer preferences, emerging technologies, and evolving industry standards. By decoding market trends, product managers gain foresight into the direction the market is heading. This strategic intelligence allows for the alignment of product development with future market demands, ensuring that the product remains relevant and competitive.

Competitor Landscape Analysis

Another integral aspect of understanding the market landscape is the thorough examination of competitor activities. Product managers scrutinize the strengths, weaknesses, opportunities, and threats posed by competitors. This competitive landscape analysis is crucial for identifying potential market gaps, differentiating the product, and positioning it strategically in the marketplace. It's a proactive step that allows for informed decision-making in the face of existing market competition.

Guiding the Product's Evolution

The insights gathered during the Understanding the Market Landscape phase serve as a guiding compass for the product's evolution. Whether it's refining features, adjusting marketing strategies, or addressing specific pain points, the knowledge gained from market research shapes the product development roadmap. This phase ensures that the subsequent stages of product management are not driven by assumptions but are grounded in a comprehensive understanding of the market environment.

Data-Driven Decision-Making

To effectively conduct market research, product managers embark on a data-driven journey. They gather, process, and interpret data from various sources, including user demographics, preferences, and pain points. By employing a data-driven approach, product managers not only understand their potential customer base but also assess the competitive landscape. It's a strategic dive into the wealth of available information, transforming abstract ideas into concrete insights.

Harvesting User Data

At the core of Data-Driven Decision-Making lies the art of harvesting user data. Product managers leverage various sources to collect a rich array of data, which includes user demographics, behavioural patterns, preferences, and pain points. The collection process may involve surveys, user feedback, website analytics, and other tools designed to paint a comprehensive picture of potential customers. By gleaning these insights, product managers move beyond assumptions and gain a concrete understanding of their target audience.

Assessing the Competitive Landscape

Data-Driven Decision-Making doesn't end with user data; it extends to a rigorous evaluation of the competitive landscape. Product managers conduct an in-depth analysis of the activities of competitors, deciphering their strengths, weaknesses, strategies, and positioning in the market. This examination provides invaluable insights for product differentiation, strategic market positioning, and the identification of gaps or opportunities in the marketplace. It's a proactive approach that steers product development in alignment with the prevailing market conditions.

The Power of Data Interpretation

However, collecting data is just the first step. Equally significant is the skill of data interpretation. Product managers meticulously process and interpret the collected data to unearth meaningful patterns, trends, and insights. It's not merely about acknowledging what the data says; it's about understanding why it behaves in a certain way. For instance, if data reveals a high drop-off rate during the onboarding process, thorough interpretation might pinpoint a specific step causing user frustration. Such insights drive informed decision-making in product development, where improvements are strategically focused.

From Abstraction to Insight

Data-Driven Decision-Making fundamentally transforms abstract ideas into actionable insights. It ensures that product managers make informed choices grounded in empirical data rather than assumptions or intuition. This data-centric approach empowers them to understand their customers on a profound level and navigate the competitive landscape with a heightened sense of strategic intelligence. Ultimately, it paves the way for well-informed decisions that drive product success in the marketplace.

Crafting the Business Case

Simultaneously, this phase involves the meticulous crafting of a compelling business case. This document serves a dual purpose: firstly, it demonstrates the potential value of the product idea, and secondly, it underscores its feasibility. The business case provides a strategic backbone for the product's journey from concept to reality. It showcases how the proposed product aligns with the company's overall strategic objectives, ensuring that it's not merely an exciting concept but a feasible endeavour that significantly contributes to the organization's success.

Demonstrating Potential Value

The business case is more than just a document; it's a persuasive narrative that demonstrates the potential value of the product idea. Within its pages, product managers meticulously articulate how the proposed product addresses specific market needs and customer pain points. This storytelling isn't mere conjecture; it's supported by the insights gained from the market research phase. By aligning the product concept with real-world market dynamics and customer preferences, the business case becomes a compelling argument for the product's significance. It goes beyond merely stating the idea's brilliance; it shows precisely why it matters.

Emphasizing Feasibility

However, a great idea alone is not enough; it must also be practical. The business case underscores the feasibility of the product, showcasing that it's not just a visionary concept but a project that can be successfully executed. It outlines the resources required, including the financial investments, human capital, and technological support needed for product development. Moreover, it addresses potential challenges and risks, emphasizing how these obstacles can be overcome. This focus on feasibility ensures that the product isn't just a pipe dream but a real, attainable goal for the organization.

Strategic Alignment

Another critical aspect of the business case is its emphasis on strategic alignment. It clearly outlines how the proposed product dovetails with the broader strategic objectives of the company. This alignment ensures that the product isn't a mere standalone project but a crucial part of the organization's vision for the future. By illustrating how the product complements and advances the company's mission, the business case positions the idea as a pivotal element of the company's success strategy.

The Financial Perspective

A well-structured business case often includes a financial perspective. This may encompass a cost-benefit analysis, which weighs the expected benefits against the projected costs. Such an analysis provides stakeholders with a transparent view of the project's financial viability. It demonstrates that the idea isn't just an exciting concept but a calculated investment that offers substantial returns. This financial perspective is a crucial element in ensuring that stakeholders, including executives and investors, can see the tangible benefits of the product concept.

In essence, the business case transforms the abstract concept of a product into a well-defined, strategic initiative. It goes beyond a mere description of an idea; it forms a solid foundation for the product's journey, showcasing its significance, feasibility, and alignment with the organization's overarching goals.

Documenting the Strategic Significance

Within the business case, product managers detail the project's scope, anticipate return on investment, and assess its potential impact on the company's market positioning. A key component of this process is the inclusion of a cost-benefit analysis, which allows stakeholders to gain a clear understanding of the project's financial viability. In this way, the business case highlights not only the creative potential of the product but also its strategic significance within the broader context of the company's goals.

Defining the Project's Scope

The business case serves as a platform for clearly defining the scope of the proposed project. It outlines the boundaries and objectives, answering questions like: What is the intended scale of the product? Which features and functionalities will it encompass? Who is the target audience, and what are their needs? By delineating the project's scope, the business case ensures that everyone involved understands the specific parameters within which the product will be developed.

Anticipating Return on Investment (ROI)

A crucial part of the business case is the anticipation of return on investment. Product managers provide stakeholders with insights into the expected financial gains associated with the product. This includes forecasting revenue generation, cost savings, and other financial metrics. By presenting a clear ROI projection, the business case provides a strong incentive for stakeholders to support the project, demonstrating the potential economic benefits it can deliver.

Assessing Market Impact

Understanding how the product will affect the company's market positioning is another vital aspect covered in the business case. Product managers analyze how the product will fit into the existing market landscape and what competitive advantages it will offer. This assessment of market impact goes beyond financial considerations and delves into how the product will influence the company's brand, reputation, and overall standing within the industry. It's an evaluation of the product's potential to be a market disruptor or an enhancer, which is vital for stakeholders to gauge.

Cost-Benefit Analysis

An integral part of the business case is the inclusion of a cost-benefit analysis. This rigorous assessment weighs the expected benefits the project will bring against the projected costs. It provides a clear financial overview, allowing stakeholders to make informed decisions regarding the project's financial viability. This analysis ensures that stakeholders are not just enticed by the product's creative potential but can see that it makes good financial sense for the organization.

The cost-benefit analysis (CBA) is a pivotal component of the business case. It's a structured evaluation that meticulously considers the financial implications of the proposed project. This rigorous assessment provides a clear and comprehensive financial overview, aiding stakeholders in making informed decisions about the project's financial viability.

The core of the cost-benefit analysis lies in its ability to weigh the expected benefits against the projected costs. It's not limited to merely listing the potential financial gains and expenditures; rather, it involves a detailed examination of how the benefits and costs align over time. By conducting this analysis, product managers, along with stakeholders, gain a deep understanding of the project's economic dynamics. One of the primary functions of the cost-benefit analysis is to provide stakeholders with the information they need to make informed decisions. It offers a basis for evaluating whether the project is financially justifiable and aligns with the organization's strategic goals. This analytical approach goes beyond enthusiasm and creative vision; it grounds the project in fiscal reality, helping stakeholders assess whether it's a sound investment.

The cost-benefit analysis plays a crucial role in harmonizing creative potential with fiscal responsibility. It ensures that stakeholders are not solely enticed by the allure of an innovative idea but can also see its financial rationale. This balance is vital for ensuring that projects are not only exciting concepts but also feasible and financially sustainable undertakings. The inclusion of a cost-benefit analysis within the business case serves as a bridge between creativity and financial prudence. It offers a framework for objectively assessing whether the innovative idea is not only exciting but also financially viable. This analytical rigor enhances decision-making, ensuring that projects are not just creative endeavours but strategic and fiscally responsible initiatives.

In summary, the business case transcends mere documentation; it's a strategic roadmap for the product's development. By outlining the project's scope, anticipating ROI, assessing market impact, and providing a cost-benefit analysis, the business case underscores the creative potential of the product within the broader context of the company's goals. It's a tool for aligning creativity with strategic vision, ensuring that innovative ideas become viable, strategic initiatives.

A Critical Juncture in Product Development

The Market Research and Business Case phase represent a pivotal juncture in the product management process. It's a stage where creativity meets practicality, serving as a bridge between imaginative ideation and the practicalities of the market. This phase transforms innovative ideas into well-informed, data-backed concepts that are strategically positioned to succeed.

The Bridge Between Ideation and Market Realities

This phase plays a crucial role in bridging the gap between the imaginative realm of generating ideas and the real-world market dynamics. It's where innovative concepts transition from abstract notions into concrete, actionable plans. By grounding these ideas in data and market insights, product managers are better prepared to navigate the complexities of the market landscape.

Data-Backed Concepts

A key outcome of the Market Research and Business Case phase is the generation of data-backed concepts. These concepts aren't whimsical or based solely on creative inspiration; they are informed by comprehensive market research. They are designed to address genuine customer needs, align with market trends, and position the product strategically in the competitive landscape.

Strategic Direction and Alignment

This critical juncture also sets the strategic direction for the product's development journey. It ensures that the product aligns with the demands of the market and the overarching objectives of the organization. It's about creating a roadmap that guides the product's evolution in a way that's not only creatively inspired but also strategically sound.

Foundation for Success

In essence, the Market Research and Business Case phase lays the foundation for the subsequent stages of product development. It's a phase that provides a clear and well-informed direction, ensuring that the product isn't just a creative concept but a well-considered endeavour that is strategically positioned for success. This phase is the compass that guides the product management process towards delivering products that resonate with the market and contribute to the organization's broader goals.

The Market Research and Business Case phase thus represents a critical juncture in the product management process. It transforms imaginative ideas into well-informed, data-backed concepts and demonstrates their strategic significance within the broader context of the company's goals. It's the bridge that connects creative ideation with the pragmatic realities of the market, setting the stage for the subsequent stages of product development and success.

Product Strategy

Product Strategy phase is about setting the stage for the product's journey. It's a forward-looking exercise that transcends the immediate development tasks, envisioning the product's evolution and its role within the broader business landscape. As the product manager crafts this strategic roadmap, they become not just a navigator of development but a visionary steering the product t The Product Strategy phase is where the foundation for the product's journey is set. It's a forward-looking exercise that goes beyond immediate development tasks, envisioning the product's evolution and its role within the broader business landscape. The product manager, in this phase, becomes not just a navigator of development but a visionary steering the product toward success.

Architectural Planning: Crafting the Blueprint

Entering the Product Strategy phase can be likened to laying out the architectural plans for a grand structure. Armed with insights from extensive market research and a solid business case, the product manager steps into the realm of strategic formulation. This phase is where the abstract notions of creative ideation begin to take concrete shape, guided by a meticulous roadmap—the product strategy.

The transition into the Product Strategy phase is akin to an architect embarking on the meticulous process of creating blueprints for a monumental structure. Just as an architect meticulously plans every detail of a building to ensure its functionality and beauty, the product manager, equipped with the wealth of insights from thorough market research and a robust business case, begins the strategic formulation of a product's future.

From Abstract to Concrete

This phase bridges the gap between the abstract, imaginative ideas generated in the earlier phases of creative ideation and the tangible reality of product development. It's here that those initial sparks of creativity take on more substantial form, transforming into a well-structured, data-driven roadmap known as the product strategy.

Strategic Formulation

Within the Product Strategy phase, the product manager undertakes a transformational role, evolving from a creative thinker into a strategic planner. They're tasked with defining the path the product will take, making critical decisions that set the course for the entire development journey. It's a phase that brings order to the chaos of innovative concepts, turning them into a structured plan that ensures the product's alignment with market demands and the company's overarching objectives.

The Product Strategy phase is where the abstract ideas of innovation gain structure and direction. It serves as the blueprint that guides the entire product development process, ensuring that creativity is channelled toward creating products that are not only visionary but also strategically poised for success.

The Compass of Product Development

The product strategy stands as the unwavering compass that guides product development through the intricate terrain of challenges and opportunities. It's a comprehensive and forward-looking plan, meticulously charted to ensure that every step in the journey is purposeful and in harmony with the dynamic interplay between the ever-evolving market demands and the overarching goals of the company.

Purposeful Navigation

Just as a ship's captain relies on a finely tuned compass to navigate treacherous waters, the product manager uses the product strategy as their guiding instrument in steering the product toward its intended destination. Every decision, every development task, and every adjustment along the way is carefully aligned with the true north defined by the product strategy.

Market Dynamics and Business Objectives

The compass of product development is designed to work in concert with the dynamic forces of market dynamics and the unchanging vision represented by the company's overarching objectives. It ensures that the product's trajectory doesn't drift aimlessly but remains resolutely on course.

A Future-Oriented Plan

The forward-looking nature of the product strategy allows it to anticipate challenges and opportunities on the horizon. It prepares the product for what lies ahead, enabling it to adapt to emerging trends, competitive pressures, and shifting customer preferences.

Establishing Clear & Measurable Objectives

At the core of the product strategy are clear objectives. These aren't mere aspirations but actionable and measurable goals that define the product's intended trajectory. Whether it's gaining a specific market share, enhancing user engagement, or achieving technological milestones, these objectives become the guiding lights steering the product's evolution.

Setting the Course with Clear Objectives

Deep within the product strategy lies the heartbeat of the product's journey is clear and measurable objectives. These aren't vague dreams or abstract hopes but tangible, achievable milestones that define the product's path. Whether it's conquering a specific market share, amplifying user engagement, or reaching technological pinnacles, these objectives are the North Stars that guide the product's evolution.

The Guiding Lights

Just as stars in the night sky have led explorers and sailors through history, these objectives act as the guiding lights for the product's development. They provide clarity and direction to every step, ensuring that the ship sails with intent and purpose, not drifting aimlessly.

Actionable and Measurable

What distinguishes these objectives is that they are actionable and measurable. They're not mere aspirations but concrete targets, complete with criteria for success. This specificity allows for a clear evaluation of progress and a means to measure how far the product has come in its journey.

Purposeful Navigation

The product strategy's role is not merely as a document but as a living compass. It ensures the product's voyage is purposeful and in harmony with the intricate interplay of market dynamics and the company's higher-level objectives. It's a dependable guide that keeps the ship of product development steadfast on its course.

Achieving Success through Purpose

In essence, the product strategy acts as the compass of product development. It doesn't just point the way; it ensures that each step is taken with intent. It's the tool that helps the ship navigate the complex waters of product creation, steering it with precision and purpose towards its ultimate destination — success.

Adaptable Guidance

Crucially, the product strategy is a dynamic document that adapts to the ever-changing nuances of the market. It's not a rigid prescription but a flexible guide, allowing for agility in response to emerging trends, competitor moves, or shifts in customer preferences. This adaptability is vital for ensuring that the product remains not just relevant but also ahead of the curve.

Rigid vs. Flexible

In the realm of product strategy, rigidity is the nemesis of adaptability. Some strategies are rigid, acting as restrictive blueprints that confine product development to a predetermined path. They offer little room for deviation. In contrast, the product strategy is like a flexible map. It doesn't prescribe a single, unalterable route but provides options and alternatives for the journey ahead. This flexibility is crucial because, in a dynamic market, adherence to a rigid plan can be a product's downfall, whereas adaptability is its greatest asset.

Responsiveness to Change

Imagine the market as a constantly shifting landscape. Competitors introduce new products, consumer preferences evolve, and unforeseen trends emerge. The adaptable product strategy thrives in this environment. It is responsive to these changes, allowing the product to pivot, adjust, and respond effectively. This agility is a vital shield against the unpredictability of the market.

Remaining Relevant

In today's fast-paced business world, relevance is often fleeting. What's in demand today may be obsolete tomorrow. It's here that the adaptability of the product strategy shines. It ensures the product doesn't just keep pace with industry developments but often stays ahead. The ability to adapt swiftly to changing circumstances is a core attribute of any product set on a path to long-term success.

Ahead of the Curve

Flexibility in the product strategy doesn't just maintain the product's relevance; it positions it as a forward-thinker. Imagine the product as an early explorer, always ready to embrace the next big trend or address the latest consumer needs. This approach propels the product towards sustained success by allowing it to continuously offer innovative solutions and stay one step ahead of the competition. It's a strategy that doesn't just follow trends; it sets them.

Alignment with Organizational Goals

The product manager must consider the broader organizational context when crafting the product strategy. How does the product contribute to the company's overall goals and strategic vision? This alignment is pivotal, ensuring that the product isn't an isolated venture but a synergistic component of the company's larger narrative.

The Bigger Picture

In the product strategy phase, the product manager becomes a bridge-builder, connecting the product's journey with the broader organizational landscape. It's not merely about creating an isolated product; it's about crafting a piece that seamlessly fits into the larger organizational puzzle.

Harmony with the Organizational Symphony

Consider an orchestra where each instrument represents a department within the organization. To create beautiful music, all instruments must play in harmony. In the same vein, for a company to thrive, all its components, including the products, must align with the organization's overarching objectives. The product strategy is like the conductor's baton, ensuring that the product's performance blends seamlessly with the organizational symphony.

Strategic Synergy

A product operating in isolation is akin to a single chess piece that doesn't contribute to the overall strategy. The product strategy shapes this chess piece, ensuring that it moves in alignment with the grand strategy set by the organization. This synergy is strategic; it's about pulling in the same direction, leveraging collective efforts, and maximizing the impact.

Shared Vision

The product strategy communicates a shared vision. It answers the question of how the product isn't just a standalone venture but a vital contributor to the company's bigger picture. This alignment is not just about the present but extends into the future, ensuring that the product remains integrated into the company's evolving narrative.

Impact and Relevance

In essence, the alignment of the product with organizational goals is what determines its impact and relevance. A misaligned product might perform well on its own, but its success is limited to its individual achievements. An aligned product, on the other hand, becomes a building block of the company's success, contributing meaningfully to the accomplishment of overarching goals. It's not just a product; it's a partner in the journey towards success.

Communication and Alignment

Furthermore, the product strategy serves as a communication tool. It's the means through which the product manager conveys the vision, objectives, and anticipated impact of the product to key stakeholders. This communication fosters alignment and buy-in across different teams, ensuring that everyone is on the same page regarding the product's purpose and direction.

The Bridge of Communication

The product strategy is more than just a document; it's a bridge of communication that connects the product manager's vision with the understanding of key stakeholders. It acts as the messenger that carries the product's purpose, objectives, and anticipated impact from the realm of ideas to the desks of those who will bring it to life.

Conveying the Vision

Consider the product manager as the architect of a magnificent structure, and the product strategy as the blueprint. Now, to bring this vision to life, the blueprint must be shared with the builders, engineers, and financiers. This is precisely what the product strategy accomplishes – it articulates the architect's vision in a language that the rest of the team can understand.

Alignment of Efforts

In the world of product development, alignment is crucial. It's like synchronizing a well-choreographed dance. Every move must be in harmony with the music, and every member of the team must be in sync. The product strategy ensures that everyone, from developers to marketers, is dancing to the same tune. It aligns their efforts towards a shared goal.

Buy-In and Commitment

The communication facilitated by the product strategy isn't just about conveying information; it's about securing buy-in and commitment. It's like a captain addressing the crew before embarking on a long journey. The crew, in this case, are the various teams and stakeholders involved in product development. They need to be on board, not just physically, but also mentally and emotionally.

One Page, One Plan

The beauty of the product strategy is that it condenses a world of ideas and plans into a single, cohesive document. This one-page plan becomes the compass for the entire journey, ensuring that everyone is not just in the same boat, but also rowing in the same direction. It's a testament to the power of effective communication in achieving alignment and, ultimately, success.

The Power of a One-Page Plan

Imagine you're embarking on a grand expedition. You have a diverse crew with various talents, a complex route to navigate, and ambitious goals to achieve. To ensure everyone is on the same page and rowing in the same direction, you need a map – a clear, concise plan that guides your journey. In the realm of product management, this map is the product strategy, often distilled into a one-page plan.

Simplicity and Focus

The beauty of a one-page plan is its simplicity. It doesn't drown your team in an ocean of details; instead, it provides a clear and focused snapshot of the product's purpose, objectives, and key strategies. It's akin to a condensed roadmap, highlighting the critical landmarks and milestones you must reach on your expedition.

Clarity of Purpose

A one-page plan is like the mission statement of your product. It clearly defines why the product exists, who it serves, and what problems it solves. Just as a captain sets the destination and purpose of a voyage, the one-page plan aligns every team member with a shared vision, fostering a sense of purpose that fuels motivation and commitment.

Strategic Direction

Your expedition needs a strategic direction. Without it, you risk drifting aimlessly. The one-page plan outlines the strategies your team will employ to achieve the product's objectives. This is your compass, providing clear guidance on how to navigate the ever-changing waters of the market and steer toward success.

Alignment and Accountability

Just as every crew member plays a vital role in the expedition's success, every team member's responsibilities are outlined in the one-page plan. This transparency ensures that each individual knows their role and how it contributes to the larger mission. It fosters a sense of accountability, much like sailors who rely on each other to keep the ship on course.

Buy-In and Enthusiasm

A one-page plan is not just a document; it's an instrument of communication that ensures everyone is not just informed but enthusiastic about the journey. Just as an inspiring captain's speech can motivate the crew, the one-page plan conveys the product manager's vision, garnering buy-in and commitment from the entire team.

Thus this one-page plan becomes the product manager's chart, the navigator's map, and the captain's speech, all condensed into a single, powerful charter. It unifies the team, provides clarity and direction, and serves as a constant reminder of the journey's purpose. With this map in hand, the expedition is not just a voyage; it's a coordinated, purpose-driven quest for success.

In essence, the Product Strategy phase is the visionary's workshop, where the product manager crafts a roadmap that transforms creative ideas into a strategic reality. It's the compass, the architectural plan, and the communicator that sets the stage for successful product development.

Creating a Robust Product Strategy

Product strategy is not a one-size-fits-all paradigm, but a thoughtful process that demands meticulous planning and execution. Creating a robust product strategy is a dynamic and iterative process, and to craft an effective strategy, we must consider a range of factors, a nuanced process that demands meticulous planning and execution and a tailored approach that should align with the specific product and market.

Articulating Product's Vision

In the world of product management, the process of articulating your product's vision is not merely a superficial exercise but a cornerstone of strategic planning. It's the North Star that illuminates the path your product will tread. Let's delve into this concept more deeply:

Defining the North Star

Your product's vision is akin to the North Star for sailors of old. It serves as a fixed point in the ever-changing business landscape, offering a consistent reference for your team. Just as sailors relied on the North Star for direction, your product's vision is the guiding light that ensures everyone knows where they're headed. It's the unchanging, unwavering objective that remains constant in a world of shifting priorities.

Aspirational and Transformative

A powerful product vision isn't merely a practical goal; it's a lofty ambition. It goes beyond solving a specific problem or addressing a particular need. Instead, it aims to be transformative, altering the very fabric of the market it operates in. It's the difference between developing a slightly better mousetrap and reimagining how we catch mice entirely. An aspirational vision sets a high bar, motivating your team to achieve more than they thought possible.

Inspiring Your Team

Your product's vision is not just a statement on paper; it's a source of inspiration. It should stir the passion and commitment of your team. When your vision is compelling and transformative, it becomes a rallying point. It inspires your team to think big, work hard, and persevere in the face of challenges. It's the answer to the question, "Why are we doing this?" — and it should be an answer that excites and energizes.

A Foundation for Decision-Making

Your product's vision becomes a touchstone for every decision you make along the product management journey. It serves as the ultimate filter, guiding choices about feature prioritization, target markets, and strategic direction. If a decision aligns with your product vision, it's likely the right one. If it doesn't, it should raise questions and prompt a re-evaluation.

In essence, articulating your product's vision is a foundational and transformative process. It's the process of defining a clear and inspiring destination for your product and its journey. Your product's vision is the unwavering North Star that guides your strategy, inspires your team, and shapes your decision-making. When it's aspirational, transformative, and resonates deeply with your team, it becomes a driving force for success in the ever-evolving market landscape.

Understand Target Customers

Deep customer understanding is the cornerstone of a successful product. Dive into the needs, pain points, and expectations of your target audience. Conduct user research, surveys, and interviews to gather insights. The more you know about your customers, the better you can tailor your product to meet their demands.

In the world of product management, understanding your target customers is like having a treasure map that leads you to success. Let's explore why this deep understanding is the bedrock of any successful product:

The Customer-Centric Approach

First and foremost, understanding your target customers is an unequivocal commitment to a customer-centric approach. It's a strategic shift that places the customer's needs, desires, and pain points at the core of your product development process. Instead of starting with the question, "What can we build?" you begin with, "What do our customers need?"

Diving into Needs and Pain Points

To truly understand your customers, you need to dive deep into their world. This means conducting thorough user research, running surveys, and engaging in insightful interviews. You're not just scratching the surface; you're peeling back the layers to reveal the core needs and pain points that your product can address. By understanding what keeps your customers up at night, you can tailor your product to provide real solutions.

Tailoring Your Product

Armed with this profound understanding, you're now equipped to tailor your product to meet the specific demands of your audience. You're not guessing or making assumptions; you're implementing features and functionalities that directly address the challenges and desires of your customers. This tailored approach sets your product apart from generic solutions and resonates deeply with your target audience.

The Competitive Edge

In the competitive landscape of today's market, deep customer understanding is a powerful differentiator. It's your secret weapon for staying ahead. While others are shooting in the dark, you're laser-focused, knowing exactly what your customers want and delivering it. This is how you gain a competitive edge that's sustainable and enduring.

Customer Loyalty and Advocacy

When your product speaks directly to the needs of your customers, something magical happens. You build not just customers but advocates. Satisfied users become loyal supporters who not only stick with your product but passionately recommend it to others. This word-of-mouth marketing is priceless and forms the foundation of long-term success.

In essence, understanding your target customers is not just a part of the product management process – it's the heart of it. It's a commitment to putting your customers first, diving deep into their world to uncover their needs, and using that knowledge to create a product that resonates with and solves the real-life challenges of your audience. This approach isn't just about building products; it's about building relationships, loyalty, and a thriving brand in today's dynamic and competitive market.

Analyze Your Competitors

Competitor analysis is essential. Identify who your competitors are and evaluate their strengths and weaknesses. Identify gaps and opportunities in the market where your product can differentiate itself. This analysis is crucial for positioning your product effectively.

Identifying Your Rivals

The first step in competitor analysis is identifying who your competitors are. These could be direct competitors, offering products or services similar to yours, or indirect competitors, who might not have identical offerings but cater to similar customer needs. By knowing your competition, you can prepare for the battle effectively.

Evaluating Strengths and Weaknesses

Competitor analysis involves a thorough examination of your competitors' strengths and weaknesses. What are they exceptionally good at, and where do they fall short? This evaluation is akin to dissecting the competition under a microscope, revealing insights that can shape your product's positioning.

Finding Market Gaps and Opportunities

Through competitor analysis, you can identify gaps and opportunities in the market. What needs are your competitors not fully addressing? Where can your product differentiate itself? By pinpointing these openings, you can tailor your product to meet unmet customer demands, making it more appealing in the market.

Effective Positioning

Positioning is all about how your product is perceived in the minds of your customers. Armed with competitor insights, you can craft a positioning strategy that highlights your product's unique strengths and sets it apart from the competition. This strategic positioning helps you stand out in a crowded market.

Strategic Decision-Making

Competitor analysis is a compass that guides your strategic decision-making. Should you focus on price, quality, or innovation? Are there specific markets or customer segments that your competitors are neglecting? These decisions become clearer when you have a comprehensive view of your competitive landscape.

Continuous Improvement

Competitor analysis is not a one-time activity; it's an ongoing process. The competitive landscape evolves, and your competitors adapt. By continuously monitoring and analyzing your rivals, you stay agile and can make real-time adjustments to your product strategy to maintain your competitive edge.

Thus competitor analysis is not merely about keeping an eye on the competition; it's a way to gain a strategic advantage. It's about understanding your rivals, learning from their successes and shortcomings, and positioning your product effectively in a crowded marketplace. This process equips you with the insights and tools needed to make informed strategic decisions and remain at the forefront of the competition, ensuring your product's success in a dynamic and ever-changing market.

Set Clear Objectives

Objectives in a product strategy are not mere placeholders; they are the North Star, the guiding light that steers your entire team toward a common destination. But what makes clear objectives so crucial in product management? Let's delve into the significance and impact of setting clear and measurable objectives:

A Common Purpose

Clear objectives provide a unified direction for your team. In the complex landscape of product development, team members can often get caught up in various tasks. Objectives serve as a shared mission statement that keeps everyone aligned and focused on the same end goal.

Measurable Progress

The effectiveness of objectives lies in their measurability. They are not vague aspirations but specific targets with quantifiable metrics. This measurability enables you to gauge progress accurately. Team members can track their contributions and see how they are contributing to the broader objectives.

Decision-Making Clarity

Clear objectives facilitate decision-making. When faced with choices or challenges, your team can refer back to the objectives as a litmus test. Will a particular action help achieve the objectives? If not, it may not be the best course of action. This clarity streamlines decision-making in the often turbulent world of product management.

Accountability and Responsibility

Objectives create a sense of accountability. When everyone knows what they are working toward, there's a greater sense of responsibility to deliver on their commitments. It fosters a culture of ownership, where each team member recognizes their role in achieving the objectives.

Strategic Adaptation

In dynamic markets, adaptation is key to success. Clear objectives allow you to adapt your product strategy effectively. If you see that you're not making progress toward your objectives, it's a signal to re-evaluate your approach. Are the objectives still relevant, or has the market landscape shifted?

Motivation and Engagement

Achieving well-defined objectives can be highly motivating. When team members see progress and the impact of their work, it fosters a sense of accomplishment and pride. This motivation can lead to higher engagement and more innovative problem-solving.

Clear objectives are the backbone of product strategy. They provide direction, measure progress, clarify decision-making, foster accountability, enable strategic adaptation, and motivate the team. Setting these objectives is not a trivial task; it's the foundation upon which you build a successful product. It's the difference between wandering aimlessly and embarking on a purposeful journey with a clearly defined destination.

Create a High-Level Product Roadmap

Your roadmap outlines the key features and milestones needed to achieve your objectives. It provides a structured path forward and helps your team understand the product's strategic direction. Your roadmap should be flexible, allowing for adjustments as you learn more about your customers and market.

A roadmap is akin to a map for a grand expedition. It outlines the path, marks significant waypoints, and guides the team to their destination – in this case, the successful development and launch of a product. The product roadmap is an invaluable strategic tool that warrants a closer look.

Key Features and Milestones

A product roadmap is not a mere to-do list; it's a dynamic blueprint. It outlines the essential features and critical milestones required to achieve your objectives. These aren't arbitrary additions but carefully selected components that align with your product's vision and customer needs.

Structured Path Forward

Imagine embarking on a journey without a map. It's a daunting prospect. Your product roadmap provides a structured path forward. It acts as a guide for your team, making the complex terrain of product development more manageable. It defines what needs to be done, in what order, and why.

Ensuring Team Alignment

A product team is a diverse ensemble of roles and responsibilities. A roadmap serves as the common language that ensures everyone is on the same page. It clarifies the strategic direction of the product, helping designers, developers, marketers, and others understand how their contributions fit into the bigger picture.

Adaptability as a Strength

In the ever-evolving landscape of product development, adaptability is a strength. A high-level roadmap should be flexible and open to adjustments. It acknowledges that as you learn more about your customers and market, your strategy may need fine-tuning. A rigid roadmap can lead to stubbornness; a flexible one leads to innovation.

Visualizing Progress

Human beings are visual creatures. A well-structured roadmap allows you to visualize your progress. It's like a treasure map where the "X" marks the spot – the spot being the completion of critical features and achievement of significant milestones. This visualization can be highly motivating for your team.

Strategic Communication

Communication is the lifeblood of effective product management. A roadmap isn't just an internal guide; it's a tool for external communication as well. It's how you convey your product's strategic direction to stakeholders, customers, and investors, fostering trust and transparency.

Thus, a high-level product roadmap is more than a schedule; it's a strategic compass. It aligns your team, visualizes your journey, allows for adaptability, and serves as a communication tool. It's the instrument that transforms your product strategy from a conceptual plan into a tangible reality.

Execution and Continuous Monitoring

Execution is crucial, but it should go hand in hand with continuous monitoring. Regularly assess your progress, gather feedback from customers, and be prepared to adapt your strategy based on market conditions and changing circumstances. Flexibility is key to success in dynamic markets.

Crafting a strategy is just the beginning of the journey. The true test of success lies in execution and the ability to adapt to the ever-changing landscape. Here, we delve into the crucial aspects of execution and continuous monitoring:

The Heart of the Strategy

Execution is the heartbeat of product strategy. It's where plans transition into action, and ideas evolve into tangible results. This phase involves coordinating team's efforts, setting development tasks in motion, and making strategic vision a reality. *Execution is where the rubber meets the road*, but it's not a solo act; it involves collaboration, communication, and meticulous planning.

The Agile Approach

In the dynamic realm of product management, flexibility is paramount. While your product strategy provides a structured path, it's essential to embrace an agile approach to execution. Agile methodology promotes adaptability, allowing team to respond swiftly to market shifts, evolving customer needs, and emerging trends. Agile sprints, regular stand-up meetings, and continuous feedback loops are your allies in this journey.

Customer-Centricity

Customers are the ultimate judges of product's success. Continuous monitoring involves gathering feedback from customers, whether through surveys, user analytics, or direct interactions. This feedback loop ensures that product remains aligned with customer needs and expectations. It's an iterative process of refining product based on real-world usage and feedback.

Market Conditions and Adaptation

Markets are not static; they're dynamic and ever-changing. product may launch into one landscape and need to navigate another. Continuous monitoring should extend beyond your customers to encompass market conditions. Keep an eye on shifting industry trends, competitive movements, and economic factors. A nimble product manager knows when to adapt the strategy to suit the current market climate.

A Learning Journey

Execution and continuous monitoring represent a learning journey. Each product launch, update, or iteration offers insights that can be invaluable for future endeavours. It's not just about the success of your current product but the accumulation of knowledge that informs future strategies. This learning journey fosters innovation and positions your team for long-term success.

Key Performance Indicators (KPIs)

In starting of my professional life I was once told by my manager, *"Anything that cannot be measured, monitored or tracked cannot be managed"*. This engraved "mantra" has been my guiding light so far.

Key Performance Indicators (KPIs) serve as guiding lights during execution and continuous monitoring. These metrics, whether related to customer acquisition, engagement, or retention, offer quantifiable data that reveals the health of your product. Regularly tracking KPIs helps you gauge the impact of your strategy, identify areas for improvement, and make data-driven decisions.

Quantifiable Assessment

KPIs provide a quantifiable means to assess your product's performance. They are the yardsticks against which you measure the effectiveness of your strategy. By attaching specific numbers or values to various aspects of your product, such as user engagement, conversion rates, or customer satisfaction, KPIs offer a clear and objective view of your product's health.

Focus and Prioritization

KPIs help in prioritizing efforts. They direct your attention to the most critical aspects of your product. Instead of getting lost in a sea of data, you can focus on KPIs that matter most to your strategy. For instance, if your

KPIs indicate a decline in user retention, you can prioritize efforts to improve this crucial aspect of your product.

Feedback and Improvement

KPIs are not just indicators; they are feedback mechanisms. Regularly tracking KPIs provides insights into how well your strategy is working. When KPIs reveal areas of underperformance or opportunities for improvement, they prompt you to take action. KPIs essentially facilitate a cycle of continuous improvement, as they highlight what's working and what requires attention.

Data-Driven Decision-Making

In the realm of product management, decisions shouldn't be based on hunches or gut feelings. KPIs foster a data-driven approach. They enable you to make informed decisions rooted in empirical evidence. If your KPIs show that a particular feature is significantly boosting user engagement, you can confidently allocate resources to enhance that feature further.

Accountability and Transparency

KPIs promote accountability and transparency within your team and organization. When KPIs are consistently monitored and shared, everyone involved in product development knows what's expected and how success is measured. This alignment fosters a sense of responsibility and ensures that every team member is working toward common objectives.

Adaptation and Flexibility

KPIs are not static. They evolve with product and strategy. As market conditions change or customer preferences shift, you can adjust your KPIs to remain aligned with your objectives. This adaptability allows you to pivot and refine your strategy based on the most current insights.

Remember, *KPIs are the pulse of your product strategy execution*. They provide a quantifiable assessment, prioritize efforts, offer feedback for improvement, enable data-driven decision-making, enhance accountability and transparency, and allow for adaptation to dynamic market conditions. The vigilant tracking of KPIs ensures that your product remains on course and well-prepared to navigate the complexities of the ever-evolving business landscape.

In summary, execution and continuous monitoring are the dynamic phases that bring your product strategy to life. Agile methodology, customer-centricity, adaptation to market conditions, and a commitment to learning are the cornerstones of success. Embrace these aspects, and you'll not only execute your strategy effectively but also position your product for enduring relevance and success. It's not a destination but a continuous journey of growth and adaptation.

Remember, creating a robust product strategy is not a one-time task but an ongoing, evolving process. It requires a commitment to staying attuned to market dynamics, customer feedback, and the competitive landscape. This adaptability and willingness to refine your strategy as needed will help you navigate the ever-changing market effectively and keep your product on a path to success. By following this suggested structured framework, one can create a robust product strategy that aligns with product's vision, resonates with target customers, and positions product effectively in the competitive landscape. It's a dynamic and iterative process that requires ongoing refinement and adjustment to navigate the ever-changing market effectively.

Product Design

Product Design phase is about shaping the product's form and function, translating ideas into a user-friendly, aesthetically pleasing, and engaging reality. It's the bridge that connects the abstract vision with the practical, hands-on development. Product managers, as conductors of this intricate process, ensure that the product's design harmonizes with both the user's desires and the strategic compass, bringing the product one step closer to market readiness.

The Essence of Product Design

The Product Design phase is a pivotal juncture in the product management process, where the intangible concept of a product transforms into a tangible reality. It's the bridge that seamlessly connects the strategic foresight laid out in the product strategy to the practical, hands-on development of the product. This phase is marked by the meticulous crafting of every detail to ensure that the product is not only functional but also user-friendly, aesthetically pleasing, and engaging.

From Vision to Form

The transition from the strategic realm of product strategy to the Product Design phase marks a pivotal moment where the abstract vision of a product takes on a tangible and concrete form. Product managers, equipped with a well-defined strategy, dive headfirst into the nitty-gritty details of product development. This is the realm of Product Design, a stage where the focus shifts from strategic planning to the practical aspects of creating a product that not only meets but also exceeds user needs and expectations.

Strategic Foundation

The journey from product strategy to design is underpinned by a solid strategic foundation. It's the strategic objectives set forth in the product strategy that guide and inform the design process. These objectives act as a North Star, ensuring that the design phase aligns harmoniously with the overarching vision.

Attention to User-Centricity

One of the primary focuses of the design phase is user-centricity. Product managers, designers, and developers collaborate closely to ensure that the product is tailored to the needs and preferences of the target audience. This involves a deep understanding of user behavior, preferences, and pain points.

Aesthetic and Functional Fusion

Product Design is where aesthetics and functionality converge. It's not just about making the product visually appealing but also about ensuring it functions effectively. The design phase seeks to strike a balance between form and function, creating a product that is not only visually captivating but also practical and efficient.

User Experience (UX) Design

At the core of the design phase lies User Experience (UX) design, a discipline that focuses on crafting an interface and functionality that provide users with a seamless and enjoyable experience. This involves intuitive navigation, visually pleasing design elements, and optimizing user interactions to ensure a positive and efficient experience.

Prototyping and Iteration

Prototyping plays a critical role in the design phase. It allows for the creation of visual blueprints that outline how the product will function and how users will interact with it. These prototypes facilitate early testing and iteration, ensuring that the final product aligns seamlessly with the objectives outlined in the product strategy.

A Dynamic and Iterative Process

The design phase isn't a one-time effort but a dynamic and iterative process. It operates as a continuous feedback loop, connecting with the earlier stages of ideation and strategy. New insights and challenges discovered during design may necessitate revisiting the product strategy, ensuring that the product remains aligned with evolving user needs and strategic objectives.

The transition from product strategy to the Product Design phase is where the visionary ideas of the product strategy begin to take shape and become tangible. It's the phase where creativity and strategic planning meet the practical requirements of product development, resulting in a user-friendly, aesthetically pleasing, and engaging product. It embodies the commitment to continuous improvement and refinement based on user feedback and the ever-evolving landscape of the market.

The Art of User Experience (UX) Design

Within the Product Design phase, a central and crucial element is the discipline of User Experience (UX) design. This discipline is dedicated to the art of shaping the product's interface and functionality in a manner that provides users with a seamless, intuitive, and delightful experience. It delves deep into the psychology and behaviour of users, ensuring that every interaction with the product is not just efficient but also a source of genuine enjoyment.

Understanding User Psychology

UX designers embark on a journey to understand the intricate workings of the human mind and how it interacts with technology. This involves studying user psychology and behaviour, gaining insights into what makes users tick and what frustrates them. By grasping the intricacies of human cognition, emotions, and preferences, UX designers can create experiences that resonate with users on a profound level.

Efficiency and Intuitiveness

At the heart of UX design lies the principle of efficiency and intuitiveness. The product should not require users to decipher complex instructions or navigate through convoluted menus. Instead, it should provide an interface that guides users naturally and effortlessly. The design should intuitively lead users to their desired actions, reducing the cognitive load and friction in their interaction with the product.

Aesthetic Pleasure

Beyond functionality, aesthetics play a pivotal role in UX design. Visual design elements should be not only functional but also aesthetically pleasing. An attractive visual design can evoke positive emotions and make the user experience more enjoyable. It's about creating a product that users not only find easy to use but also visually appealing.

Optimized User Interactions

User interactions are fine-tuned to perfection in UX design. Every button click, swipe, or tap is meticulously designed to ensure it serves a purpose and feels satisfying to the user. Optimized interactions contribute to the overall user satisfaction and the perception of a well-crafted product.

Wireframes and Prototypes

To bring the theoretical aspects of UX design into practice, product managers, designers, and developers collaborate to create wireframes and prototypes. These visual blueprints outline how the product will function and how users will interact with it. Prototyping is a crucial phase that allows for early testing and refinement based on real user feedback.

Continuous Improvement

The art of UX design doesn't stop with the initial product release. It embodies a commitment to continuous improvement and refinement. User feedback and changing market dynamics necessitate ongoing adjustments to ensure that the product remains user-centric and aligned with both the original product strategy and evolving user needs.

Remember, the art of User Experience (UX) design within the Product Design phase is a multifaceted discipline that merges an understanding of user psychology with a focus on efficiency, aesthetics, and optimized interactions. It's a holistic approach that transforms abstract ideas into a tangible reality, ensuring that every interaction with the product is a delightful and seamless experience for users. This commitment to user-centric excellence is an integral part of the journey from concept to a successful, market-ready product.

Collaboration for Visual Blueprint

In the realm of UX design, product managers collaborate closely with designers and developers to create wireframes and prototypes. These serve as visual blueprints outlining how the product will function and how users will interact with it. Prototyping plays a pivotal role in visualizing the product's user interface and features. It allows for early testing, iteration, and refinement, ensuring that the final product aligns seamlessly with the product strategy's objectives.

Imagine you're part of a product development team, and you've entered the crucial Product Design phase. Your product manager has a clear and ambitious vision for a new mobile app that will revolutionize how people manage their daily schedules. This vision involves creating an intuitive, visually appealing, and user-friendly interface that will make scheduling and task management a breeze for users.

The Essence of Product Design

You begin this phase with the product's abstract vision in mind. The abstract vision is to create a scheduling app that not only meets the functional needs of users but also delights them with its design. This is the essence of Product Design - taking the grand vision and translating it into a tangible form.

The Art of User Experience (UX) Design

A central element of the design phase is User Experience (UX) design. Your team collaborates with UX designers to create wireframes and prototypes. These visual blueprints illustrate how the app's interface will function and how users will interact with it. For example, the wireframes outline the initial layout, displaying how users can add, edit, and delete tasks. The prototypes go a step further, allowing you to click through and interact with a simulated version of the app. This helps the team visualize and refine the user experience.

Collaboration for Visual Blueprint

In the UX design process, your team holds regular meetings to discuss and refine the wireframes and prototypes. For instance, the designer suggests an innovative way to display task priorities based on user research, which results in a visual representation of task priorities that enhances user experience. These collaborative sessions lead to a shared vision of the app's design.

Early Testing and Validation

Before diving into actual development, your team uses these prototypes to conduct early testing. They invite a small group of potential users to interact with the prototype. Feedback from users reveals some issues with task categorization, prompting adjustments to the design. This early testing prevents potential problems from arising later in development.

Iteration and Refinement

Based on user feedback and continuous collaboration, your team iterates on the design. For example, users find it challenging to differentiate between personal and work-related tasks in the prototype. This feedback leads to a design refinement where task categories are color-coded, making it more intuitive for users.

By the end of the Product Design phase, you should have a well-defined, user-friendly, and aesthetically pleasing app interface. This bridge between the abstract vision of a revolutionary scheduling app and its practical design is the essence of Product Design. Collaboration and iteration have allowed you to refine the design to meet both user needs and the strategic objectives outlined in the product strategy. Your app is one step closer to becoming a reality, delighting users with its intuitive design while aligning with the broader goal of revolutionizing daily scheduling.

Convergence of Creativity and Functionality

The design phase is the juncture where creative ideas, aesthetics, and functionality come together to form a harmonious whole. It's not just about making the product visually appealing but also ensuring it functions effectively to meet user needs and strategic goals.

the convergence of creativity and functionality is where the abstract vision of a product becomes a tangible reality. Imagine you're working on a team tasked with designing a new e-commerce website. The product manager's vision is to create a visually stunning and user-friendly platform that not only attracts customers but also offers a seamless shopping experience.

Convergence of Creativity and Functionality

The product design phase is where creative ideas for the website's layout, colour schemes, and interactive features come together with the functionality of the platform. It's not just about making the website visually appealing with vibrant visuals and a user-friendly interface; it's also about ensuring the site functions effectively. This means customers can easily browse products, add items to their carts, and complete purchases. Team must strike a balance between creativity and functionality to create a harmonious whole.

User-Centered Approach

To achieve this balance, your team conducts user research to understand what your target audience values in an e-commerce site. You learn that users prefer a clean and intuitive design that allows for easy navigation and quick access to product information. This user-centered approach guides the creative elements like the layout, typography, and images, ensuring they align with users' preferences while also enhancing the website's functionality.

Interactive Features

Once you have brainstormed creative interactive features like a product recommendation engine and a user review system. These elements not only add a creative touch to the website but also serve a functional purpose. For example, the product recommendation engine uses algorithms to suggest relevant products to users, enhancing their shopping experience and increasing sales.

Mobile Responsiveness

Functionality extends to ensuring the website is responsive on various devices. With more users shopping on mobile phones, your team must creatively adapt the design to different screen sizes. This requires innovative solutions to maintain a consistent user experience regardless of the device used.

Feedback Loop

Throughout the design process, your team continuously collects feedback from users and stakeholders. This iterative approach helps identify creative and functional aspects that need refinement. For instance, based on feedback, you enhance the design of the checkout process to make it more intuitive, reducing cart abandonment rates.

Alignment with Strategy

While pursuing creativity and functionality, your team keeps the product strategy in mind. The website's design aligns with the strategic goal of increasing sales and customer retention. The aesthetics aren't just visually pleasing; they're designed to drive conversions and contribute to the company's bottom line.

As the team moves from the product strategy's visionary phase to the product design's practical implementation, the creative vision harmoniously combines with the website's functionality. The e-commerce site becomes an engaging platform that not only captures users' attention with its aesthetics but also provides them with a smooth shopping experience. It's a convergence that aligns with the broader goals of your product strategy.

An Iterative Feedback Loop

The design phase operates as a continuous feedback loop that connects with earlier stages of ideation and strategy. As product managers delve into the specifics of product design, they may uncover new possibilities or encounter challenges that require revisiting the product strategy. This iterative approach ensures that insights from the design phase inform and enhance the strategic framework, keeping the product in alignment with both user needs and strategic objectives.

Imagine you're working on a team developing a mobile app for a ride-sharing service. The product strategy focuses on providing an efficient and user-friendly transportation solution while increasing market share. As you transition into the design phase, the process unfolds as an iterative feedback loop that aligns with the earlier stages of ideation and strategy.

Uncovering New Possibilities

In the design phase, you work closely with UX designers and developers to create wireframes and prototypes for the app. During this hands-on process, your team identifies an opportunity to introduce a new feature—a real-time traffic update system that can suggest alternate routes to users based on current traffic conditions. This feature wasn't part of the initial strategy, but it's an exciting prospect.

Challenges and Revisiting Strategy

However, implementing this feature presents challenges related to data integration and potential user adoption. To address these challenges, you realize it's time to revisit the product strategy. You consult with your cross-functional team, which includes data scientists, to evaluate the feasibility and impact of this new feature. This iterative approach means that you're open to adjusting the strategic framework in response to new possibilities and obstacles that emerge during the design phase.

Alignment with User Needs and Strategy

The decision to incorporate real-time traffic updates aligns with the product's core objective of providing efficient transportation. It addresses a key user need for avoiding traffic jams and arriving at their destinations faster. Simultaneously, it supports the strategic goal of increasing market share because this feature could make your ride-sharing service more appealing to potential users.

Continuous Refinement

The iterative feedback loop doesn't stop with this strategic adjustment. As the new feature is integrated into the design, you collect feedback from beta testers and potential users. This ongoing feedback loop helps fine-tune the feature and ensures that it aligns not only with user needs but also with the broader strategy of growing the user base and outperforming competitors.

A Harmonious Convergence

Ultimately, the iterative feedback loop in the design phase becomes a mechanism for harmoniously integrating creativity and functionality. New ideas and insights from the design process not only enhance the user experience but also contribute to the overarching strategic objectives of the product. It's a process where the creative vision and the practical execution converge to create a product that resonates with users and propels the product's success.

In essence, the Product Design phase is the bridge where creativity meets practicality, shaping the product into a user-centric, visually appealing, and functionally sound reality. It's where strategic planning takes on a tangible form, and it's marked by a commitment to continuously improve and refine the product based on user feedback and evolving market conditions. The transition from the strategic realm of product strategy to the design phase is where the product's abstract vision begins to take tangible form. Product managers, equipped with a well-defined strategy, dive headfirst into the specifics of product development. This is the realm of Product Design, a stage where the focus shifts from strategic planning to the nitty-gritty details of creating a user-friendly and engaging product.

This dynamic process of development is facilitated by an iterative approach, where insights from design are fed back into the strategic framework, ensuring that the product remains aligned with both user needs and strategic goals.

Product Validation

With the product's design firmly in place, the next crucial phase in the product management process is Product Validation. This stage marks a pivotal moment in the product's journey, where the focus shifts from internal development to the critical perspective of the end-users. This is the stage where your focus shifts from internal development efforts to the eagle-eyed perspective of the end-users. Product Validation is all about meticulously testing and evaluating your product's concepts and designs to ensure they genuinely align with user needs and expectations.

The Essence of Product Validation

Product Validation is, at its core, a litmus test for your product. It acknowledges that real-world user validation is a non-negotiable checkpoint before advancing further in the product development journey. The phase of Product Validation in the product management journey is akin to a critical crossroads, transitioning your product from a well-designed concept to a practical, user-facing reality. This stage marks a pivotal moment where the focus shifts from internal development and strategic planning to the profound perspective of the end-users. Product managers, entrusted with the responsibility of shepherding the product to fruition, meticulously embark on a rigorous process of assessing the product's concepts and designs to ensure they genuinely align with user needs and expectations.

The essence of Product Validation is fundamentally rooted in the core principle of putting your product to the test – a rigorous examination by its intended audience, the users. It recognizes that real-world user validation is an indispensable checkpoint before advancing further in the product development journey.

Product Validation is a multifaceted approach, where several key practices converge to provide a holistic evaluation of whether the product effectively addresses user needs and meets their expectations. This critical phase encompasses a combination of methods that directly engage users, producing insights that prove to be invaluable for refining the product.

Gathering User Feedback: A Well of Valuable Insights

One of the cornerstone activities within Product Validation is the collection of user feedback. This can take on various forms, ranging from structured surveys to in-depth interviews or focus groups where users are encouraged to express their opinions, suggestions, and criticisms regarding the product. Their feedback forms an invaluable well of insights that product managers can draw upon to enhance the product.

By actively seeking out user feedback and listening to their voices, product managers not only showcase their dedication to user satisfaction but also gain a profound understanding of how the product is perceived and utilized by its intended audience. User feedback is the compass that guides further development, steering it toward fulfilling user needs and expectations.

In the intricate process of Product Validation, the collection of user feedback stands out as a cornerstone activity. This crucial practice unfolds in diverse forms, encompassing structured surveys, in-depth interviews, and facilitated focus groups where users are earnestly encouraged to articulate their opinions, suggestions, and criticisms regarding the product. The richness and depth of their feedback form an invaluable well of insights that product managers can seamlessly draw upon to refine and enhance the product.

Structured Surveys

Structured surveys provide a quantitative lens into user sentiment. By designing well-crafted questionnaires, product managers can systematically gather data on user preferences, satisfaction levels, and areas for improvement. This method allows for the efficient collection of a large volume of responses, providing statistical insights into the overall reception of the product.

In-Depth Interviews

In-depth interviews delve into the qualitative realm, unveiling nuanced perspectives that might escape the confines of structured surveys. These one-on-one conversations offer a deeper understanding of individual user experiences, preferences, and pain points. Through open-ended questions, product managers can uncover hidden insights and emotions that contribute to a more comprehensive view of the user landscape.

Focus Groups

Focus groups create a dynamic environment for collaborative discourse. Users, brought together in a facilitated setting, not only express their individual opinions but also engage in discussions with fellow participants. This method fosters the exploration of diverse viewpoints and the emergence of collective insights. The interactive nature of focus groups can reveal shared patterns of user behaviour and expectations.

Active Listening

Actively seeking out user feedback is not merely a procedural step but a testament to the dedication of product managers to ensure user satisfaction. By providing a platform for users to voice their thoughts, product managers cultivate a direct line of communication with their audience. This engagement transcends the quantitative realm of structured surveys, delving into qualitative aspects through in-depth interviews and focus groups.

Understanding User Perception - A Profound Insight

Listening attentively to the voices of users becomes a conduit for gaining a profound understanding of how the product is perceived and utilized by its intended audience. The spectrum of user feedback, spanning from positive endorsements to constructive criticisms, paints a comprehensive picture of the user experience. Each piece of feedback becomes a unique data point, contributing to the mosaic of insights that guides further development.

User feedback operates as more than just a compass; it's a dynamic force steering the trajectory of product development. It serves as a guiding light, illuminating the path toward meeting and exceeding user needs and expectations. This iterative process, driven by user feedback, ensures that the product evolves in tandem with the ever-changing landscape of user preferences and market dynamics. As a result, the product becomes not merely a creation of the development team but a coalescence of user-driven enhancements that propel it toward optimal user satisfaction and success in the market.

The Crucial Role of Testing

Testing is another vital element within the Product Validation phase. It involves the real-world application of the product by users under controlled conditions, providing a systematic assessment of how the product performs when wielded by its target audience. Testing stands as a pivotal and non-negotiable element within the Product Validation phase, bringing the theoretical aspects of product development into the practical realm. This rigorous process involves the hands-on, real-world application of the product by users under controlled conditions. The objective is clear: to systematically assess how the product performs when wielded by its target audience.

Putting the Product to the Test

Testing shifts the focus from conceptual evaluations to the tangible experience of end-users. It mimics real-world scenarios, allowing users to interact with the product as they would in their daily lives. This method provides a comprehensive understanding of how the product functions when subjected to the diverse usage patterns and expectations of its intended audience.

Navigating User Experience

In the context of a mobile app, a common testing approach is usability testing. During this process, users are observed as they navigate the app and interact with its features. The testing environment is carefully controlled, enabling the identification of user experience nuances, challenges, and areas of friction. This method provides practical insights into how intuitive the app is, whether users can easily accomplish their tasks, and if there are any stumbling blocks in the user journey.

Identification of Usability Issues

The primary aim of testing is to unveil any usability issues, obstacles, or bugs that may impede the seamless interaction between the user and the product. Usability issues can range from navigation difficulties to inefficient task completion, and even unexpected system crashes. Through testing, product managers gain a first-hand look at how users experience and interact with the product, allowing for the identification and subsequent resolution of these potential roadblocks.

Iterative Refinement

Testing is not just a one-time assessment; it initiates an iterative process of refinement. The insights garnered from testing become a catalyst for making informed decisions about enhancing the product. Product managers use this feedback loop to iteratively refine the user interface, improve performance, and address any issues that surfaced during testing. This dynamic approach ensures that the product evolves in response to user feedback, aligning more closely with user expectations and needs.

User-Centric Development: Minimizing Risks

The crucial role of testing extends beyond identifying issues; it is a strategic imperative for user-centric development. By actively involving users in the testing process, product managers minimize the risks associated with launching a product that may not resonate with its audience. Testing serves as a proactive measure to ensure that the product, when introduced to the market, not only meets but exceeds user expectations.

Testing is the crucible where the theoretical meets the practical, and user experience is validated in the crucible of real-world usage. It is a meticulous and indispensable phase that empowers product managers to fine-tune their creations, ensuring that the final product aligns seamlessly with user needs and expectations. Through rigorous testing, the product not only emerges stronger but also more attuned to deliver optimal user satisfaction and success in the market.

The Significance of User Experience (UX) Assessment

Furthermore, Product Validation is a pivotal moment for evaluating the User Experience (UX) offered by the product. UX design goes beyond aesthetics; it encompasses a comprehensive evaluation of how the product's design and functionality impact the user's experience. The validation process allows product managers to assess whether the product is indeed intuitive, efficient, and satisfying to use, or if there are areas that necessitate refinement.

Product Validation represents a critical juncture for evaluating the User Experience (UX) that the product delivers. Beyond mere aesthetics, UX design encompasses a holistic evaluation of how the product's design and functionality influence the user's overall experience. It's a process that allows product managers to assess whether the product excels in being intuitive, efficient, and ultimately satisfying to use, or if there are areas that warrant refinement. In this context, the user's perspective becomes the touchstone for evaluating how well the product aligns with their expectations and offers a delightful experience.

Going Beyond Aesthetics

UX assessment delves deep into the product's user interface and functionality. It evaluates how well the product guides users to their goals, how smoothly they can navigate its features, and how efficient and enjoyable each interaction is. It's about more than just visual appeal; it encompasses the entire journey a user takes when engaging with the product.

Assessing Intuitiveness

One vital aspect of UX assessment is evaluating the intuitiveness of the product. An intuitive product minimizes the learning curve for users and enables them to understand and use it effectively right from the start. A well-designed, intuitive product reduces frustration and enhances user satisfaction.

Evaluating Efficiency

Efficiency is another critical dimension. Users should be able to accomplish their tasks quickly and with minimal effort. This efficiency not only saves users time but also contributes to a positive perception of the product. An efficient product streamlines user interactions and optimizes the user's workflow.

User Satisfaction and Enjoyment

The end goal of UX assessment is ensuring that users not only find the product efficient and intuitive but also enjoyable to use. A delightful experience not only leads to increased user satisfaction but can also contribute to user loyalty and positive word-of-mouth recommendations.

User-Centric Focus - Aligning with User Expectations

By evaluating the UX, product managers align the product with user expectations. It's about ensuring that the product not only functions as intended but does so in a manner that resonates with its intended audience. This user-centric focus minimizes the risk of launching a product that may fall short of user expectations or cause frustration, both of which can have detrimental effects on its success in the market.

Refinement for User-Centric Success

The insights gained through UX assessment are instrumental for refinement. Areas that need improvement or adjustment can be identified and addressed, resulting in a product that genuinely aligns with user needs and expectations. By integrating this user feedback into the product's development, product managers make data-driven decisions that lead to a more user-friendly and ultimately successful product. The user's perspective becomes the touchstone for evaluating how well the product aligns with their expectations and offers a delightful experience.

User Experience (UX) assessment during Product Validation is an essential step that ensures the product excels in providing an intuitive, efficient, and satisfying experience for users. It's a process that emphasizes user-centric development, aligning the product with user expectations and minimizing the risk of user dissatisfaction. Through UX assessment and subsequent refinement, the product is poised for optimal user satisfaction and success in the market.

Ultimately, Product Validation is a milestone that safeguards the product's journey. It mitigates the risk of launching a product that may not resonate with users or meet their demands. It's a commitment to user-centric product development, ensuring that the product doesn't just exist but thrives in serving its intended audience. By actively engaging users in the validation process, product managers create a feedback-driven ecosystem that leads to a more refined, user-friendly, and ultimately successful product.

Product Launch

The culmination of extensive effort, creative ideation, strategic planning, and rigorous validation, the Product Launch phase is the grand moment in the product management process. This stage is all about taking meticulously crafted product from the confines of development and putting it into the hands of eagerly awaiting users. It's the pivotal juncture where the abstract becomes tangible, and creation becomes accessible to the market.

Product managers embark on this exciting journey with a validated product in hand, one that has been meticulously tested and refined based on user feedback and insights. The product, at this stage, embodies the solution to a specific need or challenge identified in the market. The product manager's role now shifts towards ensuring that this solution is not just introduced but also embraced and accepted in the market.

Product Launch is an intricate process that involves several critical steps, each contributing to the successful introduction of the product. One of the initial and pivotal considerations in this phase is defining the marketing strategies. This involves answering questions like, how do we create awareness about the product? What message do we want to convey to our audience? Which channels are most effective for reaching our target customers? Crafting a compelling and resonant narrative is paramount. The product's story, conveyed through marketing, should encapsulate its value, uniqueness, and its potential to address specific customer needs.

Since the Product Launch phase stands as the crescendo in the symphony of product management, marking the transition from concept and development to the tangible reality presented to eager users, becomes the pivotal juncture where abstract ideas transform into palpable products, ready to conquer the market.

Embarking on the Momentous Journey

In this thrilling phase, product managers embark on a journey, armed with a product that has been rigorously tested, refined based on user feedback, and represents the solution to a specific market need. Their role transitions from internal development to ensuring that this solution is not merely introduced but embraced and accepted by the market.

The Product Launch phase is an exciting journey for product managers. At this point, they enter the phase with a product that has undergone rigorous testing and refinement based on user feedback. This product represents a solution to a specific need in the market. The product manager's role transitions from an internal developer to a strategic orchestrator, ensuring the product's successful introduction to the market.

The Validated Product

The product manager begins this phase with a product that has successfully passed the validation phase. This product has been meticulously tested and refined, guaranteeing that it effectively addresses user needs and expectations.

From Development to Market Acceptance

The pivotal transition in this phase is from focusing on internal product development to ensuring that the product is embraced and accepted in the market. This is a shift from being a custodian of development to a strategic facilitator of the product's entry into the market.

The Essence of the Journey

This phase embodies a journey that product managers embark upon. It's a journey where a validated and refined product becomes a tangible reality accessible to the market. The product manager's mission is to guide this journey to success.

Examples and References

- *The launch of the iPhone by Apple is an iconic example of a successful product launch where the transition from product development to market acceptance was expertly orchestrated.*
- *The introduction of new car models by companies like Tesla showcases the journey of bringing an innovative product to market and creating acceptance among consumers*
- *Case studies of successful product launches, such as the launch of Airbnb's "Experiences" or the unveiling of new gaming consoles by companies like Sony and Microsoft, provide references for this phase.*

The Product Launch phase is a thrilling journey where product managers transition from being custodians of development to strategic facilitators of market acceptance. They embark on this journey with a validated product in hand, equipped with a clear understanding of user needs and the solution the product offers to the market.

Crafting Strategic Marketing Initiatives

Defining marketing strategies becomes paramount. Questions arise: How do we create awareness? What message should resonate with our audience? Which channels will be most effective in reaching our target customers? Crafting a compelling and resonant narrative takes center stage. This narrative, conveyed through marketing, should encapsulate the product's value, uniqueness, and its potential to meet specific customer needs. Defining marketing strategies is of paramount importance. Questions arise regarding how to create awareness, the messaging that will resonate with the audience, and the most effective channels for reaching target customers. Crafting a compelling narrative that encapsulates the product's value, uniqueness, and its potential to meet specific customer needs is central to this phase.

Defining Marketing Strategies

In the Product Launch phase, product managers are tasked with defining marketing strategies. This entails making decisions about how to introduce the product to the market, create awareness, and engage with the target audience effectively.

Creating Awareness

One of the primary goals of marketing strategies in this phase is to create awareness about the product. This involves ensuring that the product and its value proposition are visible to the intended audience.

Messaging that Resonates

To effectively communicate the product's value, the messaging used must resonate with the audience. It should address their needs and concerns while highlighting the unique aspects of the product.

Channel Selection

Choosing the right channels for marketing and communication is critical. It involves deciding where and how the product will be promoted and made accessible to potential customers.

Narrative Crafting

Crafting a compelling narrative is central to the Product Launch phase. This narrative serves as the story of the product, conveying its value, uniqueness, and how it fulfils specific customer needs.

Examples and References

- *The launch of the Tesla Model 3 involved crafting a narrative that emphasized its affordability, sustainability, and advanced technology, resonating with environmentally conscious consumers.*

- *The marketing campaign for the iPhone, including its iconic "There's an app for that" slogan, is an example of a narrative that highlighted the product's capabilities and resonated with a tech-savvy audience.*
- *Successful product launches by companies like Coca-Cola, Nike, and Google offer references for effective marketing strategies.*

Distribution Channels & Accessibility: Local vs. Global Context

Simultaneously, the choice of distribution channels becomes a pivotal decision. Product managers must decide how and where the product will be available. The choice of distribution channels is inherently linked to the product's nature, the target audience, and the overall business strategy. For example, digital products might be distributed through app stores, while physical products could leverage retail partnerships or e-commerce platforms. The aim is to ensure efficient and effective access for the intended audience.

In the context of product launch, the selection of distribution channels is influenced by a complex interplay of local and global factors. This section delves into how these considerations differ when addressing local and global markets.

Product managers are pivotal in navigating the intricate landscape of distribution and accessibility. They play a central role in ensuring that products are not only readily available to the target market but also accessible and usable by a diverse range of consumers. Here's a comprehensive guide on what product managers should be cognizant of and integrate into their strategies:

Understanding Distribution Dynamics

Ensuring a product reaches its intended audience effectively and efficiently is a multifaceted task. Product managers should be aware of and incorporate the following key considerations:

Channel Diversity

A successful product manager will strive to make the product available through a diverse range of channels. This involves balancing both online and offline retailers to maximize the product's reach. Whether through e-commerce platforms, app stores, or traditional brick-and-mortar stores, a comprehensive presence is essential.

Efficient Order Fulfilment

Product managers need to prioritize efficient order fulfilment. This means ensuring that the product is easy to order and receive. Customers should have access to fast and reliable shipping options, creating a positive and convenient buying experience.

Affordability and Accessibility

A product's success often hinges on its affordability and accessibility. Successful product managers will find ways to make their product accessible to customers from various income levels. This could involve pricing strategies, discounts, or partnerships to ensure a broad range of consumers can benefit from the product.

Product Accessibility Considerations

In an increasingly diverse and inclusive market, product accessibility is paramount. Here are essential aspects product managers should consider:

Design for All

A product should be designed to be accessible to everyone, including people with disabilities. This means incorporating features that make it user-friendly for individuals with visual, hearing, or mobility impairments. Accessibility features can range from high-contrast colors for text to keyboard navigation and compatibility with screen readers.

Multilingual Documentation

Product managers should provide clear and concise instructions in multiple languages. This ensures that language barriers don't hinder the product's usability. Multilingual documentation caters to a more diverse customer base and facilitates a better user experience.

Responsive Customer Support

Building a responsive customer service team is vital. Customers often have questions, issues, or concerns, and a dedicated customer support team can address these promptly. This responsiveness is crucial for maintaining customer satisfaction and resolving problems effectively.

Tailoring Strategies for Product Types

Different types of products require tailored distribution strategies. Product managers should consider the nature of their product and the market it serves. Here's how they can do this:

Digital Products

For digital products such as software, e-books, or online courses, a comprehensive online presence is paramount. This involves leveraging digital platforms, app stores, and e-commerce websites to ensure global accessibility. Strategic partnerships with online retailers can also expand the product's reach. Digital products often benefit from subscription models, which provide a steady revenue stream and foster customer loyalty. Security is crucial to ensure secure digital distribution. Robust digital rights management (DRM) systems and encryption techniques can safeguard against piracy and unauthorized access.

Material Goods

Physical or material goods, especially those with global demand, benefit from local distribution partnerships. These partnerships streamline the distribution process, reduce shipping costs, and navigate local regulations effectively. Efficient supply chain management is vital for material goods. This involves optimizing manufacturing processes, inventory management, and transportation logistics to ensure timely delivery and minimize costs. Capitalizing on e-commerce platforms enhances accessibility for material goods. Establishing a strong presence on platforms like Amazon, Alibaba, or regional e-commerce giants facilitates direct-to-customer sales and broadens market reach.

Perishable Goods

Products with a limited shelf life, such as fresh produce, pharmaceuticals, or flowers, require specialized distribution strategies. Cold chain logistics, which maintain a temperature-controlled supply chain from production to delivery, are imperative to preserve product quality and safety. Establishing localized distribution hubs near target markets reduces transit times for perishable goods, ensuring freshness upon delivery and quick responses to market demand fluctuations. Real-time tracking and monitoring, often facilitated by technology such as IoT sensors and GPS tracking, provide visibility into the location and condition of goods throughout the distribution process.

Holistic Strategies

Effectively managing distribution and accessibility strategies goes beyond tailoring approaches for different product types. Successful product managers incorporate cross-cutting strategies that enhance their product's reach and appeal. These strategies include:

Customer-Centric Approach

Regardless of the product type, a customer-centric approach remains foundational. Understanding customer preferences, addressing pain points, and offering a seamless purchasing experience contribute to successful distribution. Products that prioritize user satisfaction are more likely to succeed in the market.

Digital Marketing Integration

Integrating distribution strategies with digital marketing efforts is crucial in the modern market. For all product types, a compelling online narrative, social media engagement, and targeted advertising contribute to brand visibility and product desirability. Effective digital marketing strategies can significantly impact a product's accessibility and reach.

Sustainability Initiatives

Sustainability is an increasingly important consideration for consumers and regulators alike. Implementing eco-friendly packaging, optimizing transportation routes to reduce the carbon footprint, and incorporating sustainable practices into the supply

In terms of means and methods, local markets necessitate comprehensive market research to understand and adapt to local preferences. Establishing regional partnerships with local distributors and ensuring efficient logistics and courier services are imperative in a diverse country like India. On the global stage, the focus is on understanding regional market nuances, devising strategies for international shipping, and establishing global partnerships to reach customers worldwide.

In summary, the choice of distribution channels is a strategic decision that varies significantly between local and global contexts. Understanding local and global customer preferences and ensuring accessibility and efficiency are pivotal to a successful product launch. Moreover, aligning distribution strategies with the broader business strategy remains a crucial factor, irrespective of the market scale.

Timing: A Critical Element

Timing is another critical aspect of the Product Launch phase. Knowing when to introduce the product is crucial. Product managers must consider factors like market conditions, the competitive landscape, and broader economic trends. Timing is also intricately connected to understanding customer behaviour and preferences, which can vary by region, demographics, or industry. Launching at the right moment can significantly impact the product's success.

The timing of a product launch plays a crucial role in its overall success. Product managers must meticulously assess various factors to determine the ideal moment to introduce their product to the market. Here's a closer look at why timing is such a critical element in the Product Launch phase:

Market Conditions

Before launching a product, it's vital to evaluate the current state of the market. Are there any external factors, such as economic conditions, industry trends, or cultural shifts, that could influence your product's reception? For example, launching a luxury product during an economic downturn might not yield optimal results.

Competitive Landscape

An awareness of your competitors is key. Product managers should analyze what other companies in the same space are doing. If similar products are set to launch around the same time, it might be wise to adjust your launch date to avoid direct competition or to differentiate your product more effectively.

Customer Behaviour and Preferences

Understanding your target audience is paramount. Customer behaviour and preferences can vary significantly based on demographics, geographic locations, and even cultural factors. Conducting market research to gain insights into when your potential customers are most active or likely to make purchasing decisions can inform your launch timing.

Region-Specific Considerations

If your product has a global reach, be mindful of time zone differences and regional holidays. A well-timed launch that considers these factors can ensure that your product receives attention worldwide without any time-related barriers.

Seasonal and Trend-Based Timing

Some products have seasonal relevance. For instance, launching a new line of winter jackets in the summer might not yield the best results. Similarly, if your product aligns with specific trends or events (e.g., back-to-school season or holiday shopping), timing your launch to coincide with these trends can boost its reception.

Adaptability and Flexibility

While thorough planning is essential, it's also important to be adaptable. In a fast-paced market, unforeseen circumstances or opportunities might arise. Product managers should be ready to adjust their launch timeline if needed.

Ultimately, the timing of a product launch is about capitalizing on the most favourable conditions and maximizing its potential for success. It requires a deep understanding of the market, consumers, and the competitive landscape. By carefully considering these factors, product managers can strategically time their product's entry into the market to achieve the best possible outcome.

Comprehensive Go-to-Market Strategy

A successful product launch necessitates a comprehensive go-to-market strategy. This strategy includes various elements, from sales enablement to training, to ensure that everyone involved in the product's introduction is well-prepared and aligned with overarching launch objectives.

A comprehensive go-to-market (GTM) strategy is an essential component of a successful product launch. It encompasses a wide range of elements designed to ensure that the product's introduction into the market is well-prepared and that all stakeholders are aligned with the overarching launch objectives. Let's delve into the details of what makes up a comprehensive GTM strategy:

Market Analysis and Segmentation

From a product manager's perspective, the initial step in a comprehensive go-to-market (GTM) strategy involves in-depth market analysis and segmentation. They collaborate closely with marketing and research teams to gain insights into customer needs and the competitive landscape. The product manager's goal is to identify niche market segments where the product can provide unique value, tailoring the strategy to these specific customer groups for an increased chance of success.

Customer Profiling

Active participation in creating customer personas is a key responsibility of a product manager. They provide insights into the product's features and benefits that align with customer pain points, ensuring these personas guide informed decisions throughout the product development process. These profiles serve as the foundation for understanding customers and their specific requirements.

Value Proposition

The product manager takes responsibility for crafting a compelling value proposition. They work closely with the product development team to ensure that the unique features and benefits are integrated into the product. Their role is to communicate these value points effectively to both internal teams and external customers, emphasizing the distinctive advantages the product offers.

Positioning and Messaging

Collaboration with the marketing team is pivotal in developing clear product positioning and messaging strategies. In their role, the product manager ensures that the product's unique attributes are prominently highlighted in the messaging. This not only sets the stage for successful marketing but also helps create a strong brand presence in the market.

Channel Strategy

Selecting the right distribution channels is a product manager's responsibility. They consider factors like the product's nature and the target audience while making informed decisions. Collaboration with the sales and distribution teams is essential to ensure that the chosen channels are not only feasible but also align with the overall strategy, ensuring the product reaches its intended customers effectively and efficiently.

Pricing Strategy

Setting an optimal price point is a critical aspect of the GTM strategy. As a product manager, they work on pricing strategies that reflect the product's value while considering customer affordability. Their role is to balance profitability with market competitiveness, ensuring that the pricing strategy resonates with the target audience.

Sales Enablement

Equipping the sales team with the necessary knowledge and resources is paramount. The product manager provides them with in-depth product knowledge and sales collateral, ensuring that they are well-prepared to present the product to customers. Collaboration with sales teams to address their specific needs and challenges is an ongoing task to ensure a successful product launch.

Marketing and Promotion

Collaboration with the marketing team is pivotal in the GTM strategy. The product manager works closely to develop a marketing plan that aligns with the value proposition. Ensuring that the content calendar accurately reflects the product's features and benefits is a significant part of their role. Effective marketing and promotion are key to creating anticipation and excitement around the product.

Customer Support and Service

Overseeing the customer support strategy is a critical aspect of the GTM strategy. The product manager ensures that customers have access to the support they need. Collaboration with the customer support team is essential to provide a seamless post-launch experience, ensuring that any issues are addressed promptly.

Measuring Success

Setting key performance indicators (KPIs) for success is a critical task for the product manager. They focus on measurable objectives such as sales targets, customer acquisition rates, and customer satisfaction. In collaboration with the analytics and reporting teams, they track these metrics to evaluate the success of the GTM strategy and make data-driven adjustments.

Flexibility and Adaptability

Remaining agile and ready to adapt the strategy in response to changing market conditions is part of the product manager's role. Collaboration with cross-functional teams is vital to ensure that the organization can pivot when necessary. The product manager fosters a culture of adaptability and innovation within the organization.

Cross-Functional Collaboration

Collaboration is the cornerstone of a successful GTM strategy. The product manager ensures that all teams, including product development, marketing, sales, and customer support, understand the strategy. Their role includes actively seeking input and feedback from these teams to enhance the GTM strategy continuously. This cross-functional alignment is key to a smooth and well-coordinated product launch.

In summary, a comprehensive go-to-market strategy is a multifaceted plan that covers market analysis, customer profiling, value proposition, messaging, channel strategy, pricing, sales enablement, marketing, customer support, measurement, adaptability, and collaboration. A well-executed GTM strategy is pivotal in ensuring a product launch that resonates with customers and achieves its objectives.

Creating Anticipation and Excitement

Successful product launches extend beyond mere market entry; they spark anticipation, excitement, and an understanding of why the product matters. Engaging with the audience in a way that resonates and compels them to embrace the innovation is the essence of a triumphant launch.

From the perspective of a product manager, creating anticipation and excitement is not just about introducing the product to the market; it's about building a buzz and a sense of anticipation among the target audience. This involves several key considerations and strategies:

Engaging Storytelling

The product manager plays a pivotal role in crafting a compelling narrative around the product. They need to convey the story of why the product matters, its journey from inception to development, and the problems it aims to solve. Storytelling can capture the audience's imagination and create an emotional connection to the product.

Teaser Campaigns

Product managers can collaborate with the marketing team to design teaser campaigns. Teasers offer sneak peeks, glimpses, or cryptic hints about the product, generating curiosity and anticipation. These campaigns often include teaser videos, images, or cryptic messages shared on social media or through email marketing.

Product Demonstrations

Hosting live product demonstrations or webinars can be an effective way to showcase the product's features and benefits. The product manager ensures that these demonstrations are informative and engaging, allowing potential customers to see the product in action and understand its value.

Influencer Partnerships

Collaborating with industry influencers or thought leaders can amplify the reach of the product. Product managers identify key influencers relevant to the product's niche and work on partnerships that involve product endorsements, reviews, or co-creation content.

Beta Testing and Early Access

Providing early access to a select group of customers or running a beta testing program can generate excitement. This not only involves the audience in the product's development but also creates a sense of exclusivity, making customers feel like valued contributors.

Contests and Giveaways

Organizing contests or giveaways can be a fun way to engage the audience and create anticipation. Product managers work with the marketing team to design and execute these campaigns, offering the chance to win the product or exclusive merchandise.

Countdowns and Launch Events

Countdowns to the product launch, whether on a website or through social media, build anticipation. Additionally, organizing virtual or live launch events can be a grand finale that engages the audience. Product managers plan these events to ensure they align with the product's unique selling points.

Engaging Content

The product manager collaborates closely with content creators to develop engaging content that showcases the product's benefits. This content can take various forms, such as blog posts, videos, podcasts, or interactive infographics, and is distributed across relevant channels.

Social Media Engagement

Leveraging social media platforms is crucial. Product managers work with social media managers to engage with the audience through polls, Q&A sessions, behind-the-scenes content, and interactive posts. This not only creates excitement but also provides an avenue for direct interaction.

User Testimonials and Pre-launch Reviews

Sharing early user testimonials or pre-launch reviews can build trust and excitement. Product managers ensure that these testimonials highlight the positive impact of the product on real users.

From the product manager's perspective, creating anticipation and excitement involves carefully orchestrating these strategies and maintaining a consistent narrative that emphasizes the product's value and relevance. It's about capturing the audience's attention, maintaining their interest, and ultimately compelling them to embrace the innovation.

The Bridge to Market Existence

The Product Launch phase serves as the bridge between the product's development journey and its tangible existence in the real world. It signifies the realization of the product's potential and the commencement of its journey to make a positive impact on the lives of users. By orchestrating this phase with care and precision, product managers pave the way for the product to make a resounding entry into the market, setting the stage for its success. This phase is the grand unveiling where innovation meets reality, and the product begins its journey to make a meaningful mark in the world. In the eyes of the product manager, this phase is not just an event but a carefully orchestrated process that requires meticulous planning and execution. It serves as the grand unveiling, where innovation takes its first steps into reality, and the product embarks on its quest to make a meaningful mark in the world.

As the product takes its first steps into the market, the product manager's careful orchestration of this phase sets the stage for the product's success. It is the moment when innovation meets reality, and the journey of making a positive impact begins. Through meticulous planning, a compelling narrative, and a deep understanding of the market, the product manager paves the way for the product to make a resounding entry into the market.

The successful execution of the Product Launch phase is a testament to the efforts, creativity, and strategic planning that went into product development. The product manager's role is to ensure that this unveiling is met with enthusiasm, anticipation, and a deep understanding of why the product matters. This requires engaging with the audience in a way that resonates and compels them to embrace the innovation.

This phase is where the product's potential transforms into tangible existence, and its journey to create a meaningful footprint in the world begins. By carefully orchestrating this phase, product managers pave the way for the product to make a resounding entry into the market, setting the stage for its success.

Product Evaluation

The post-launch phase of Product Evaluation marks a pivotal juncture in the product management process. Far from being the end of the journey, it represents the beginning of a continuous quest for excellence and improvement. Product managers transition their focus from the development and launch phases to a critical task — assessing the product's performance. This phase involves a systematic approach to collect, analyze, and interpret data, feedback from customers and stakeholders, and determining whether the product is meeting its defined objectives and making the desired impact.

Data Collection for Comprehensive Assessment

Data collection in the Product Evaluation phase is not just about gathering information haphazardly; it's a strategic and well-planned endeavour. Product managers aim to collect data that provides a comprehensive view of how the product is performing in the real world. This data serves as the foundation for informed decision-making and iterative product improvement.

Diverse Data Points

Product managers cast a wide net in their data collection efforts. They aim to capture diverse data points that collectively paint a vivid picture of the product's interaction with the market and users. This involves collecting quantitative data, qualitative feedback, and various performance indicators. The goal is to understand not just the "what" but also the "why" behind the product's performance.

Key Performance Indicators (KPIs) as Guidance

Key Performance Indicators (KPIs) play a pivotal role in the data collection process. These are specific metrics that have been predefined to help gauge the product's success. The selection of KPIs depends on the product's nature and objectives. For instance, in a digital service, KPIs might include metrics like user retention rates, conversion rates, or average revenue per user. In a physical product, KPIs could be related to sales figures, customer satisfaction scores, or market share.

Examples of Performance Metrics

User Adoption Rates

This metric tracks how quickly and extensively users are adopting the product. It measures the rate at which new users are signing up, installing, or subscribing to the product. A high adoption rate suggests that the product is appealing and valuable to users.

Customer Satisfaction Scores

Customer feedback and satisfaction are paramount. Metrics like Net Promoter Score (NPS) or Customer Satisfaction Score (CSAT) provide insights into how well the product meets user expectations. High satisfaction scores indicate a positive user experience, while low scores may signal issues that need attention.

Revenue Growth

For products with a revenue component, tracking revenue growth is crucial. It reflects the product's ability to attract paying customers or upsell to existing ones. Steady revenue growth is often a sign of a healthy product.

Churn Rate

In subscription-based models, the churn rate measures how many customers cancel their subscriptions. A high churn rate can indicate dissatisfaction or issues with the product that need to be addressed.

Conversion Rates

In e-commerce or online services, conversion rates indicate the percentage of users who complete a desired action, such as making a purchase. Optimizing conversion rates is essential for driving revenue.

Customized Metrics for Specific Products

The choice of performance metrics isn't one-size-fits-all. Product managers tailor the metrics to the specific goals and nature of their product. For example, a product focused on user engagement may prioritize metrics related to user interactions, while a product with a revenue generation goal may emphasize metrics tied to sales and profitability.

In essence, data collection and performance metrics provide product managers with a quantitative and qualitative understanding of how their product is performing in the market. This data-driven approach empowers them to make informed decisions, identify areas for improvement, and drive the product towards continued success and relevance in a competitive landscape.

Feedback and Stakeholder Involvement

Feedback is another invaluable resource in the Product Evaluation phase. It provides a direct channel to understand how the product is perceived, what users appreciate, and where improvements are needed. Feedback mechanisms are designed to gather insights from customers, including structured surveys and open-ended communication. It's equally important to involve stakeholders, including internal teams, to obtain a 360-degree view of the product's performance.

The Value of Feedback

Feedback is a fundamental element in the ongoing assessment of a product. It serves as a direct conduit to gain insights into the product's performance and user satisfaction. Here are some key aspects of its importance:

User Perception

Feedback helps product managers understand how the product is perceived by its users. Whether users find the product valuable, user-friendly, and efficient or if there are pain points that need to be addressed.

Identifying Appreciated Aspects

It sheds light on what users appreciate about the product. This can include specific features, functionalities, or aspects of the user experience that resonate with the target audience.

Detecting Areas for Improvement

Feedback is equally valuable for identifying areas that require improvement. Users can highlight issues, difficulties, or shortcomings in the product that might have gone unnoticed during development and launch.

User Engagement

It provides insights into user engagement and whether users are actively using the product, which is crucial for assessing long-term success.

Collecting Feedback

Effective feedback mechanisms are designed to gather information from users and stakeholders systematically. Here's how it's typically collected:

Structured Surveys

Product managers often use structured surveys with predefined questions. These surveys can cover various aspects of the user experience, including usability, satisfaction, and specific features.

Open-Ended Communication

In addition to structured surveys, open-ended communication channels are crucial. This includes feedback forms, customer support channels, and direct communication with users. These channels allow users to express their thoughts, suggestions, and concerns in their own words.

The Role of Stakeholders

Stakeholders, both internal and external, play a critical role in the evaluation process. Involving various stakeholders ensures a holistic view of the product's performance:

Internal Teams

Internal stakeholders, such as marketing, sales, and customer support teams, often have valuable insights into user feedback and market dynamics. They interact closely with customers and are attuned to their needs and concerns.

External Partners

External stakeholders like business partners or third-party vendors may also provide input on the product's performance, especially in cases where there are collaborative efforts or dependencies.

360-Degree View

Involving stakeholders ensures that the evaluation process considers multiple perspectives. It's not solely reliant on user feedback but also factors in the insights, expertise, and interests of various stakeholders.

Collaborative Decision-Making

Stakeholder involvement fosters a collaborative environment where product managers can work together with other teams to address issues, make improvements, and align the product's direction with broader organizational goals.

Feedback and stakeholder involvement in the Product Evaluation phase create a robust framework for understanding the product's strengths, weaknesses, and opportunities for enhancement. It's a dynamic process where user insights and stakeholder perspectives converge to guide the product's evolution and ensure that it remains aligned with user needs and market demands.

Data Analysis and Diagnostic Insights

The evaluation process goes beyond the raw collection of data. It involves a rigorous analysis to draw meaningful insights. Product managers sift through the data to identify patterns, trends, and anomalies. This analysis helps in understanding not only how the product is performing but why it is behaving in a certain way. For example, a decline in user engagement may be attributed to a specific feature or design element. This kind of diagnosis is crucial for informed decision-making.

Data analysis is a pivotal step in the Product Evaluation phase. It's not merely about collecting data; it's about uncovering the story behind the numbers and metrics. Here's why data analysis is essential:

Identifying Patterns and Trends

When product managers analyze the collected data, they're looking for patterns and trends. This might include identifying periods of increased or decreased user activity, changes in user preferences, or shifts in market conditions.

Understanding User Behaviour

Data analysis delves into understanding user behaviour. It helps answer questions like why users are or aren't engaging with the product, what features are popular, and where users tend to drop off in their interactions with the product.

Diagnostic Insights

While data can tell you "what" is happening, diagnostic insights uncover the "why" behind the observed data. It's about understanding the reasons and causes that lead to certain outcomes. Here's how diagnostic insights play a pivotal role:

Feature Performance

Data analysis can reveal how specific product features are performing. If, for instance, user engagement is declining, diagnostic insights can pinpoint whether it's due to a particular feature not meeting user expectations or encountering usability issues.

Design Element Impact

If there's a noticeable shift in user behaviour, such as decreased retention or conversion rates, diagnostic insights can help identify the design elements that might be influencing these changes. It could be related to the user interface, navigation, or visual design.

User Feedback Validation

Diagnostic insights validate user feedback. For example, if users have provided feedback about difficulties in completing a specific task within the product, data analysis can validate whether there's a consistent trend indicating the same problem.

Root Cause Analysis

Data analysis can lead to root cause analysis. For instance, if there's a decline in customer satisfaction scores, diagnostic insights can uncover whether it's linked to customer support response times, product performance issues, or other factors.

Informed Decision-Making and Improvement

Diagnostic insights are crucial for informed decision-making. Once product managers understand the "why" behind the data, they can make strategic choices to drive product improvement. This may involve:

Prioritizing Changes

Understanding the root causes allows product managers to prioritize changes or updates that are most likely to have a positive impact on the product.

Iterative Development

Based on diagnostic insights, product managers may initiate iterative development. This could involve refining features, redesigning elements, or optimizing the user experience based on user behaviour.

User-Centric Approach

Diagnostic insights align product development with a user-centric approach. Decisions are made based on data and user feedback, ensuring that product changes directly address user needs and pain points.

In summary, data analysis in Product Evaluation is not a standalone process; it's a pathway to diagnostic insights. It helps product managers understand not only what's happening but why it's happening. These insights are the foundation for data-driven decisions and product enhancements that keep the product aligned with user expectations and evolving market dynamics.

Goal Comparison and Corrective Actions

One of the primary objectives of Product Evaluation is to compare the actual product performance against the predetermined goals and objectives. Product managers revisit the product strategy and initial expectations to assess whether the product is on track. Deviations are noted, and if the product is falling short of its goals, this phase is where corrective actions are initiated. It might involve revising strategies, redefining objectives, or refining specific features.

Goal comparison is a fundamental component of Product Evaluation, and it plays a pivotal role in ensuring the product remains on track and aligned with its initial objectives. Here's how it works:

Objective Reassessment

Product managers begin by revisiting the product's strategy and its initial objectives. This step is crucial because it ensures that the product's direction is in line with what was originally planned.

Quantitative Metrics

To assess goal alignment, quantitative metrics and key performance indicators (KPIs) are vital. Product managers rely on these metrics to measure the actual product performance against the set goals.

Qualitative Assessments

In addition to quantitative metrics, qualitative assessments are essential. These might include customer feedback, user satisfaction scores, and other subjective insights that offer a more nuanced view of the product's performance.

Deviations Identification

When assessing goal alignment, product managers must identify any deviations. Deviations signify that the product is not meeting its defined objectives. Here's what product managers look for:

Performance Shortfalls

These are the most evident deviations, such as not achieving revenue targets, falling short of user adoption goals, or missing out on customer satisfaction benchmarks.

User Feedback Alignment

Deviations can also manifest in user feedback. If users consistently report issues or express dissatisfaction in areas that were outlined as objectives, this misalignment is a significant deviation.

Competitive Landscape Consideration

Changes in the competitive landscape can also result in deviations. For instance, if a new competitor enters the market, the product's objectives may need to be adjusted.

Corrective Actions: Realigning the Product

When deviations are identified during Product Evaluation, it's essential to initiate corrective actions. These actions are designed to realign the product with its objectives and get it back on track. Here's how corrective actions are implemented:

Revising Strategies

Corrective actions can involve revising the overall product strategy. For example, if the market conditions have changed, it may be necessary to adapt the product's positioning or target audience.

Redefining Objectives

In some cases, it might be necessary to redefine objectives. This could include setting new, more attainable goals based on the product's current performance and the evolving market landscape.

Feature Refinement

If deviations are related to specific features or functionalities, corrective actions might involve refining or reengineering these aspects of the product to better meet objectives.

User-Centric Adjustments

Corrective actions should always prioritize user-centric adjustments. Addressing user needs and preferences is fundamental to getting the product back on course.

Iterative Development

Corrective actions often lead to iterative development. Product managers use insights gained during the evaluation to implement changes, updates, or improvements that address the identified deviations.

In short, the goal comparison and corrective actions in the Product Evaluation phase are essential for maintaining the product's alignment with its objectives. They provide product managers with a mechanism to recognize when deviations occur and take proactive steps to realign the product and ensure it continues to meet user needs and market dynamics effectively.

Iterative Development

In the continuous quest for excellence, Product Evaluation often leads to iterative development. Insights gained from data and feedback are used to refine the product. This could involve updates, new feature implementations, or even a major product overhaul based on user feedback and data-driven findings. Product managers are committed to continuous improvement, ensuring that the product remains competitive and valuable in the market.

Iterative development is a key aspect of Product Evaluation, representing the commitment to continuous improvement. This approach acknowledges that a product is not static; it should evolve and adapt to changing user needs, market dynamics, and emerging technologies.

Gathering Insights and Data

The process of iterative development begins with the collection of insights and data. Product managers leverage various sources, including user feedback, performance metrics, and market trends. These inputs provide a comprehensive understanding of how the product is currently performing.

Refining the Product

With insights in hand, product managers embark on the journey of refining the product. This can take various forms:

Updates

Minor updates might address issues, fix bugs, or improve existing features. For example, if users report difficulties with a particular user interface element, product managers may release an update to enhance its usability.

New Feature Implementations

Based on user feedback and identified needs, new features or functionalities may be implemented. This expansion enriches the product's capabilities and aligns it more closely with user expectations.

Major Overhauls

In some cases, iterative development might involve a major product overhaul. This is a strategic move often triggered by significant shifts in the market or user behaviour. For instance, the advent of a new technology might prompt a complete revamp of the product to remain competitive.

User-Centric Approach

Throughout the iterative development process, a user-centric approach is paramount. Product managers continuously seek to address user needs, preferences, and pain points. User feedback is a guiding light, illuminating the path toward product improvements.

Agile Methodologies

Iterative development often aligns with agile methodologies, which emphasize flexibility and adaptability. Agile practices involve short development cycles, frequent testing, and a willingness to embrace change. This allows product managers to respond swiftly to new insights and adapt the product accordingly.

Continuous Learning and Adaptation

The iterative development approach is underpinned by a commitment to continuous learning and adaptation. Product managers understand that the product's journey is ongoing, and they remain open to evolving strategies and tactics to ensure its success.

Competitive Edge

Iterative development is not only about meeting existing user needs but also staying ahead of the competition. By proactively addressing emerging trends and user demands, a product can maintain its competitive edge and remain a relevant choice in the market.

Market Relevance

In the fast-paced world of technology and innovation, staying relevant is essential. Iterative development ensures that the product remains a valuable and impactful part of the market's landscape, effectively serving the needs of users.

Iterative development in Product Evaluation is a dynamic and adaptive approach. It involves a commitment to continuous improvement based on data-driven insights and user feedback. By refining the product through updates, new feature implementations, or even major overhauls, product managers ensure that the product remains competitive and valuable in the ever-evolving market.

Stakeholder Alignment and Communication

Transparent communication and stakeholder alignment are critical in the Product Evaluation phase. The findings and insights derived from the evaluation process are shared within the organization, ensuring that all relevant parties are informed about the product's performance. This fosters a shared understanding of the product's status and potential courses of action. Effective communication is crucial to get buy-in from stakeholders and to facilitate collaborative decision-making.

In the Product Evaluation phase this aspect is crucial in creating a shared understanding of the product's performance, making informed decisions, and achieving buy-in from all relevant parties. Let's explore the significance of stakeholder alignment and effective communication in this phase:

Shared Insights and Understanding

One of the primary objectives of stakeholder alignment and communication is to ensure that all key stakeholders have access to the same insights and data. This shared understanding of the product's performance is essential for making informed decisions. It prevents information silos and aligns everyone with the same set of facts, allowing for consistent assessments.

Informed Decision-Making

In the complex landscape of product management, decisions are rarely made in isolation. Multiple teams and individuals, each with their expertise and perspectives, are involved. Effective communication ensures that these stakeholders are aware of the insights derived from the Product Evaluation phase. Armed with this information, they can actively participate in the decision-making process.

Buy-In from Stakeholders

Stakeholder alignment fosters buy-in from individuals and teams who play a crucial role in the product's future. When stakeholders are well-informed and understand the rationale behind decisions, they are more likely to support and actively engage in the actions that follow. This buy-in is fundamental for executing any changes or improvements identified during the evaluation.

Collaborative Courses of Action

Transparent communication opens the door to collaborative decision-making. It allows stakeholders to share their perspectives, insights, and concerns. By engaging in discussions and debates, teams can collectively determine the most appropriate courses of action. Collaborative decision-making often leads to more well-rounded solutions and better outcomes.

Feedback Integration

Effective communication is a two-way street. It's not only about sharing findings but also about gathering feedback and input from stakeholders. Stakeholders, including internal teams, may have valuable insights to contribute based on their experiences and areas of expertise. This feedback integration enhances the overall quality of the decision-making process.

Strategic Adaptation

In a rapidly evolving market, the ability to adapt strategically is paramount. By ensuring that all stakeholders are aligned and informed, product managers are better positioned to assess the need for strategic adaptations. These adaptations might involve pivoting the product strategy, exploring new market opportunities, or responding to shifting user needs.

Crisis Management

In some cases, the Product Evaluation phase may uncover critical issues or challenges. Effective communication and stakeholder alignment are essential for swift and efficient crisis management. It allows teams to respond to urgent matters in a coordinated and organized manner, minimizing potential damage.

Feedback Loop

The communication process between product managers and stakeholders often establishes a feedback loop. This loop can be instrumental in ensuring that the insights gained during Product Evaluation are effectively applied to product improvement. It enables a continuous cycle of assessment, adaptation, and refinement.

The stakeholder alignment and effective communication are not ancillary activities in Product Evaluation but are integral to its success. This alignment creates a shared understanding, fosters buy-in from stakeholders, and enables collaborative decision-making. It ensures that the product's performance insights are leveraged effectively and that the product remains responsive to evolving market dynamics and user needs.

Ongoing Commitment

Product Evaluation is not just a phase but an ongoing commitment. It represents the compass guiding product managers to navigate the ever-changing landscape of market dynamics and user needs. Through data-driven insights and customer feedback, product managers are poised to steer the product's journey towards excellence, ensuring that it remains a valuable and impactful part of the market's landscape. This ongoing commitment is vital to maintaining a competitive edge and responding to evolving customer demands and market conditions.

Product Evaluation is not a finite phase; it signifies an ongoing commitment by product managers. This unwavering dedication serves as a compass, guiding product managers as they navigate the ever-changing landscape of market dynamics and evolving user needs. Here, we delve into the significance of this continuous commitment in product management:

Adaptation to Market Dynamics

Market dynamics are in a perpetual state of flux. Consumer preferences, competitive forces, and economic conditions continuously evolve. Product managers committed to ongoing evaluation are better equipped to adapt their products to these changing dynamics. They can identify shifts in the market, anticipate emerging trends, and make the necessary adjustments to remain competitive.

Responsiveness to User Needs

User needs and expectations are not static. As technology advances and societal demands change, products must evolve to address these shifts. Continuous evaluation allows product managers to stay attuned to user feedback and evolving needs. It enables them to proactively implement improvements and new features that enhance the product's value and relevance.

Continuous Improvement

Excellence in product management is not a one-time achievement but an ongoing pursuit. By continually evaluating the product's performance, product managers can identify areas that require enhancement. This might involve refining existing features, streamlining user experiences, or introducing innovations that set the product apart in the market.

Competitive Edge

In today's fiercely competitive landscape, maintaining a competitive edge is essential for sustained success. Ongoing product evaluation enables product managers to not only keep up with competitors but also to outpace them. By staying ahead of industry trends and delivering continuous product enhancements, they can solidify their position in the market.

Proactive Issue Resolution

Product Evaluation is instrumental in early issue detection. Product managers who are committed to ongoing evaluation can swiftly identify problems or challenges and initiate solutions before they escalate. This proactive approach helps prevent crises and ensures a seamless user experience.

Market Relevance

Relevance is key to product longevity. An ongoing commitment to evaluation ensures that the product remains relevant to its target audience. By responding to shifting market demands and staying aligned with customer expectations, the product continues to hold value for its users.

Feedback Integration

The feedback loop established through ongoing product evaluation is a valuable asset. It allows product managers to integrate customer insights and stakeholder feedback into their decision-making processes. This integration is instrumental in driving product improvements, ensuring that the product aligns with user preferences.

User-Centric Approach

An ongoing commitment to evaluation is inherently rooted in a user-centric approach. Product managers prioritize understanding and addressing the needs and desires of their user base. This approach enhances user satisfaction and fosters loyalty, as users recognize the product's responsiveness to their feedback.

Sustainability

Maintaining a product's relevance and value over time contributes to its sustainability. An ongoing commitment to product evaluation is a sustainable practice in itself. It safeguards the product against obsolescence and positions it for long-term success.

In essence, Product Evaluation transcends a singular phase; it embodies an enduring commitment that lies at the core of effective product management. This perpetual dedication involves vigilance towards market dynamics, responsiveness to evolving user needs, and vigilance towards emerging trends. This persistent commitment acts as the propelling force behind securing a product's lasting significance and influence within the constantly shifting market landscape. Anchored in data-driven insights and continuous customer feedback, it empowers product managers to chart a course towards product excellence, preserving its status as a valuable and influential entity within the market's ever-changing terrain.

Product Iterations

In the dynamic realm of product management, the journey doesn't conclude with the launch of a product; it's an ongoing expedition of evolution and refinement. This phase, known as Product Iterations, is where product managers harness the insights gathered during the evaluation phase to drive a process of continuous improvement. Data-driven insights, customer feedback, and a commitment to excellence are the cornerstones of this iterative approach, ensuring that the product remains not only relevant but competitive in an ever-evolving market landscape.

Data-Driven Refinements

In the dynamic realm of Product Iterations, the intelligent and strategic use of data stands as the bedrock upon which meaningful refinements are built. At the heart of this phase, product managers delve deep into the wealth of data that has been meticulously collected during the evaluation phase. This data encompasses an array of key performance indicators (KPIs), user usage patterns, and behavioural insights. However, the aim goes beyond merely understanding how the product has been performing; it's about unravelling the intricate "why" behind its behaviour. This profound understanding of the "why" empowers product managers to make data-driven decisions that lead to meaningful improvements.

Consider a scenario where a product manager is examining user behaviour within a mobile application. Through data analysis, they uncover that a significant number of users are dropping off during the onboarding process, which is a critical phase for user retention. However, the magic happens when they move beyond this observation. The product manager delves deeper, scrutinizing the data to identify the specific point within the onboarding process where users disengage. It could be a particular step that poses challenges, like a cumbersome account creation process or a lack of clear instructions. This meticulous analysis transforms data into actionable insights.

The "why" is essential because it unravels the narrative behind user actions. It's not just about recognizing that users are dropping off; it's about understanding the reasons that underlie their decisions. In this example, the product manager's data-driven insights highlight a particular friction point within the onboarding process. Armed with this knowledge, they can confidently collaborate with the development and design teams to streamline that specific step, ultimately enhancing the user experience and boosting retention rates.

In essence, data-driven refinements are not arbitrary adjustments; they are the result of a precise and methodical process. Product managers act as detectives, poring over data to uncover the stories it tells. They seek patterns, trends, and anomalies within the data that provide critical insights into user behaviour. These insights go beyond surface-level observations; they enable product managers to pinpoint the root causes of issues, identify areas for improvement, and make refinements that lead to a more refined product.

Moreover, data-driven refinements are not isolated events but part of an iterative cycle. Product managers continuously revisit and analyze data, tracking the impact of their refinements. It's a process of learning and adaptation, where each iteration builds upon the insights gained from the previous one. This approach ensures that the product remains aligned with user needs and competitive within the market.

Data-driven refinements are driven by curiosity, precision, and a commitment to excellence. They illustrate the power of data in the hands of skilled product managers, who use it as a compass to navigate the path of continuous improvement and innovation. In the ever-evolving landscape of product management, these refinements are not just about optimizing the product but about sculpting a user experience that resonates and excels.

User-Centric Enhancements

In the larger context of product management, the wisdom of data-driven decisions is complemented by the invaluable voice of the customer. While data provides a wealth of quantitative insights, the qualitative feedback from users stands as an equally vital source of information. It's the convergence of these two dimensions that empowers product managers to create truly user-centric enhancements.

Gathering user feedback is a multifaceted endeavour. Product managers employ various channels to capture the voice of the customer. Structured surveys serve as a structured and systematic approach to understanding user perspectives. These surveys are carefully designed to extract specific insights, ranging from satisfaction levels to feature requests. They act as a reliable source of data to gauge user sentiments and experiences.

In addition to surveys, interactions with customer support play a pivotal role. These interactions offer a direct line of communication with users who are encountering challenges or seeking assistance. They provide a rich source of feedback, often highlighting immediate pain points and issues. Product managers carefully catalogue these interactions, identifying recurrent themes and areas that demand attention.

Furthermore, the user-centric approach extends to various touchpoints where users engage with the product. This can encompass a wide spectrum, from social media discussions and online reviews to in-app feedback mechanisms. Product managers are adept at scouring these touchpoints for user comments, suggestions, and discussions related to their product.

But what truly sets user-centric enhancements apart is the attentive and empathetic approach product managers take toward this qualitative feedback. They don't merely skim the surface; they dive deep to understand the intricacies of user perceptions. User comments aren't just data points; they are narratives that provide insights into individual journeys, needs, and desires.

This user feedback unveils the full spectrum of the user experience. It showcases areas of delight where the product excels and areas of frustration where it falls short. It brings to light unmet needs and latent desires that users may not express through their actions alone. This holistic understanding is what guides product managers to craft enhancements that truly resonate with their audience.

Consider a scenario where user feedback reveals consistent frustration with a product's navigation. While quantitative data may indicate a high bounce rate at a particular stage, the qualitative feedback delves into the reasons behind this behaviour. Users may express their challenges with finding specific features or confusion about the navigation structure. Armed with this feedback, product managers can collaborate with UX designers to revamp the navigation, making it more intuitive and user-friendly.

The user-centric enhancements are the bridge between user expectations and data-driven refinements. They are the result of a conscientious process where user feedback is synthesized with data insights. This blend of qualitative and quantitative information paints a holistic picture of the user experience. Product managers then navigate this landscape, making informed decisions that improve the product based on both user behaviours and desires.

User-centric enhancements are not isolated actions; they are part of an iterative cycle of improvement. Product managers continuously revisit user feedback, track the impact of their enhancements, and gather further insights. This iterative approach ensures that the product remains closely aligned with user needs, resulting in a more satisfying and user-friendly experience.

In essence, user-centric enhancements embody the commitment of product managers to create products that not only meet market demands but also resonate deeply with the people who use them. They highlight the user's voice as the guiding star, ensuring that the product continually evolves to provide value, delight, and satisfaction..

Prioritizing Improvements

In the journey of product management, the path to enhancement is often paved with a multitude of potential improvements, each vying for attention. However, not all feedback or data insights can be addressed immediately. Prioritization is the cornerstone of wise decision-making, ensuring that resources are allocated judiciously, timelines are met, and the product's overarching goals are upheld. It's a process of discernment and strategy that culminates in a well-crafted roadmap for iterations, focusing on enhancements that deliver the most significant value to both users and the product's performance.

Product managers are confronted with a constant influx of suggestions, observations, and data-driven insights that point towards possible improvements. These suggestions can range from fixing minor user interface glitches to the introduction of game-changing features. The challenge lies in deciding which enhancements should be pursued and in what order.

One of the guiding principles of prioritization is the potential impact of an improvement. Product managers meticulously assess the extent to which a particular enhancement can benefit users and enhance the product's performance. They seek to understand how addressing a specific issue or introducing a new feature can elevate the user experience and contribute to the product's overarching goals. For instance, a feature that streamlines a complex process, making it more efficient for users, might have a more substantial impact than minor cosmetic changes.

However, potential impact is only one facet of the prioritization process. It's intricately intertwined with the availability of development resources and project timelines. Product managers need to consider the capacity of their development team and the existing commitments and priorities within the organization. They must weigh the potential impact against the feasibility of implementation within the defined timeframes.

Additionally, prioritization extends beyond individual improvements to encompass the holistic vision of the product. Product managers maintain a clear understanding of the product's overarching objectives and strategy. Enhancements that align with these goals are given precedence, as they contribute not only to immediate user satisfaction but also to the long-term success of the product.

In the process of prioritization, product managers often employ various frameworks and methodologies. One commonly used approach that categorizes features and improvements into Must-Have, Should-Have, Could-Have, and Won't-Have categories. This categorization helps in clearly defining what needs to be addressed urgently versus what can be deferred or discarded.

The result of the prioritization process is a strategic roadmap for iterations. This roadmap outlines a sequence of planned enhancements, each positioned to address specific user needs, improve the user experience, and align with the product's strategic objectives. It provides clarity not only for the product team but for all stakeholders, helping everyone understand the order of priority and the rationale behind it.

The prioritization process is not static; it's an ongoing endeavour. As new feedback is gathered and data insights are obtained, the roadmap evolves. Product managers continuously reassess and adjust their priorities based on changing circumstances, market dynamics, and user expectations.

Ultimately, prioritization is an art of discernment that allows product managers to navigate the complex landscape of potential improvements. It's a strategic dance of weighing potential impact, resources, timelines, and alignment with overarching goals. By making informed decisions about which enhancements to pursue, product managers ensure that their efforts are focused on those that deliver the most significant value to both users and the product's performance.

Agile Development

Product Iterations are the lifeblood of a dynamic and evolving product. They keep it in tune with user needs, market trends, and technological advancements. In this continuous journey of improvement, agile development stands as the trusty engine that propels the product forward. The agile model offers a flexible and adaptive framework that allows for incremental and continuous changes to the product. It's the very antithesis of large, infrequent updates, ensuring that enhancements are smaller, more frequent, and deeply responsive to the ever-evolving landscape of user needs and market dynamics.

One of the fundamental strengths of agile development lies in its responsiveness. In a rapidly changing world, where new technologies, competitors, and user expectations emerge regularly, the ability to adapt swiftly is a significant advantage. Agile development acknowledges that not all user needs or market trends can be predicted far in advance. It accepts that the best ideas and insights often emerge when users begin interacting with a product. As such, it enables product managers to respond to emerging opportunities and challenges promptly.

Incremental, frequent updates are essential for another critical reason: user satisfaction. Large, infrequent updates can lead to user frustration, as they might have to wait for a considerable amount of time to see their needs addressed or new features introduced. In contrast, agile development ensures that users can experience ongoing enhancements, which keeps them engaged and satisfied. Users are more likely to stick with a product that continually evolves to meet their needs and expectations.

Moreover, agile development minimizes the risks associated with large updates. When a product undergoes infrequent and massive changes, the potential for problems and disruptions is higher. In contrast, agile development's incremental approach allows for better control and testing of each enhancement before it's integrated. This reduces the likelihood of major issues that can lead to downtime, frustration, or loss of users.

From a product manager's perspective, agile development offers improved project management and resource allocation. Smaller, incremental changes are more manageable, easier to plan, and less likely to result in resource bottlenecks. It enables product managers to maintain a steady and predictable pace of improvement, ensuring that the product remains on a trajectory of growth and success.

In short, agile development is the beating heart of iterative progress. It aligns perfectly with the spirit of Product Iterations, where the journey is ongoing, and improvement is constant. This approach enables product managers to adapt to shifting market dynamics, respond to user needs, and enhance user satisfaction while minimizing risks and maintaining effective project management. It ensures that the product not only stays competitive but thrives amidst change.

Continuous Evolution

At the heart of Product Iterations lies a fundamental commitment to perpetual evolution. It's not merely a one-time endeavour but a deeply ingrained mindset that becomes an integral part of the product management process. Each iteration cycle serves as a building block, standing on the foundation of the last, and forming a continuous narrative of refinement and enhancement. In essence, it's a dynamic journey characterized by growth, adaptation, and a relentless pursuit of aligning the product with the ever-evolving needs and expectations of its users.

This iterative philosophy is grounded in the acknowledgment that the journey of product development is an ongoing and dynamic process. It doesn't culminate in a single, definitive release but is rather a series of responsive steps taken in sync with the feedback, data, and experiences gathered from the users. The very essence of iterations lies in the ability to learn from past efforts, both successes and challenges, and to channel that knowledge into informed decisions for the future.

With each iteration, product managers not only refine features and functionalities but also fine-tune the overall strategy. The iterative approach enables a product to stay relevant and competitive in a landscape where change is constant. It's about embracing uncertainty and being responsive to emerging opportunities and challenges. This mindset of continuous improvement fosters a culture of adaptability within the product team, where learning and evolution are not just encouraged but inherent in the process.

The commitment to continuous evolution through iterations is also a commitment to the users. It signifies a dedication to delivering a product that consistently meets and exceeds user expectations. By actively seeking and incorporating user feedback, iterating becomes a means of co-creation with the user community. It's a collaborative process where the product team and users engage in a dynamic dialogue, ensuring that the product remains a valuable and indispensable part of the user's experience.

Moreover, Product Iterations contribute to the resilience of a product. In a landscape that is prone to rapid changes in technology, market dynamics, and user preferences, the ability to iterate becomes a strategic advantage. It allows the product to pivot when necessary, seize emerging opportunities, and navigate challenges with agility. This adaptability is not just a feature of the product; it's a quality ingrained in the very fabric of its development process.

Now we know that the Product Iterations are not just about refining features; they are about fostering a mindset of continuous evolution. It's a commitment to learning, adapting, and staying in harmony with the ever-changing landscape of user needs and market dynamics. This iterative philosophy transforms product development from a linear process to a dynamic and responsive journey of growth.

Collaboration and Communication

Product Iterations thrive in an ecosystem of collaboration and communication, where a symphony of minds works together to create harmonious progress. These iterative endeavours are not isolated pursuits but instead a dynamic interplay between product managers, development teams, designers, and a spectrum of stakeholders. The essential fuel that powers this collaborative engine is effective communication, a vital conduit for sharing insights, rationale, and the profound impact of each iteration.

Effective collaboration stands as the backbone of successful Product Iterations. This collaborative spirit begins at the very inception of the product management process. When identifying areas for improvement or new features, product managers engage in open discussions with development teams to outline the technical feasibility and constraints. Designers bring their creative perspectives into the mix, ensuring that each iteration not only addresses functional aspects but also enhances the overall user experience.

However, collaboration isn't just about technical aspects; it extends to a holistic view of the product. Various stakeholders, including marketing, sales, and customer support teams, offer invaluable insights based on their interactions with users. Their feedback is a goldmine of real-world experiences that help in crafting iterations that align with user needs and market demands.

In this symphony of collaboration, effective communication emerges as the harmonious conductor. It is the medium through which the insights, findings, and objectives of each iteration are conveyed to all participants. This transparency is invaluable, as it ensures that everyone involved in the product development journey remains aligned with the goals and progress of the product.

For instance, when an iteration aims to improve the onboarding process for an app, effective communication is vital in conveying the reasons behind this decision. It may be based on user feedback that highlighted specific pain points. The product manager collaborates with designers to visualize enhancements and with development teams to understand the technical aspects of implementation. Clear and open communication allows all stakeholders to comprehend the purpose and significance of the iteration, leading to a shared vision and commitment to its success.

Effective communication thus always serves as a bridge between the data-driven insights and the decisions made during iterations. It is through communication that product managers convey the reasoning behind prioritizing certain improvements and the potential impact they will have on the product's performance and user satisfaction. This insight fosters a sense of ownership and empowerment among the product development team, as they can clearly see how their contributions align with the product's overarching objectives.

In the context of stakeholders, effective communication keeps marketing and sales teams well-informed about upcoming iterations and improvements. This allows them to align their strategies, messaging, and customer interactions with the evolving product. For customer support teams, it provides a deeper understanding of how the product is changing and equips them to assist users more effectively.

In conclusion, the nexus of collaboration and communication is at the heart of successful Product Iterations. It's a symphony where the collective wisdom and insights of various roles come together to create iterative progress. Effective communication ensures that this symphony is in harmony, with all participants well-informed, aligned, and committed to the journey of iterative improvement.

In summary, Product Iterations epitomize the spirit of agility and evolution in product management. It's the phase where data and user insights drive refinements, keeping the product relevant, competitive, and aligned with the dynamic market landscape. The commitment to continuous improvement ensures that the product isn't just a static creation but a vibrant, ever-evolving part of the market's tapestry.

Part 3: Managing Technology Products

Product managers who oversee technical products and services play a pivotal role in ensuring their success in the market. Managing such products involves a unique set of challenges and responsibilities that require a blend of technical knowledge, strategic thinking, and effective communication thus a distinctive and pivotal role. They are at the helm of products that rely on intricate technological foundations, and their responsibilities are a unique blend of technical prowess, strategic acumen, and adept communication skills. This section delves into the multifaceted role of these product managers, highlighting the key aspects that define their journey.

Understanding the Technology Stack

Product managers must possess a foundational understanding of the technology stack that underpins their products. This includes awareness of the programming languages, frameworks, and infrastructure used in the development process. They should comprehend the core architecture and how various components, services and API subsystems interact. While not expected to be experts, a working knowledge enables effective communication with the technical team, streamlining decision-making and issue resolution.

In the contemporary landscape influenced by emerging technologies like Industry 4.0, product managers overseeing technical products and services have assumed an even more central role in ensuring product success. This challenging endeavour necessitates a unique amalgamation of technical expertise, strategic insight, and effective communication. Here are the critical aspects of managing technical products and services, taking into account the evolving technological frontier of Industry 4.0, encompassing areas like Site Reliability Engineering, DevOps, Cloud Computing, and Distributed Systems and Architecture.

Embracing Emerging Technologies

In the context of Industry 4.0, characterized by the integration of digital technologies into various industries, product managers must remain at the forefront of emerging technologies. This necessitates a proactive approach to learning about innovations like artificial intelligence, the Internet of Things (IoT), blockchain, and augmented reality. An understanding of these technologies and their potential applications is crucial to making informed decisions about product features and roadmaps.

In the context of Industry 4.0, product managers are increasingly called upon to embrace emerging technologies that are reshaping the landscape of technical products and services. This proactive approach to technology involves keeping a keen eye on innovations like artificial intelligence (AI), the Internet of Things (IoT), blockchain, and augmented reality. It's not merely about awareness; it's about understanding how these technologies function and the potential they hold.

AI, for instance, is revolutionizing industries by enabling predictive maintenance, where machine learning algorithms analyze data to predict equipment failures before they occur. IoT is providing real-time insights from connected machinery, enhancing operational efficiency. Blockchain is being used for transparent and secure supply chain management, and augmented reality is altering the way we interact with digital information.

The importance lies in comprehending how these technologies can be woven into product strategies. Product managers need to explore the practical applications of these innovations within their products, whether it's offering new features that leverage AI for personalized recommendations or optimizing operational efficiency using real-time data from IoT devices. These technologies have the potential to not only improve existing product features but also open doors to entirely new avenues of innovation.

Mastering Technical Fundamentals

In navigating the complex terrain of Industry 4.0, where the integration of digital technologies is redefining the product landscape, product managers must equip themselves with a strong foundation in technical fundamentals. This foundational knowledge is not about coding but about understanding the technological underpinnings of their products. It involves awareness of programming languages, cloud computing platforms, and core infrastructure components.

Product managers don't need to write lines of code, but they should have a working knowledge of languages like Python, Java, or JavaScript. In the era of microservices and containerization, they should grasp concepts such as Docker containers for encapsulating applications and Kubernetes for orchestrating and managing containers. These technologies are critical for scalability and flexible deployment.

Moreover, in the realm of distributed systems and architecture, where large volumes of data are processed, product managers should understand the dynamics of systems like Apache Kafka for real-time data streaming or Apache Cassandra for distributed databases. It's not about becoming experts but about having the ability to converse with technical teams, streamline decision-making, and identify potential challenges.

In the dynamic landscape of Industry 4.0, characterized by the pervasive integration of digital technologies, product managers must arm themselves with a profound understanding of technical fundamentals. This doesn't imply writing code but rather gaining a comprehensive comprehension of the technological bedrock that supports their products. This understanding spans several key areas:

Programming Languages

Product managers aren't expected to be coders, but a basic familiarity with programming languages is invaluable. Languages like Python, Java, or JavaScript are commonly used in software development. Knowing the principles of these languages helps product managers engage in technical discussions with development teams and facilitates better decision-making.

Microservices and Containerization

In the era of microservices architecture, understanding concepts like containerization is vital. Docker, for instance, is a popular containerization platform that encapsulates applications and their dependencies. Kubernetes, on the other hand, is a powerful tool for orchestrating and managing containers at scale. A grasp of these technologies enables product managers to make informed decisions about scalable deployment and efficient resource utilization.

Distributed Systems and Architecture

Industry 4.0 often relies on distributed systems that handle substantial data volumes and transactions. Apache Kafka, a distributed streaming platform, is employed for real-time data streaming. Apache Cassandra, a distributed NoSQL database, is used for managing large amounts of data across multiple commodity servers. Product managers should understand these technologies, not as experts but to foster effective communication and decision-making within their technical teams.

Mastering technical fundamentals equips product managers with a broad technical vocabulary and foundational knowledge. This knowledge allows them to engage in meaningful conversations with technical teams, streamline decision-making, and anticipate potential technical challenges, ensuring that their products align with the rapidly evolving landscape of Industry 4.0.

Managing Distributed Systems

Industry 4.0 has ushered in a reliance on distributed systems and architectures that can efficiently handle vast amounts of data and transactions. Understanding how these systems operate is a fundamental requirement for product managers as they navigate this complex terrain.

This comprehension extends to critical concepts like load balancing, sharding, and data consistency.

In the landscape of Industry 4.0, characterized by a reliance on distributed systems and architectures that efficiently handle significant data volumes and transactions, product managers must navigate a complex terrain. Here are the key facets of managing distributed systems, as an example..

Load Balancing

In Industry 4.0, ensuring that workloads and data are evenly distributed across multiple servers is paramount. This is achieved through load balancing. Load balancing technologies are essential for maintaining system performance and uptime. Product managers need to understand the principles and mechanisms of load balancing, as it directly impacts a product's ability to handle concurrent users and data processing efficiently.

Sharding

The concept of sharding, a database partitioning technique, is crucial in managing large datasets. Sharding involves breaking a database into smaller, more manageable pieces called "shards." Each shard is stored on a separate server. This approach enables better data distribution and retrieval performance, especially when dealing with vast amounts of data. Product managers must understand how sharding works and its implications for database scalability and performance.

Data Consistency

Ensuring data consistency, especially in the context of distributed databases, is a complex challenge. Distributed systems often involve multiple data sources, and maintaining data integrity and reliability across these sources is critical. Understanding mechanisms for data consistency, such as strong consistency or eventual consistency, is essential. This knowledge empowers product managers to make informed decisions about product architecture, data storage, and access methods.

An example of how this knowledge is applied in practice is when designing a real-time data analytics platform that relies on a distributed database for storing and processing vast volumes of data. The ability to grasp, communicate, and make decisions regarding these technical intricacies is invaluable for product managers in the dynamic world of Industry 4.0. It ensures that their products are technically robust and capable of addressing the data and workload challenges that characterize this era. Such knowledge empowers product managers to make informed decisions about product architecture, for instance, when designing a real-time data analytics platform that relies on a distributed database for storing and processing vast volumes of data. The ability to understand and communicate these technical intricacies is invaluable for product success in the world of Industry 4.0.

Cloud Computing Expertise

In today's technological landscape, cloud computing is the linchpin of many technical products and services. The ability to harness cloud platforms, hyperscale's, private and public hybrid clouds, edge datacenters and interconnection and interoperability etc is vital for product managers. Understanding cloud infrastructure, as well as concepts like serverless computing and containerization technologies, is crucial.

Cloud Platform Diversity

The cloud computing ecosystem is vast and diverse. It includes hyperscale cloud providers like AWS, Azure, Google Cloud, private clouds, public clouds, hybrid clouds, edge data centers, and various interconnection and interoperability solutions. Product managers need to understand the nuances of these cloud platforms to select the most suitable one for their products. Each of these platforms has its strengths and use cases, and choosing the right one can significantly impact a product's performance and scalability.

Cloud Infrastructure

A fundamental component of cloud computing expertise is understanding cloud infrastructure. Product managers should be well-versed in the architecture and services offered by their chosen cloud platform. This includes knowledge about virtual machines, storage solutions, content delivery networks (CDNs), and networking capabilities. Cloud infrastructure knowledge is vital for making informed decisions regarding resource allocation, data storage, and network configurations.

Serverless Computing

The concept of serverless computing is transforming how applications are developed and deployed. Product managers need to understand serverless computing, which abstracts server management and allows developers to focus on code without worrying about the underlying infrastructure. This technology is particularly useful in scenarios where rapid development and scaling are required. Product managers can leverage serverless computing to develop applications efficiently, without the complexities of traditional server setups.

Containerization Technologies

Containers, such as those managed by Docker and orchestrated by Kubernetes, have become integral to modern software development. They enable consistent application deployment and scaling across different environments. Product managers should grasp containerization technologies and their implications for product development. This knowledge helps in making informed decisions about application deployment, resource utilization, and portability.

In summary, cloud computing expertise equips product managers with the knowledge and skills needed to make informed decisions about cloud platforms, infrastructure, serverless computing, and containerization technologies. This expertise is pivotal in ensuring that technical products and services are not only well-conceived but also technically robust, scalable, and capable of addressing the dynamic demands of the modern digital landscape.

Product managers must comprehend these cloud platforms and clous based services etc to make informed decisions regarding infrastructure. Consider a scenario where an e-commerce product needs to scale up rapidly during holiday seasons. Understanding the capabilities of these cloud platforms enables product managers to set up auto-scaling configurations to handle increased traffic efficiently. They can also leverage serverless computing, which abstracts server management, to develop applications without the complexities of traditional server setups.

Site Reliability Engineering (SRE)

Site Reliability Engineering (SRE) is a set of principles and practices central to ensuring the reliability and performance of modern technical products. As the tech landscape evolves in the era of Industry 4.0, it's essential for product managers to grasp these SRE concepts.

In the ever-evolving landscape of Industry 4.0, Site Reliability Engineering (SRE) principles and practices play a central role in ensuring the reliability and performance of modern technical products. Here's a detailed exploration of why SRE concepts are vital for product managers:

Service Level Indicators (SLIs) and Service Level Objectives (SLOs)

SRE focuses on the establishment of Service Level Indicators (SLIs) and Service Level Objectives (SLOs). SLIs are specific metrics that quantify aspects of system reliability and performance, such as the percentage of successful user logins or the response time for database queries. SLOs, on the other hand, set specific targets for these metrics within defined time frames. For example, an SLO might establish a target of 99.9% successful user logins within one second. Product managers need to work closely with technical teams to define these SLIs and SLOs, as they directly relate to the expected performance and reliability of the product.

These concepts are essential for defining and maintaining product reliability. For instance, in a product that relies on real-time data processing, product managers can work with technical teams to establish SLOs for data latency. If data processing exceeds the defined SLO, it's an early indicator of performance issues and informs proactive measures to maintain product reliability.

Error Budgets

The concept of error budgets is a fundamental element of SRE. Error budgets define the acceptable error rate or deviation from the defined SLO before a service is considered unavailable or unreliable. This concept provides a quantitative measure of how much downtime or performance degradation is tolerable. Product managers must collaborate with technical teams to establish and manage error budgets. For example, if a product experiences excessive downtime or data latency, it may consume a portion of the error budget. This prompts proactive measures to restore reliability and performance.

To illustrate the practical relevance of SRE concepts, consider a scenario where a product relies on real-time data processing. Product managers can work with technical teams to establish SLOs for data latency. If the data processing consistently exceeds the defined SLO, it serves as an early indicator of potential performance issues. The deviation from the SLO triggers an examination of the error budget, and product managers can initiate measures to maintain or restore product reliability. These measures may include optimizing data processing workflows, scaling infrastructure, or improving system architecture.

SRE concepts are pivotal for product managers as they facilitate the quantification of reliability and performance expectations. These metrics empower product managers to proactively manage and maintain product reliability in a dynamic and evolving technological landscape. By aligning technical teams with SRE principles, product managers can ensure that products meet or exceed the defined SLOs, delivering a reliable and high-performance user experience.

In conclusion, in the Industry 4.0 era, product managers must collaborate with technical teams to establish and maintain SLIs, SLOs, and error budgets to ensure that modern technical products are reliable and performant, meeting the expectations of users and the evolving technological landscape.

DevOps Practices

DevOps has become a cornerstone practice in modern software development and operations, emphasizing collaboration between development (Dev) and IT operations (Ops). As product managers navigate the intricate landscape of product delivery, grasping DevOps is fundamental for ensuring the seamless and efficient deployment of their products.

Continuous Integration (CI)

Continuous Integration focuses on the frequent and automated merging of code changes into a shared repository. This practice is instrumental in detecting issues early in the development process. Product managers should understand that CI ensures that each code change is promptly integrated into the central codebase. This not only encourages a more collaborative environment but also reduces integration challenges that can arise from long development cycles.

Continuous Delivery (CD)

Continuous Delivery is all about the automated deployment of code to production environments. This practice guarantees that the deployment process is reliable and efficient. Product managers should appreciate that CD automates the steps involved in moving code from development to the production environment, making the entire process more streamlined and less error-prone. It promotes a reliable and efficient product delivery process.

Automation

Automation is a core component of DevOps, involving the use of scripts and tools to streamline various tasks, including testing, deployment, and infrastructure provisioning. Product managers should recognize that automation significantly reduces manual interventions and the potential for human error. For instance, automated testing procedures ensure that the product functions as expected without requiring exhaustive manual testing.

Product managers play a pivotal role in facilitating efficient collaboration between development and operations teams through their understanding of DevOps practices. Consider an e-commerce product that frequently introduces updates and additional features. In this scenario, the utilization of CI/CD pipelines automates the testing and deployment of new code changes. This not only accelerates the release cycle but also minimizes the likelihood of errors in the production environment.

In the dynamic and fast-paced world of product management, an understanding of DevOps practices equips product managers to ensure the timely, reliable, and error-free delivery of products. By fostering collaboration between development and operations teams, product managers contribute to the efficiency and effectiveness of product delivery, ultimately enhancing the user experience and the product's overall success.

In summary, DevOps is not just a technical concept; it is a set of principles and practices that form the backbone of modern software development and operations. Product managers who embrace DevOps principles can optimize the delivery process, improve the reliability of product releases, and reduce the chances of errors in production environments, all of which are pivotal for product success in today's tech landscape.

In the ever-evolving landscape of product management, where technology and innovation continue to drive the market, mastering these technical fundamentals is paramount. Product managers who embrace these principles stand better equipped to navigate the complex terrain of Industry 4.0, foster cross-functional collaboration, and make informed, data-driven decisions. These competencies empower them to ensure that their products not only meet the demands of the modern tech industry but also resonate with customers, delivering tangible value in the digital age and demonstrate technical acumen necessary to lead their products through the complexities of Industry 4.0, to ensure that the products remain resilient, adaptive, and at the forefront of innovation.

Risks and Challenges for Skill Development

Reskilling and upskilling resources to meet the demands of Industry 4.0 can be challenging. Product managers should be aware of potential roadblocks in terms of resource availability, time constraints, and cost. They should also consider how to provide resources with the training and education they need to adapt to the evolving technological landscape.

Resource Availability

Resource availability poses a notable challenge when it comes to reskilling and upskilling in the context of Industry 4.0. Product managers often find themselves in a delicate balancing act as they allocate resources for training and development. The scarcity of skilled personnel for specific technical roles, particularly in emerging technologies, can make the reskilling process all the more demanding. A critical consideration is the commitment of time - a precious commodity - for both the product manager and the team. Engaging in skill development implies dedicating time not only to learning but also to applying new skills, which can potentially impact ongoing projects.

Time Constraints

Time constraints are a significant impediment to reskilling efforts. Product managers juggle multiple responsibilities in their quest to manage product development, market strategies, and team leadership. In the fast-paced landscape of Industry 4.0, staying updated with the latest technologies is essential. However, balancing these ongoing duties with the time required for reskilling can be a challenging endeavour. Product managers must strategize and prioritize to ensure that they can dedicate ample time to skill development without compromising their core responsibilities.

Cost of Training

The cost associated with training is another critical challenge in the journey of reskilling. Many high-quality training programs, courses, and resources come at a financial expense. These costs encompass training materials, enrolment in courses, or even hiring experts to provide in-house training. While investing in skill development is vital for staying competitive in the tech-driven environment, product managers must be cognizant of the budgetary implications of such investments. They need to weigh the costs against the potential benefits and make informed decisions regarding the allocation of financial resources for upskilling efforts.

Strategic Approaches for Reskilling

While the challenges of reskilling and upskilling are indeed real and multifaceted, they are far outweighed by the potential benefits. Staying at the forefront of technological advancements is a competitive advantage in the world of product management, particularly in the dynamic landscape of Industry 4.0. By addressing these challenges strategically and proactively, product managers can position themselves and their teams for success in this era of technological transformation and beyond. To address these challenges effectively, product managers can employ several strategic approaches:

Plan Strategically

Developing a well-thought-out strategic plan is paramount. This plan should outline the specific skills needed and how resources will be allocated to support skill development. A strategic approach ensures that reskilling efforts are aligned with the product's requirements and the organization's goals.

Prioritize Skills

In the rapidly evolving landscape of Industry 4.0, not all skills are of equal importance. Product managers should prioritize the acquisition of skills that are most critical for their product and industry. This prioritization ensures that the time and resources invested in reskilling have a direct and tangible impact on the product's success.

Explore Cost-Effective Options

Cost-effective training options should not be overlooked. In the age of the internet, there is a wealth of valuable training materials available at little to no cost. These resources include online courses, webinars, open-source educational materials, and community forums. Product managers can explore these budget-friendly options to enhance their skills and knowledge without straining the organization's financial resources.

Create a Learning Culture

Fostering a culture of continuous learning within the organization is invaluable. Product managers can set the tone for learning by encouraging team members to pursue skill development. This includes creating an environment where learning is not just an individual effort but a collective commitment. Opportunities for knowledge sharing, peer learning, and mentorship should be encouraged.

Utilize Internal Resources

Leveraging the internal expertise within the organization can be a cost-effective and efficient means of skill development. Encouraging team members to share their knowledge and expertise, act as mentors, and provide in-house training can create a mutually beneficial learning environment.

Recognizing that the tech landscape will continue to evolve is essential. Product managers should make an ongoing commitment to learning and adaptation. The skills acquired today might become outdated in the future, and staying at the forefront of technological advancements is a competitive advantage in the world of product management. Therefore, product managers should view skill development as an integral part of their long-term product management strategy and be prepared to adapt and evolve continuously.

Operational Management Across Layers

In the rapidly evolving landscape of product management, the role of a product manager extends beyond ideation and development; it encompasses the essential task of operational management. To ensure that a technical product or service thrives in the dynamic realm of Industry 4.0, product managers must be proficient in overseeing the various operational layers. These operational layers can be likened to a complex urban ecosystem, where different infrastructure components, like transportation networks and utilities, require meticulous supervision.

Product managers need to oversee operational aspects spanning the infrastructure, application, and database layers. This includes ensuring that the infrastructure is robust, the application is optimized, and the database is scalable and secure. It's akin to managing a complex urban ecosystem with different layers of infrastructure, from transportation networks to utilities, each requiring diligent oversight.

Infrastructure Layer Management

At the base of this operational ecosystem lies the infrastructure layer, akin to the foundation of a city's physical infrastructure. Product managers must ensure that the technological infrastructure supporting their products is robust and resilient. This involves managing servers, networks, data centers, and cloud services. The infrastructure must be capable of withstanding unexpected surges in traffic, maintaining uptime, and scaling to meet growing demands. Just as a city's utilities need to be reliable, product infrastructure must be designed to keep the product running smoothly, even during peak usage.

In the multifaceted world of product management within Industry 4.0, operational management at the infrastructure layer is akin to constructing and maintaining the fundamental infrastructure of a city. Much like the urban planner responsible for ensuring that a city's utilities and services run smoothly, the product manager's role is to create and maintain a technological backbone that is robust, reliable, and capable of providing uninterrupted support to their products.

Robustness and Reliability

Just as a city's utilities are expected to offer unwavering service, a product's infrastructure must exhibit resilience and reliability. Product managers are tasked with ensuring that the underlying components of their product's infrastructure, such as servers, networks, data centers, and cloud services, are not only dependable but also prepared to handle fluctuations in demand. Whether it's a sudden surge in user traffic or an unforeseen technical issue, robust infrastructure should remain unfazed and continue to provide consistent service. A product's reliability plays a vital role in user trust and satisfaction.

Scalability and Resilience

Product managers are like architects who plan for the expansion of a city to accommodate a growing population. Similarly, they must anticipate the expansion of their product's user base and ensure the infrastructure is scalable. Scalability involves the capability to seamlessly handle increasing loads, whether due to the organic growth of users or planned marketing efforts. Planning for scalability ensures that the product can cater to a broader audience without compromising performance. Additionally, resilience is essential; it involves the capacity to absorb unexpected shocks without critical failures. By establishing redundancy and failover mechanisms, product managers guarantee that the infrastructure can recover swiftly from disruptions, much like how a city's utilities respond to outages and emergencies.

Alignment with Business Goals

While building and maintaining the technological infrastructure, product managers must constantly align their efforts with overarching business objectives. Just as city planners ensure that the urban infrastructure supports the economic and social goals of the city, product managers make certain that their infrastructure serves the product's strategic objectives. This alignment may involve optimizing for cost-efficiency, ensuring high availability, or supporting specific features or capabilities crucial for market competitiveness.

Continuous Improvement

Similar to the way cities undergo constant upgrades to meet modern standards, product managers must continuously improve their infrastructure. The technological landscape is ever-evolving, with new trends and challenges emerging regularly. Product managers need to keep their infrastructure up to date, whether by adopting new technologies, implementing security measures, or optimizing performance. This forward-thinking approach guarantees that the product's technological backbone remains reliable, resilient, and in line with current industry standards.

Application Layer Optimization

Above the infrastructure layer sits the application layer, analogous to the various services and applications that serve as the heart of a city's daily life. Product managers are responsible for ensuring that these applications are optimized for performance and user experience. This entails working closely with development and engineering teams to streamline code, enhance efficiency, and minimize bottlenecks. It also involves coordinating the release of updates and new features to align with user expectations and market demands.

In the intricate landscape of product management within Industry 4.0, the application layer functions much like the vibrant services and applications that are at the heart of a city's daily life. Product managers are entrusted with the crucial responsibility of ensuring that these applications, which are central to the product's functionality, are meticulously optimized to deliver exceptional performance and an impeccable user experience. This task involves closely collaborating with development and engineering teams to fine-tune the product's code, enhance operational efficiency, and eliminate performance bottlenecks. Furthermore, it entails orchestrating the release of updates and innovative features that seamlessly align with user expectations and the ever-changing dynamics of the market.

Performance Optimization

Just as a city's core services must run efficiently to ensure the well-being of its residents, product managers must guarantee the optimal performance of the product's applications. This process involves a deep understanding of the technical intricacies of the applications, which product managers leverage to identify performance bottlenecks and streamline operations. Through performance profiling, code optimization, and the removal of redundancies, they work alongside the development and engineering teams to enhance the product's speed, responsiveness, and resource utilization.

User Experience Enhancement

Similar to how a city's services are tailored to enhance the quality of life for its citizens, product managers focus on elevating the user experience. They meticulously examine the product's usability, accessibility, and overall feel, ensuring that it aligns with user expectations and industry standards. This involves conducting user experience testing, gathering user feedback, and collaborating with design and development teams to refine the product's interface, features, and functionality. Product managers are champions of the end user, working diligently to create a seamless and delightful product experience.

Strategic Feature Releases

Just as a city adapts its services to meet the evolving needs of its residents, product managers strategically coordinate the release of updates and new features. They carefully analyze market trends, user feedback, and the competitive landscape to prioritize feature development. By managing the product roadmap, they ensure that new functionalities are introduced at the right time and in a way that resonates with the target audience. Timely releases contribute to the product's competitiveness, user satisfaction, and long-term success.

User-Centric Approach

In the spirit of making a city's services user-centric, product managers maintain an unwavering focus on the end user. They are the voice of the user within the cross-functional team, ensuring that every decision aligns with user needs and expectations. This approach includes conducting user research, defining user personas, and consistently gathering feedback to refine the product. Product managers champion user satisfaction as the ultimate goal.

The application layer management in the context of modern product management is about optimizing the heart of the product's functionality, akin to the daily services and applications that define a city's life. It revolves around enhancing performance, perfecting the user experience, strategically introducing new features, and maintaining a user-centric perspective. Just as a city relies on the quality of its services to enhance the lives of its citizens, a product relies on the excellence of its applications to ensure user satisfaction and a competitive edge in the ever-evolving landscape of Industry 4.0. It is the product manager's role to ensure that these applications not only meet user needs but also exceed their expectations.

Database Layer Scalability and Security

In the intricate realm of product management within Industry 4.0, the database layer functions much like the data management systems that are essential for any modern city. Just as a city must ensure the integrity, accessibility, and scalability of its data systems, product managers bear the responsibility of addressing database issues to guarantee data integrity, maintain effective access control, and ensure robust scalability. They collaborate closely with database administrators to ensure that the product's databases have the capacity to efficiently manage expanding datasets, offer stringent data security to safeguard user information, and deliver consistent, reliable performance. In an age where data breaches can have severe consequences, preserving the security and integrity of user data emerges as an overarching concern.

The database layer, much like the data management systems in a city, must be both scalable and secure. Product managers need to address database issues related to data integrity, access control, and scalability. They work alongside database administrators to make certain that databases can efficiently handle growing datasets, provide data security to protect user information, and offer reliable performance. In an era where data breaches can be detrimental, safeguarding user data is of paramount importance.

Data Integrity Assurance

The sanctity of data integrity is fundamental to both a city's data systems and the product's databases. Product managers are entrusted with the task of maintaining data accuracy, consistency, and reliability. This entails developing and enforcing data integrity policies and best practices, working closely with database administrators to implement data validation measures, and overseeing the management of data quality. By ensuring that the database stores and retrieves information accurately, product managers maintain user trust and the reliability of the product.

Access Control Implementation

Just as access to sensitive city data is stringently regulated, product managers focus on implementing access control mechanisms to safeguard the product's databases. They collaborate with security experts and database administrators to define user roles, permissions, and authentication processes. The aim is to prevent unauthorized access, data breaches, and potential misuse of sensitive information. Through access control, product managers shield user data from both internal and external threats, contributing to the product's overall security.

Scalability Planning

Product managers must take a proactive stance on database scalability, ensuring that the product's data infrastructure can seamlessly expand with growing datasets. This involves strategizing with database administrators to employ efficient data partitioning, clustering, and replication techniques that facilitate scalability. As the product attracts more users and accumulates a larger volume of data, it's imperative that the database can handle these increases without compromising performance. Scalability planning is the key to preventing data bottlenecks and outages as the product grows.

User Data Security

In an era where data breaches and privacy concerns are pervasive, safeguarding user data is of paramount importance. Product managers work in tandem with security experts and database administrators to enact encryption, data masking, and other advanced security measures to protect sensitive user information. In today's digital age, where data breaches and privacy anxieties loom large, the protection of user data emerges as a paramount responsibility for product managers. These custodians of product success collaborate closely with a cadre of security experts and database administrators to create an airtight fortress around sensitive user information. This mission to ensure data security involves implementing a multi-faceted approach that includes encryption, data masking, and meticulous adherence to data protection regulations, all aimed at securing user trust, preserving brand reputation, and upholding legal compliance.

Implementing Encryption

Encryption serves as one of the foundational pillars of user data security. Product managers, in partnership with security experts and database administrators, implement encryption protocols to transform user data into an unreadable format that can only be decrypted with the appropriate decryption keys. This end-to-end encryption is essential in safeguarding data both in transit and at rest. It ensures that even if unauthorized access occurs, the data remains indecipherable and thus useless to malicious actors.

Utilizing Data Masking

In scenarios where there is a need to share data with certain parties, data masking techniques come into play. Product managers and security experts work together to apply data masking that replaces sensitive user information with fictitious or scrambled data. This allows essential functionalities, such as testing and analytics, to continue without exposing real user data. The use of data masking ensures that sensitive user information remains confidential, even in situations where sharing or analysis is required.

Ensuring Regulatory Compliance

A pivotal aspect of user data security involves strict adherence to data protection regulations. Product managers have the responsibility of staying up-to-date with the ever-evolving legal landscape governing user data, which includes laws like GDPR, CCPA, HIPAA, and various industry-specific regulations. They collaborate with legal teams and compliance officers to ensure the product complies with these regulations. Compliance is not just a matter of legal obligation but is also central to maintaining trust, reducing legal risks, and preserving brand reputation.

Monitoring and Incident Response

Security is an ongoing endeavour. Product managers, alongside security experts, set up robust monitoring systems that continuously track and analyze data access and usage. This proactive stance allows for the early detection of unusual activities or potential breaches. Moreover, they establish well-defined incident response protocols to react swiftly and effectively to any security incidents, minimizing the impact on user data.

Educating Teams and Users

User data security is a collective effort. Product managers are responsible for educating internal teams and users about best practices for data security. They develop training programs, conduct awareness sessions, and provide clear guidelines for data handling. Raising awareness ensures that all stakeholders understand their roles in maintaining data security.

In conclusion, data security is becoming a multi-dimensional endeavour, and mandates collaboration between product managers, security experts, and database administrators. The joint efforts of these stakeholders encompass encryption, data masking, compliance with data protection regulations, continuous monitoring, incident response, and education. In an era marked by heightened data concerns, these efforts are not just about safeguarding data; they are about preserving user trust, bolstering brand reputation, and adhering to legal standards. Just as a city must protect the sensitive information of its citizens, product managers must secure the data that users entrust to their product, providing an essential foundation for its success in the data-driven landscape of Industry 4.0.

To conclude the discussion in this section, we acknowledge that operational management across these layers requires a comprehensive understanding of the product's architecture, technology stack, and business objectives. Just as urban planners must ensure a city's different infrastructure components work in harmony, product managers orchestrate the technical elements that underpin modern products and services. By meticulously overseeing the infrastructure, optimizing applications, and ensuring secure and scalable databases, product managers contribute to the sustained success of their products in the ever-evolving landscape of Industry 4.0.

Managing technical products and services in the era of Industry 4.0 is a complex and multifaceted task. Product managers must stay attuned to emerging technologies, comprehend the technology stack, communicate effectively with cross-functional teams, and streamline decision-making. They should also be well-versed in aspects like SRE, DevOps, and cloud computing, and navigate the challenges of skilling and operational management. This comprehensive knowledge ensures that product managers remain at the forefront of innovation, enabling their products to thrive in the ever-evolving technological landscape. Just as city planners ensure a metropolis functions seamlessly, product managers orchestrate the technical elements that underpin modern products and services, from infrastructure to applications and beyond.

Working with Cross-Functional Teams

Effective collaboration with cross-functional teams is pivotal in product management. Product managers need to foster clear communication and synergy among disciplines such as engineering, design, marketing, and more. This entails defining objectives, aligning priorities, and maintaining a shared vision. Successful product managers are adept at bridging gaps between technical and non-technical team members, ensuring a cohesive approach to product development and delivery. The ability to bridge gaps and facilitate effective communication across diverse disciplines, including engineering, design, marketing, and more, is the hallmark of successful product managers. Here, we delve into the critical aspects of working with cross-functional teams and the significance it holds in modern product management.

The Art of Clear Communication

The foundation of productive cross-functional collaboration is clear and transparent communication. Product managers act as the linchpin in ensuring that information flows seamlessly between different teams. They must convey product objectives, goals, and requirements, making sure that each team comprehends its role in the broader context. This communication encompasses not only disseminating information but also actively listening to the concerns and suggestions of each team.

Clear and transparent communication serves as the cornerstone of productive cross-functional collaboration in the realm of product management. Product managers, akin to linchpins, play a pivotal role in ensuring the seamless flow of information across diverse teams. Here, we delve into the intricacies of this art of clear communication and the vital role it plays in driving successful product development.

Conveying Product Objectives and Goals

At the heart of clear communication is the ability to convey product objectives and goals effectively. Product managers serve as the torchbearers of the product's mission, ensuring that every team comprehends its role in the broader context. This involves articulating the product's purpose, its envisioned impact on users, and the strategic goals it aims to achieve. By painting a vivid picture of the product's destination, product managers guide each team on the path to success.

Translating Requirements into Actionable Tasks

Clear communication goes beyond lofty goals; it extends to translating these goals into actionable tasks. Product managers break down the high-level product strategies into granular requirements for various teams. This involves defining technical specifications for the engineering team, elucidating user experience expectations for designers, and outlining marketing strategies for the marketing team. The ability to transform abstract concepts into concrete tasks is the hallmark of an effective product manager.

An Open Ear to Concerns and Suggestions

Successful product managers are not just skilled at conveying information; they are equally adept at listening. They create an environment where each team feels heard, and their concerns and suggestions are valued. This two-way communication fosters a sense of ownership and engagement among team members. It opens the door to innovative ideas and solutions, often arising from the frontline experts who execute the tasks. Listening becomes a means of continuous improvement and adaptation.

Navigating Complex Technical Terrain

Product managers often find themselves navigating the complex technical terrain, especially when interacting with engineering teams. Here, the ability to comprehend and convey technical details in a comprehensible manner to non-technical teams is a distinctive skill. Simultaneously, they must translate business objectives and user needs into technical requirements for the engineering team. This bridging role ensures that all teams are on the same page and working cohesively.

Holistic Vision Transmission

Beyond individual tasks, clear communication includes transmitting a holistic vision of the product. Product managers convey not only what needs to be done but also why it is essential. They narrate the story of the product, its value proposition, and the problems it aims to solve. This holistic vision serves as a guiding star, aligning teams with the overarching product mission.

In short, the art of clear communication is an indispensable asset in the arsenal of product managers. They ensure that product objectives and goals are effectively transmitted, requirements are translated into actionable tasks, concerns and suggestions are heard, technical complexities are navigated, and a holistic vision is conveyed. As linchpins of cross-functional collaboration, product managers drive teams forward, harmonizing their efforts and guiding them towards the collective goal of successful product development. Just as a conductor leads an orchestra, product managers orchestrate the symphony of cross-functional collaboration that results in exceptional products.

Defining Objectives and Priorities

Successful product managers are adept at setting clear objectives and aligning priorities. This often involves translating high-level product strategies into actionable tasks for various teams. Whether it's delineating the technical requirements for an engineering team, outlining the user experience for designers, or defining the marketing strategy for the marketing team, product managers act as the guiding force in ensuring that each team's efforts harmonize to achieve the overarching product goals.

defining clear objectives and aligning priorities is akin to setting the course for a successful journey. The role of a product manager becomes even more pivotal in translating high-level product strategies into actionable tasks for diverse teams. Here, we delve into the art of defining objectives and priorities and how adept product managers act as the guiding force to ensure a harmonious and goal-oriented product development process.

Translating Vision into Action

High-level product strategies and visions often serve as the guiding star for product managers. Their primary responsibility lies in breaking down these overarching strategies into actionable and tangible objectives. This involves delineating specific tasks, milestones, and goals that each team must strive towards. Product managers take on the role of translators, ensuring that the vision is not a distant dream but a well-defined roadmap.

Different Strokes for Different Folks

A hallmark of effective product managers is their ability to speak multiple languages – that of engineering, design, marketing, and more. They recognize that different teams have varied areas of expertise and requirements. For the engineering team, product managers define precise technical requirements. Designers receive instructions related to user experience and aesthetics. The marketing team gains clarity on the target audience, messaging, and promotional strategies. Product managers play the role of a multi-linguist, ensuring that each team receives information in a form that resonates with their expertise.

Alignment of Efforts

In the orchestration of cross-functional teams, product managers serve as conductors, ensuring that each instrument plays in harmony. By defining objectives and aligning priorities, they prevent the discord that can arise from disjointed efforts. This alignment is vital to create a symphony of productivity, where every team's contributions synchronize to produce the desired product.

The North Star Principle

Objectives and priorities should not exist in a vacuum. Product managers ground these objectives in the overarching product strategy, creating a North Star for all teams to follow. This principle ensures that every objective is not only a task to be completed but a step towards fulfilling the product's mission. It maintains the focus on the bigger picture and the ultimate goal.

Adaptation and Evolution

While setting objectives is a structured process, adept product managers remain flexible. They recognize that the product development landscape is not static. Changes in market dynamics, user feedback, or emerging trends can necessitate a re-evaluation of objectives and priorities. Being receptive to adaptation is crucial in steering the product on the most promising course.

In summary, defining objectives and priorities is both an art and a science in product management. Product managers excel at translating high-level strategies into actionable tasks for diverse teams. They act as translators, aligning efforts across different areas of expertise. They anchor objectives in the overarching product strategy, maintaining a clear focus on the ultimate goal. Simultaneously, they remain flexible, adapting to changes and ensuring that the product's course remains true. Just as a captain charts the course for a ship, product managers steer the product development journey towards success, keeping it on the path to its destination.

Maintaining a Shared Vision

In the dynamic world of product management, having a shared vision is paramount. Product managers are responsible for cultivating a collective understanding of the product's purpose, value, and its potential to meet user needs. This shared vision becomes the guiding star that leads the cross-functional teams forward and ensures that everyone is on the same page, working towards a common goal, and fully comprehends the product's significance in the market. Product managers bear the responsibility of not only defining this vision but also fostering a collective comprehension of the product's essence, its value, and its capacity to address user needs. This shared vision serves as the lodestar, illuminating the path for cross-functional teams, aligning their efforts, and instilling a profound awareness of the product's significance in the market.

The Visionary's Role

Product managers are the torchbearers of the product's vision. They hold the vision aloft, ensuring that it radiates clarity, purpose, and an unwavering commitment to addressing user needs. In essence, they paint a vivid picture of what the product stands for and what it aims to achieve. This vision transcends mere functionality; it encompasses the product's potential to make a difference in the lives of users.

A Unified Understanding

The true strength of a shared vision lies in its capacity to unite diverse teams, each with its own expertise and priorities. Product managers are adept at articulating the vision in a manner that resonates with engineers, designers, marketers, and every other stakeholder. This shared understanding is akin to a universal language, ensuring that every team is aligned with a common goal. It bridges gaps and forges connections, encouraging a symphony of efforts.

Purpose in Action

A shared vision is not a static concept but a dynamic force. It propels teams into action by answering the fundamental question of "why." Why does this product exist, and why is it essential? It steers the collective effort by providing the "what" and "for whom." What needs to be done, and for whom is it being done? In this manner, the vision brings clarity to every task and purpose to every role.

Significance in the Market

A shared vision extends beyond internal teams; it extends to the market. Customers, partners, and stakeholders should also perceive the product's value and purpose in a unified manner. Product managers are the conduits for this external alignment. They ensure that the messaging, branding, and communication mirror the shared vision. This alignment fortifies the product's position in the market, fostering trust and relevance.

Adaptability and Evolution

While a shared vision provides a clear path, adept product managers recognize the need for adaptation. The product development landscape is not static, and external factors continually change. The shared vision remains unwavering, but the route to achieving it may need adjustments. Adaptability ensures that teams can navigate challenges and harness opportunities while staying true to the vision.

The cultivation and maintenance of a shared vision is the cornerstone of effective product management. Product managers are not just keepers of this vision; they are its custodians, ensuring it shines brightly and is understood by all. They utilize this shared vision as a unifying force, aligning the diverse expertise of cross-functional teams. It is not merely a vision but a call to action, infusing purpose into every endeavour.

This vision extends to the market, reinforcing the product's significance. While the vision remains constant, its path may evolve, reflecting the adaptability of product managers in the face of change. In the journey of product management, the shared vision is the North Star of success, always guiding the way.

Bridging Technical and Non-Technical Worlds

One of the most distinctive aspects of modern product management is the need to bridge the gap between technical and non-technical team members. Product managers often find themselves at the intersection of these two worlds. They must possess the ability to translate complex technical jargon into layman's terms for non-technical teams while communicating the business and user needs effectively to the technical teams. This bridging role is instrumental in ensuring that all aspects of product development move forward cohesively, one of the most remarkable feats lies in bridging the profound chasm that often separates the technical and non-technical dimensions of a project. Product managers emerge as the linchpins, the connectors, and the translators who navigate the intricate terrains of these two worlds. Their unique role requires the dexterity to translate complex technical intricacies into plain language for non-technical teams, all while ensuring that the business and user needs resonate with technical teams. This bridging role is more than a mere job description; it is an art that harmonizes the multifaceted aspects of product development into a coherent symphony.

Translators of Technical Complexity

Technical teams are fluent in the intricate dialect of programming languages, algorithms, and system architectures. They sculpt the product's backbone with lines of code, making it function seamlessly. But this technical poetry can often sound like gibberish to non-technical stakeholders. Product managers act as linguistic bridges, converting these technical intricacies into a language that everyone can comprehend. They break down complex systems into digestible explanations, turning intricate algorithms into relatable stories.

Amplifiers of Business and User Needs

On the flip side, product managers need to convey the essence of business goals and user needs to technical teams with the utmost precision. They articulate the "what" and "why" of the project, answering questions like, "What problem are we solving, and why is it crucial?" These managers act as the storytellers of user personas, ensuring that every line of code resonates with the end-users' aspirations.

Synthesizers of Diverse Perspectives

In essence, product managers are the synthesizers who blend an array of perspectives and requirements into a harmonious solution. They navigate the complexities of engineering, design, marketing, and customer support, fusing them into a unified vision. This role involves setting clear objectives, aligning priorities, and ensuring that everyone is on the same page. It involves sculpting a shared vision that serves as a guiding light for every team member, irrespective of their technical prowess.

Problem Solvers and Diplomats

The bridging role extends beyond mere translation. Product managers are also adept problem solvers and diplomats. When technical challenges seem insurmountable, they work with engineers to find innovative solutions. When non-technical stakeholders question the rationale behind a particular feature, these managers diplomatically explain its importance. They navigate these diverse waters, fostering a sense of trust and collaboration.

Adaptability as a Superpower

In the dynamic world of product management, adaptability is a superpower. As technical landscapes shift, product managers stay updated with emerging technologies, ensuring that their translation remains accurate. They pivot strategies and redefine the vision when necessary, adeptly steering the project through turbulent waters.

The role of a product manager as a bridge between the technical and non-technical worlds is nothing short of remarkable. It involves translation, amplification, synthesis, problem-solving, and diplomacy. It is a role that thrives on adaptability and clear communication. The success of a product often hinges on the efficacy of this bridging function. The product manager is the conductor of a complex orchestra, ensuring that each instrument, whether technical or non-technical, plays in harmony, producing a symphony that resonates with users and fulfils business objectives.

Creating a Cohesive Approach

The ultimate goal of working with cross-functional teams is to establish a cohesive approach to product development and delivery. It's akin to conducting an orchestra where different instruments (teams) play in harmony to produce a beautiful symphony (product). Product managers guide this orchestration, ensuring that every element works in synchrony, meeting deadlines, and upholding quality standards. Orchestrating the efforts of cross-functional teams is akin to conducting a symphony. Each team member, akin to a musical instrument, contributes their unique notes to create a harmonious and beautiful product.

Product managers assume the role of the conductor, guiding the performance to ensure that every element works in synchrony, meets deadlines, and upholds quality standards. Their ultimate goal is to establish a cohesive approach to product development and delivery, where the cacophony of diverse skills and perspectives transforms into a melodious symphony.

Defining the Score

Much like a conductor sets the musical score, product managers delineate the product roadmap and objectives. They lay out a strategic plan that defines the project's trajectory, what needs to be achieved, and the roles of each team. This roadmap serves as the musical notes that every team member follows.

Harmonizing Diversity

The magic of a symphony arises from the diversity of musical instruments, each contributing a unique sound. Similarly, cross-functional teams bring together individuals with diverse skills and perspectives – from developers to designers, marketers, and more. Product managers recognize the value in this diversity and harmonize it to create a balanced product. They ensure that every team's work complements and enriches the overall outcome.

Aligning Priorities

A symphony can only be enchanting when every instrument is attuned to the same pitch. Product managers are responsible for aligning the priorities of various teams. They ensure that everyone comprehends how their work fits into the bigger picture, thus avoiding conflicting interests. By doing so, they create a clear path forward, where all the "instruments" play in harmony.

Maintaining Tempo

Just as a conductor maintains the tempo of a piece, product managers keep the project on track. They set deadlines and milestones, ensuring that the work progresses as per the predefined schedule. This involves a delicate balance between pushing teams to meet their commitments and being flexible when challenges arise.

Quality Assurance

In an orchestra, the conductor listens keenly to ensure that every note is played with precision. Similarly, product managers are the quality assurance officers of the project. They oversee the work of different teams to ensure it meets the defined quality standards. This involves reviewing code, designs, marketing strategies, and all other facets of the product.

Communication as the Baton

Much like a conductor uses a baton to communicate with the orchestra, product managers use effective communication to guide the teams. They must be articulate in conveying the vision, addressing concerns, and resolving conflicts. They are the central point of communication, ensuring that every team is on the same page.

Solving Discord

In any symphony, there might be moments of discord. It's the conductor's role to resolve these discrepancies and bring the orchestra back into harmony. Similarly, when conflicts or issues arise within cross-functional teams, product managers act as mediators. They diplomatically resolve disputes and foster a spirit of collaboration.

Adaptability and Innovation

A symphony conductor may adapt the tempo or introduce new elements for innovation. Product managers likewise stay adaptable and innovative. They are open to change, iterate on strategies, and incorporate new ideas to improve the product. This ensures that the project remains fresh and aligned with evolving market demands.

In conclusion, product managers are the conductors of cross-functional teams. They wield the baton of clear communication, set the tempo of progress, and maintain quality standards. By harmonizing the diversity of skills and perspectives, they guide the teams in achieving a cohesive approach to product development and delivery, transforming the varied efforts into a harmonious and impactful product symphony.

The art of working with cross-functional teams is fundamental in modern product management. Product managers serve as the nexus of communication, setting clear objectives, and fostering a shared vision among diverse teams. They bridge the gap between the technical and non-technical realms, ensuring a cohesive and productive approach to product development. Just as a conductor orchestrates a symphony, product managers harmonize the efforts of various teams to create products that resonate with users and succeed in the market.

Managing Technical Risks

Identifying, assessing, and mitigating technical risks is a critical aspect of a product manager's role. This involves a proactive approach to foreseeing potential challenges, whether they are related to scalability, security, or other technical aspects, one of the key responsibilities of a product manager is to navigate the treacherous waters of technical risks. These risks encompass a spectrum of challenges, from scalability issues to security concerns. However, the hallmark of an adept product manager lies in their proactive approach to identify, assess, and ultimately mitigate these risks, ensuring the project's smooth sailing. They are akin to navigators steering a ship through stormy seas, employing risk management strategies and contingency plans to reach the desired destination.

Product managers should implement risk management strategies, contingency plans, and regular assessments to ensure the project stays on course. Their ability to navigate technical risks is essential in preventing roadblocks and maintaining the product's trajectory.

Risk Anticipation

A pivotal aspect of a product manager's role is akin to that of an experienced ship navigator who possesses the unique ability to anticipate and navigate potential hazards before they escalate into insurmountable obstacles. In this context, the hazards are technical risks that can impede a project's progress or even lead to its downfall. Similar to a seasoned navigator who can spot looming icebergs in the distance, a proficient product manager doesn't simply react to issues as they arise. Instead, they exhibit proactive foresight by actively seeking out and identifying potential challenges that might unfold in future.

Much like a navigator scanning the horizon for signs of impending danger, a product manager maintains a vigilant stance in risk assessment. They are constantly on the lookout for telltale signs that could signal potential issues, some of which might not be immediately obvious. For instance, they might foresee scalability bottlenecks looming on the horizon as the user base grows. This proactive anticipation involves a deep understanding of the product's architecture, usage patterns, and the market landscape.

Another critical aspect of risk anticipation is the identification of security vulnerabilities within the product's architecture. Just as a navigator scans the water for submerged threats, the product manager conducts thorough assessments of the product's security posture. They consider factors such as the architecture's susceptibility to cyber threats, data breaches, or unauthorized access. Their proactive approach allows them to uncover potential weak points and take the necessary steps to fortify the product's defenses.

The essence of risk anticipation lies in the product manager's ability to maintain constant vigilance, much like a navigator's unwavering watchfulness on the open sea. They engage in meticulous risk assessment, using their industry knowledge, experience, and intuition to detect early warning signs of impending challenges. By proactively seeking out these technical risks, they can address them before they evolve into significant roadblocks. This approach prevents costly delays and disruptions, steering the project towards a successful destination. In the world of technical product management, the product manager's role is to be the vigilant navigator who not only reads the current conditions but also anticipates and prepares for the storms that lie ahead.

Risk Assessment

Upon identifying potential technical risks, a product manager embarks on the crucial phase of risk assessment, akin to a seasoned navigator thoroughly studying a sea chart to understand the depths and potential hazards along the planned route. Employing methodologies like the PI (Potential and Impact) matrix, the product manager engages in a meticulous process, evaluating each identified risk, gauging its severity, and considering an array of factors that influence its impact. This comprehensive assessment is integral to the risk management process, as it equips the product manager with the insights needed to prioritize risks and allocate resources effectively.

Employing the PI Matrix

The Potential and Impact (PI) matrix, much like a navigator's sea chart, equips product managers with a structured tool to classify and prioritize risks. This conceptual framework breaks down risks into four distinct quadrants based on their likelihood and potential consequences, offering a comprehensive view of their significance. The Potential Axis (X) measures the likelihood of a risk occurring, while the Impact Axis (Y) quantifies the potential damage it could inflict. By categorizing risks into quadrants, product managers can efficiently allocate resources and prioritize their response.

The top-right quadrant houses high-priority risks with both a high potential for occurrence and significant impact. These are deemed critical and require immediate attention and robust mitigation strategies. Risks in the top-left quadrant have a high potential for occurrence but lower impact, necessitating monitoring but not immediate action. Meanwhile, risks in the bottom-right quadrant have a lower potential for occurrence but could result in substantial damage; they also require proactive risk reduction measures. Lastly, the bottom-left quadrant encompasses risks with low potential and low impact, considered less critical and managed with lower urgency. The PI matrix, similar to a navigator's sea chart, guides product managers in impactful decision-making and efficient resource allocation, ensuring that risks are addressed with the appropriate level of attention and urgency.

Severity Evaluation

The first task in risk assessment is to determine the severity of each risk, much like a navigator grading the potential dangers of underwater obstacles. The product manager evaluates how serious each risk is by considering its Potential and Impact. Risks that have the potential to severely disrupt the project or have far-reaching consequences are identified as high-severity risks.

Likelihood of Occurrence

Just as a navigator assesses the probability of encountering certain weather conditions on the journey, a product manager evaluates the likelihood of each identified risk occurring. This includes considering factors that might increase or decrease the probability of the risk manifesting. Risks that have a high likelihood of occurrence are given special attention.

Extent of Damage

In the risk assessment process, the product manager also delves into the potential extent of damage each risk could cause, akin to a navigator considering how underwater obstacles might impact the ship. They consider how the risk might affect various aspects of the project, from timeline disruptions to budget overruns and compromised product quality. Risks that have the potential to cause substantial damage are flagged as critical.

This multifaceted evaluation process, including the use of the PI matrix, allows the product manager to assign a level of significance to each risk. Risks are categorized based on their severity, likelihood, and extent of damage, providing a structured framework for addressing them. This framework is akin to a navigator marking treacherous waters on a chart, enabling the product manager to steer the project away from the most perilous risks while providing guidance for managing less critical ones.

Effective risk assessment, incorporating advanced tools like the PI matrix, not only aids in risk prioritization but also informs the creation of mitigation and contingency plans. By understanding the nature and potential impact of each risk, the product manager can develop strategies to either prevent or minimize these risks. Furthermore, it enables them to allocate resources efficiently, ensuring that the most critical risks are addressed with the utmost attention. Just as an experienced navigator uses detailed sea charts to navigate through challenging waters, a proficient product manager relies on a thorough PI matrix-based risk assessment to chart a course through complex technical challenges, ultimately guiding the project to its intended destination.

Risk Mitigation

Mitigating technical risks is a product manager's primary objective. They formulate risk mitigation strategies that act as safety nets. For instance, if a scalability risk is identified, they might plan for a flexible infrastructure that can readily expand with user demand. If it's a security concern, they might implement robust encryption and authentication protocols.

Principles of Effective Risk Mitigation

During my project management professional certification, I leant risk management as one of the strong pillars of project management, these fundamental help me today to simply and augment few strategies effectively. As we explore paradigm of technical project management, is still stay relevant as the role of a product manager today extends beyond mere product development and encompasses a comprehensive approach to risk management, ensuring that potential challenges are proactively identified and addressed. Effective risk mitigation, the cornerstone of project success, is guided by a set of fundamental principles.

Principle 1: Risk Identification

At the core of effective risk mitigation lies the critical principle of risk identification. Product managers are not just project managers; they are navigators steering through the uncertain waters of technical project execution. They are skilled in identifying and anticipating potential risks that could disrupt the project. This proactive approach involves a deep understanding of the project's technical intricacies, allowing product managers to foresee vulnerabilities and threats.

Principle 2: Risk Analysis

Once identified, risks must undergo a comprehensive analysis. This analysis quantifies the likelihood of each risk materializing and evaluates the potential impact it could have on the project. Risk analysis serves as the bedrock for prioritizing risks, enabling product managers to allocate resources effectively.

Principle 3: Risk Mitigation Planning

Following risk analysis, the next fundamental principle is risk mitigation planning. Product managers craft specific strategies for each identified risk. These strategies act as customized roadmaps for pre-emptively addressing potential issues. Just as a navigator charts the safest route through treacherous waters, these strategies guide product managers in steering their projects to success.

Principle 4: Risk Monitoring and Control

Effective risk mitigation is an ongoing process that requires vigilant monitoring and control. The project's risk landscape is ever-changing, and product managers must continuously assess it. This dynamic approach involves seeking out new challenges and continuously evaluating the effectiveness of existing mitigation strategies as the project unfolds.

Principle 5: Contingency Planning

In addition to risk mitigation, product managers establish contingency plans to address 'what if' scenarios. These plans are akin to lifeboats in stormy seas, serving as guides for navigating unexpected situations or emergencies. Contingency planning enhances the project's resilience and adaptability in the face of unforeseen challenges.

Risk Mitigation Strategies

The application of risk mitigation strategies is a testament to the proactive nature of successful project management. These strategies encompass deliberate approaches to managing risk, ensuring that potential challenges are addressed systematically.

Strategy 1: Risk Avoidance

Risk avoidance is the art of steering clear of potential hazards. Product managers make strategic decisions to eliminate elements or technologies that pose significant risks. By taking this approach, they aim to reduce the likelihood or impact of a risk by avoiding situations that could lead to adverse consequences.

Strategy 2: Risk Transfer

Risk transfer involves shifting the responsibility for a risk to a third party. Through contracts, agreements, or insurance, product managers ensure that another entity, such as a specialized vendor, takes on the financial or operational burden of managing the risk. While the risk remains, its management is entrusted to a capable partner.

Strategy 3: Risk Acceptance

In some scenarios, product managers opt to accept certain risks. This approach is chosen when the impact of a risk is minimal, the cost of mitigation outweighs potential damage, or the risk is beyond the product manager's control. It involves acknowledging the risk's existence and preparing to manage its consequences should it materialize.

The interaction between these principles and strategies forms a robust framework for navigating the complex landscape of technical project management. Effective risk mitigation is a dynamic, multifaceted process that is essential for ensuring project success.

Let us look at some practical approaches in line with what we discussed till now, a product manager can adopt few best practices to automatically mitigate few risks by design, they are..

Redundancy and Failover Mechanisms

In the realm of technical risk mitigation, redundancy and failover mechanisms are like a ship having multiple sails. Product managers recognize that certain components within a project are critical to its functionality. In anticipation of potential failures, they deploy redundancy mechanisms to ensure that backup systems or resources can seamlessly take over when needed. This approach serves as a safety net, minimizing downtime, and maintaining the project's continuity, even in the face of technical hiccups.

For example, in a web application, redundancy might involve the deployment of multiple servers that can instantly replace one another if any experience issues. If a server fails, another takes over, ensuring uninterrupted service. This strategy is not limited to hardware; it can also apply to data storage, network connections, and various other project components. By preparing for the worst-case scenario, product managers add robustness to the project, preventing disruptions and enhancing its overall reliability.

Rigorous Testing and Quality Assurance

Product managers recognize that the journey to a successful project is often fraught with technical challenges. To mitigate these risks, they embark on a meticulous journey of their own, characterized by rigorous testing and quality assurance. Just as a seasoned navigator inspects every inch of a ship before setting sail, product managers ensure that their projects are thoroughly tested to withstand potential challenges.

Comprehensive testing is conducted throughout the project's development, encompassing various phases. Unit testing evaluates individual components for correctness and functionality. Integration testing assesses the interactions between different parts of the project to ensure they work together harmoniously. User acceptance testing puts the project in the hands of the end-users to verify its suitability and effectiveness.

Much like a ship's crew checks and rechecks every component for seaworthiness, product managers are diligent in their testing efforts to uncover potential issues and vulnerabilities. By identifying these challenges early, they have the opportunity to address and rectify them, reducing the risk of performance issues or failures during the project's execution. Rigorous testing serves as an early warning system, ensuring that the project sails smoothly and safely through the often tumultuous waters of technical development.

Robust Security Measures

Security is a paramount concern in the realm of risk mitigation. Product managers understand the importance of securing their projects against external threats and potential breaches, much like securing valuable cargo on a ship. Encryption and access control protocols are fundamental security measures used to fortify a project's defenses.

Encryption involves the transformation of data into a secure code, making it unreadable to unauthorized individuals or systems. This process is akin to storing precious cargo in a locked and sealed container. Access control protocols define who can access specific components of the project and what actions they can perform, adding another layer of protection.

For example, in a project dealing with user data, product managers implement encryption to safeguard sensitive information such as passwords and personal details. They also establish access control rules that specify who can access this data and what they can do with it. These security measures ensure that even if a breach occurs, the impact is minimized, and the project's integrity remains intact. Security protocols are an essential component of risk mitigation, shielding the project from external threats and ensuring its safe passage.

Contingency Planning

Effective risk mitigation goes beyond identification and analysis; it entails the development of contingency plans, which serve as strategic roadmaps for addressing unforeseen 'what if' scenarios. Much like a navigator equips their vessel with lifeboats to navigate the uncertainties of the open sea, product managers craft contingency plans to maintain a project's adaptability and resilience.

Contingency planning is rooted in a proactive approach that envisions potential disruptions, whether arising from technical issues, security breaches, or other unexpected events. By contemplating these scenarios in advance, product managers create a structured response system to swiftly address challenges. The fundamental purpose of contingency planning is to ensure that the project can adapt and continue even in the face of challenging conditions.

Regular Risk Assessment

One of the fundamental principles of risk mitigation is the understanding that risks are not static entities; they evolve as a project progresses. Effective risk mitigation demands an ongoing vigilance, much like a navigator who continuously monitors changing weather patterns during a voyage. Product managers engage in regular risk assessments to ensure the risk landscape is up-to-date.

Regular risk assessments encompass the identification of new challenges that may arise during the project's course. By constantly evaluating the effectiveness of current risk mitigation strategies, product managers adapt and refine their approaches as needed. This dynamic approach guarantees that emerging risks are addressed promptly and that mitigation strategies remain relevant and effective throughout the project's lifecycle.

Effective Communication

Clear and transparent communication is the anchor of risk management. In the context of technical project management, product managers act as both navigators and communicators. They relay technical risks, their assessments, and mitigation strategies to relevant stakeholders, ensuring that the entire team is informed and aware of potential challenges.

Effective communication creates a shared understanding of risks and fosters collaboration among team members. It ensures that everyone is prepared to fulfil their roles in addressing identified challenges. This approach aligns the team's efforts and prevents misunderstandings or gaps in the risk management process.

Preventing Roadblocks

Navigating the intricate path of technical project management requires an approach that prevents potential roadblocks from derailing the project. Product managers, much like skilled navigators, proactively identify and mitigate risks before they escalate to the point of becoming significant obstacles.

In essence, effective risk mitigation is akin to clearing obstacles from the project's path, ensuring that it maintains its trajectory. By addressing risks in their early stages, product managers prevent costly delays, disruptions, or even project failure. This proactive approach is instrumental in maintaining the project's course toward success, much like a navigator ensuring the vessel safely reaches its destination through vigilant planning and risk management.

Skill and Expertise

Navigating technical risks requires a deep understanding of the product's technology stack. Product managers need to be well-versed in the technical aspects to comprehend the intricacies of potential risks. This might entail upskilling in relevant technical domains. The core of managing technical risks lies in having a deep understanding of the product's technology stack, its architecture, and the broader technical landscape. Product managers must not only sail on the surface but also dive into the depths of technical intricacies.

Technical Proficiency and its Significance

Having a profound technical proficiency serves as the compass guiding a product manager through the turbulent waters of project management. This proficiency is not merely beneficial; it's often essential. It's akin to a ship captain's knowledge of the depths and currents of their chosen route.

Navigating technical risks necessitates understanding the technology stack that underpins the project. This includes awareness of programming languages, data management systems, infrastructure components, and the interaction of various subsystems. A product manager must grasp not only what each component does but how they interact and influence each other.

The Value of Upskilling and Learning

Just as a ship captain must adapt to changing sea conditions, product managers might need to upskill in relevant technical domains as the technology landscape evolves. The ability to steer the project clear of technical risks often requires a commitment to continuous learning and improvement.

For instance, in a world where cloud computing is central, gaining expertise in cloud platforms, serverless computing, or containerization technologies becomes a necessity. The ability to harness these tools empowers a product manager to make informed decisions and better comprehend potential risks and their implications.

The Navigator's Journey of Learning

The journey of learning never truly ends for a product manager. It's an ongoing commitment to understanding the evolving technology that underpins their product. This commitment might entail formal training, workshops, self-study, or collaboration with technical experts. Much like ship captains who continuously improve their knowledge of navigation and seamanship to keep their crew and cargo safe, product managers must continuously refine their technical proficiency to ensure they can safely steer their project through the intricacies of the technical landscape.

In conclusion, skill and expertise are fundamental to effective risk management in technical project management. Much like a seasoned ship captain who understands the intricacies of navigation and seamanship, product managers must possess a deep technical proficiency to comprehend the complexities of their product's technology stack. Upskilling and continuous learning are integral to this process, ensuring they remain adept navigators in the ever-evolving technological landscape, guiding their projects to safe and successful destinations.

Staying Up-to-Date on the Latest Trends

Let us keep the discussion going from as a navigators journey of learning and discuss the "How" part of the learning since Product managers need to stay abreast of the latest technological trends and industry developments almost on daily basis and remain engaged with this ongoing learning process that equips them to make informed decisions that enhance their products. They can do this by attending industry conferences, webinars, workshops, or pursuing further education. Being well-versed in emerging technologies, from artificial intelligence to blockchain, allows product managers to identify opportunities for innovation and maintain a competitive edge in the market. Thus staying up-to-date on the latest technological trends and industry developments is not a luxury but a necessity. Product managers are akin to captains steering their ships through uncharted waters, and their ability to navigate these trends can spell the difference between success and stagnation.

The Ongoing Learning Journey

Product managers understand that learning is a lifelong journey. They are committed to remaining at the forefront of technological advancements. This commitment is not a one-time effort but an ongoing process that equips them to make informed decisions and continuously enhance their products.

Industry Conferences and Events

One of the primary avenues for staying informed is through participation in industry conferences and events. These gatherings serve as lighthouses, beaming knowledge about the latest trends and innovations. Product managers eagerly attend conferences, symposiums, and seminars that provide insights into emerging technologies, best practices, and success stories.

Webinars and Workshops

In addition to physical events, webinars and workshops offer valuable opportunities for learning. They are like compasses guiding product managers through the ever-changing tides of industry advancements. Webinars, in particular, allow them to gain insights from experts without geographical constraints.

Further Education

Product managers are also avid proponents of further education. They recognize that knowledge is a beacon that illuminates the path to innovation. Pursuing advanced degrees, certifications, or specialized training in areas like data analytics, artificial intelligence, or cybersecurity enables them to delve deeper into the technological domains that shape their products.

The Mosaic of Emerging Technologies

Being well-versed in a mosaic of emerging technologies is a hallmark of successful product managers. They understand that these technologies, whether it's artificial intelligence, blockchain, or the Internet of Things, are the winds that fill their sails. These innovations present opportunities for efficiency, automation, and differentiation.

Identifying Opportunities for Innovation

Knowledge of emerging technologies is not just about being informed; it's about recognizing opportunities for innovation. Product managers keenly understand how these technologies can be harnessed to create better, more competitive products. They see the potential to streamline processes, enhance user experiences, and open new frontiers of value.

Maintaining a Competitive Edge

In the fast-paced realm of product management, maintaining a competitive edge is of paramount importance. Staying updated on technological trends enables product managers to respond swiftly to market shifts, adapt their strategies, and keep their products at the forefront.

Adaptive Leadership

Being informed about emerging technologies is not just about making products better; it's about leading effectively. Product managers demonstrate adaptive leadership by guiding their teams through technological transformations. They provide the vision and direction necessary to leverage these trends successfully.

The Navigator's Compass

In the realm of technical project management, product managers are akin to seasoned navigators. Their success in managing complex technical projects depends on their deep understanding of the technological waters they navigate. These professionals don't need to write code, but they must grasp the fundamentals of their project's technology stack. It includes essential awareness of programming languages, cloud platforms, infrastructure components, and how they interact. This understanding is like a ship captain's knowledge of their vessel and the seas they traverse.

This journey of mastering technical fundamentals is continuous and evolving, similar to the lifelong voyage of a skilled navigator. Just as mariners need to stay updated on changing weather patterns and navigation techniques, product managers must remain attuned to shifting technological trends. Their commitment to knowledge equips them to make informed decisions, spot opportunities, and maintain a competitive edge.

Upskilling is an essential part of a product manager's toolkit, equivalent to a navigator learning to operate new navigational equipment. It involves gaining expertise in relevant technical domains, such as cloud platforms, serverless computing, and containerization technologies. These skills enable product managers to anticipate potential risks and make informed decisions to steer their projects safely.

The navigator's commitment to lifelong learning and adaptability finds its parallel in the product manager's commitment to continuous improvement. They recognize that learning is not a destination but a journey, and it's this journey that equips them to master the dynamic seas of innovation. Just as a skilled navigator keeps their skills sharp to navigate treacherous waters, product managers navigate the ever-evolving technological landscape through continuous learning and adaptation.

In conclusion, the mastery of technical fundamentals and the commitment to lifelong learning are the navigator's compass for product managers. Just as skilled navigators steer their ships through stormy seas, product managers chart a course toward success through continuous learning and adaptation. These principles serve as a profound philosophy in the world of technical project management, guiding product managers through the complex and ever-changing waters of their field.

The future of product management

Product management is a dynamic discipline, constantly evolving to meet the ever-changing needs of consumers and businesses. As we peer into the future of product management, several key tenets and trends are emerging, shaping the way products are conceived, developed, and delivered to market.

Customer-Centricity as the North Star

The future of product management is firmly anchored in customer-centricity. Product managers are increasingly placing the customer at the core of their strategies. They seek to understand not only what customers want but why they want it, delving deep into their pain points and motivations. With this approach, product managers are poised to create products that genuinely resonate with users. The compass guiding the future of product management points firmly toward customer-centricity. In this ever-evolving landscape, product managers are redefining their approach by placing the customer at the nucleus of their strategies. It's not just about what customers want, but why they want it, delving deep into their pain points, desires, and motivations. With this approach, product managers are poised to create products that not only fulfil needs but also genuinely resonate with and enrich the lives of users.

A Shift in Perspective

The fundamental shift towards customer-centricity represents a departure from traditional product development approaches. It transcends merely focusing on features and functions to comprehending the holistic customer experience. Product managers are no longer satisfied with surface-level feedback; they strive to uncover the underlying drivers of customer behaviour. This new perspective opens doors to innovation and differentiation.

Understanding the 'Why?'

To be customer-centric is to ask why. Product managers seek to understand not only what customers are asking for but the motivations and challenges driving these requests. This depth of understanding allows for the development of solutions that address the root causes of problems, rather than just the symptoms.

Personalization and Customization

Customer-centric product managers are embracing personalization and customization. They recognize that one size rarely fits all. Tailoring products to specific customer segments or even individual preferences is becoming the norm. This level of customization not only enhances user satisfaction but also builds a strong emotional connection between the product and its users.

Feedback Loops and Continuous Improvement

In the era of customer-centricity, feedback loops are lifelines. Product managers establish mechanisms for ongoing communication with customers. They actively seek feedback, analyze it meticulously, and translate it into action. This process of continuous improvement is a cornerstone of customer-centric product management.

Empathy and User-Centered Design

Product managers are becoming empathetic problem solvers. They immerse themselves in the world of their users, often employing design thinking principles. By walking in the shoes of their customers, they gain insights that drive product innovation.

Competitive Advantage

Customer-centricity isn't just a philosophy; it's a competitive advantage. Products that genuinely address user needs and aspirations are more likely to succeed in the market. By forging deep connections with their customers, product managers are also building brand loyalty and advocacy.

Agility and Flexibility

The path of customer-centricity is marked by agility and flexibility. Product managers understand that customer needs can change rapidly. They are ready to pivot and adapt, ensuring their products remain relevant in a dynamic market.

The North Star of Product Management

In essence, customer-centricity has become the North Star of product management. It guides product managers through the complexities of the digital age, ensuring that the products they conceive, develop, and deliver are not just functional but deeply meaningful to the people they serve. This approach is instrumental in forging a future where products are not mere commodities but integral parts of customers' lives, addressing their needs, desires, and aspirations in profound ways.

Data-Driven Decision Making

Data has become the lifeblood of product management. As we step into the future, the role of data in shaping product strategies will only intensify. Product managers harness data analytics and insights to make informed decisions, track product performance, and gain a competitive edge. They understand that data is not just a by-product but a strategic asset.

In the futuristic and modern product management, data has emerged as the lifeblood, the compass, and the guiding star. As we boldly step into the future, the significance of data in shaping product strategies becomes even more pronounced. Product managers recognize that data is not a by-product but a strategic asset, an invaluable resource that fuels informed decisions, tracks product performance, and provides the competitive edge needed to thrive.

Data Analytics as a Superpower

Data analytics has become the superpower of product managers. It empowers them to gain insights into user behaviour, market trends, and product performance. By sifting through mountains of data, they extract meaningful patterns, uncover hidden opportunities, and foresee potential pitfalls.

Customer Insights and Personalization

In the era of data-driven decision making, understanding customers goes beyond surface-level demographics. Product managers dive into the intricacies of customer behaviour, preferences, and feedback. This depth of understanding allows for hyper-personalization, tailoring products to individual preferences and needs.

Market Intelligence and Trend Spotting

Data isn't just about customers; it's about the market as a whole. Product managers utilize data to gain a deep understanding of industry trends, competitive landscapes, and emerging technologies. This intelligence enables them to position their products strategically and proactively respond to market dynamics.

Iterative Development and Optimization

Data-driven product managers embrace iterative development. They don't wait for a major release to make changes. Instead, they continuously optimize their products based on real-time data. This agility ensures that the product remains in sync with user expectations.

Measuring Success and ROI

Key performance indicators (KPIs) have become the compass by which product managers navigate. They meticulously track KPIs related to user adoption, engagement, retention, and revenue growth. These metrics guide them in assessing the success and return on investment (ROI) of their products.

A/B Testing and Experimentation

Experimentation is a way of life for data-driven product managers. A/B testing and other experimentation techniques allow them to make data-backed decisions about feature changes, user interface improvements, and more. This scientific approach minimizes risks and maximizes positive outcomes.

Data Security and Ethics

With great data comes great responsibility. Product managers are acutely aware of data security and ethical considerations. They ensure that user data is handled with the utmost care, in compliance with privacy regulations, and that ethical concerns related to data usage are addressed.

Predictive Analytics and Machine Learning

The future of data in product management includes predictive analytics and machine learning. Product managers harness these technologies to foresee user trends, automate decision-making processes, and unlock new dimensions of product innovation.

Data-Driven Culture

In essence, data has given rise to a data-driven culture in product management. It's no longer just a task; it's a way of thinking. Product managers, engineers, designers, and marketers all speak the language of data. This culture fosters collaboration, innovation, and a laser focus on delivering value to users.

Strategic Decision Making

Data-driven decision making isn't about being data-driven for the sake of it. It's about making strategic decisions that steer products toward success. It's about ensuring that every feature, every enhancement, and every change is rooted in data, making the product not just functional but deeply meaningful to its users.

As we march into the future, the role of data in product management continues to evolve. It's not just a tool; it's the cornerstone upon which successful products are built. In this data-centric world, product managers who can harness the power of data are poised to not only navigate the complexities of the digital age but to thrive and innovate in ways previously unimaginable.

Cross-Functional Collaboration

As we venture into the future, the walls that once separated different departments within organizations are rapidly crumbling. In this era of dynamic change and innovation, product managers are positioned at the forefront of fostering cross-functional collaboration. They understand that the success of a product is no longer the sole responsibility of one team but rather the result of a synergistic effort involving multiple departments. Product managers are evolving into expert bridge builders, ensuring that all stakeholders work cohesively towards a common goal.

The Demise of Silos

Traditionally, organizations operated within silos, with departments working in isolation. This approach is increasingly becoming obsolete. Product managers are breaking down these silos, facilitating communication, and encouraging collaboration among teams that were once separated by figurative and sometimes literal walls.

The Role of the Product Manager as an Orchestrator

Product managers are taking on the role of orchestrators. They conduct the cross-functional orchestra, bringing together the unique skills and expertise of teams spanning engineering, design, marketing, sales, and more. They harmonize these diverse voices to create a symphony, with the product at its center stage.

Aligning Objectives and Priorities

In a world of cross-functional collaboration, alignment is key. Product managers ensure that the objectives and priorities of different teams are in harmony. They create a shared vision that guides the actions of each team member. This shared vision is not limited to achieving short-term goals but extends to fulfilling the broader mission of the product and organization.

Synergy in the Product Development Cycle

Cross-functional collaboration extends throughout the product development cycle. Product managers ensure that every decision, from feature prioritization to design choices and go-to-market strategies, reflects the collective expertise and goals of all involved teams. This synergy results in products that are not just functional but holistic and well-rounded.

Customer-Centricity through Cross-Functionality

While departments like engineering and design focus on technical aspects and user experience, product managers ensure that the customer remains at the heart of the product. Cross-functional collaboration allows for a 360-degree view of customer needs and preferences. This customer-centric approach leads to products that genuinely resonate with users.

Adaptability and Resilience

The landscape of business is constantly evolving. In such a dynamic environment, cross-functional collaboration equips organizations to adapt rapidly to changes. Product managers, as the proponents of collaboration, ensure that the organization remains resilient and capable of pivoting as needed.

Effective Communication and Conflict Resolution

Cross-functional collaboration requires effective communication and conflict resolution. Product managers excel in facilitating open dialogue, ensuring that diverse viewpoints are considered, and resolving conflicts constructively. They maintain a balance between healthy discourse and maintaining a cohesive team dynamic.

The Global Workforce and Remote Collaboration

In an increasingly global and remote workforce, cross-functional collaboration takes on new dimensions. Product managers are adept at harnessing technology and strategies for effective collaboration across time zones and borders. They build virtual bridges that connect team members regardless of their physical location.

The Future of Innovation

In essence, cross-functional collaboration is not just a trend; it's the future of innovation. The most ground breaking products emerge from the fusion of diverse skills and perspectives. Product managers understand that the collective genius of cross-functional teams will drive innovation and keep organizations at the forefront of their industries.

As we embrace the future, product managers are the linchpins in this collaborative revolution. Their ability to unite teams, align objectives, and foster a culture of cross-functional collaboration will not only define the success of products but also shape the future of work itself. In this world where collaboration knows no boundaries, product managers are the visionary leaders guiding their teams to create products that transcend expectations and redefine industries.

Rapid Iteration and Agile Practices

The future of product management is characterized by agility. Product managers are embracing rapid iteration, allowing them to respond swiftly to market changes and customer feedback. Agile methodologies are becoming the norm, enabling teams to be flexible, adaptive, and responsive to evolving requirements.

In the ever-evolving landscape of product management, the future is undeniably characterized by agility. Product managers are at the forefront of this transformative journey, where rapid iteration and agile practices have become the guiding principles of success. This shift towards agility enables product managers and their teams to respond swiftly to market changes, evolving customer feedback, and the dynamic demands of the digital age.

The Agile Revolution

The future of product management represents a fundamental shift towards agility. Gone are the days of rigid, linear product development processes that left little room for adaptation. Instead, product managers are pioneering the Agile revolution, a methodology that has rapidly gained prominence across industries.

Iterate, Iterate, Iterate

Central to this transformation is the concept of rapid iteration. Product managers are no longer bound by static, unchanging plans. They understand that the most successful products are the result of a continuous cycle of development, feedback, and refinement. In the world of rapid iteration, product managers are in a perpetual state of improvement.

Responsiveness to Customer Feedback

Agile practices empower product managers to respond to customer feedback with unprecedented agility. In the past, feedback might have languished in lengthy development cycles. Today, product managers can swiftly integrate valuable insights from customers into their products, ensuring that user needs remain central to the development process.

Flexibility and Adaptation

In this future landscape, flexibility and adaptation are not merely advantageous qualities; they are the essential traits of a successful product manager. The ability to pivot, adjust, and reorient product development strategies based on emerging requirements is paramount. The inflexible product manager of the past has no place in this new world of agility.

Collaboration and Cross-Functionality

Agile practices demand collaboration and cross-functionality. Product managers work in unison with multifaceted teams, fostering a culture of open communication, shared objectives, and collective responsibility. Agile teams are not confined by departmental silos; they are united by a shared vision and a commitment to delivering value.

The Agile Manifesto

Product managers embrace the Agile Manifesto, valuing individuals and interactions, working products, customer collaboration, and responding to change. While processes and tools are essential, the focus remains on individuals and their interactions. The goal is not to be bound by rigid processes but to work with agility to deliver working products that satisfy customers.

Iterative Innovation

Rapid iteration leads to iterative innovation. Product managers understand that the most ground breaking products are those that continually evolve in response to changing market dynamics. By embracing agility, they ensure that their products remain at the forefront of innovation.

Risk Mitigation

Agile practices also play a crucial role in risk mitigation. By frequently assessing and adapting to changes, product managers are more capable of foreseeing and addressing potential issues. This proactive approach reduces the risk of costly failures and setbacks.

Maintaining Relevance

In a world where technology and consumer preferences are in a constant state of flux, rapid iteration and agile practices are the means by which product managers maintain the relevance of their products. They keep products aligned with market needs, customer expectations, and emerging trends.

The Future is Change

In the future of product management, the only constant is change. Product managers are the pioneers of this Agile transformation, leading their teams towards iterative, flexible, and customer-centric practices. This transformation ensures that products not only meet the needs of today but also remain responsive to the challenges and opportunities of tomorrow. The journey towards agile product management is not an option; it's a necessity, and product managers are its vanguards.

Personalization and AI Integration

Products of the future will be hyper-personalized. Artificial intelligence (AI) and machine learning will be integral in tailoring product experiences to individual users. Product managers will leverage AI to analyze user data, predict preferences, and deliver personalized features and content, creating deeper connections with customers.

As we peer into the future, it becomes evident that personalization, supercharged by Artificial Intelligence (AI), is set to redefine the landscape of product management. Product managers of tomorrow will navigate a world where AI integration is integral in tailoring product experiences to individual users, ushering in an era of unprecedented personalization.

AI-Powered Personalization

One of the defining features of the future of product management is AI-powered personalization. Traditional, one-size-fits-all approaches are being replaced by finely tuned, individualized experiences. AI algorithms and machine learning models act as the architects of these tailored journeys.

Data-Driven Decision Making

Product managers have embraced the power of data-driven decision making, and AI is at the heart of this transformation. AI systems are adept at analyzing vast amounts of user data, providing insights into behaviour, preferences, and patterns that were once challenging to uncover. This deep understanding of users is invaluable.

Predictive Insights

AI's ability to predict user preferences is a game-changer. Product managers harness the predictive capabilities of AI to anticipate what users want even before they explicitly express it. These predictive insights allow product managers to deliver features and content that resonate with users on a profound level.

User Engagement and Retention

Personalization, driven by AI, is not merely a luxury but a necessity for user engagement and retention. Products that understand users, cater to their specific needs, and offer a personalized journey are more likely to foster lasting connections. In the era of hyper-personalization, customer loyalty is forged through a profound understanding of individual preferences.

Content Recommendations

AI powers content recommendations that are uncannily accurate. Whether it's suggesting the next video to watch, the next book to read, or the next song to listen to, AI algorithms excel at predicting what will captivate a user's interest. Product managers utilize these recommendations to keep users engaged and satisfied.

Conversational Interfaces

Conversational AI, in the form of chatbots and virtual assistants, plays a pivotal role in the future of personalization. These intelligent interfaces engage users in natural conversations, offering help, guidance, and product-related information on an individual basis. They are the personification of personalized customer service.

Customized Features

The product features of the future are not static but customizable. Users have the freedom to shape their product experience based on personal preferences. AI-driven customization empowers users to tailor their interface, settings, and features to align perfectly with their needs.

Product Evolution

AI not only enables personalization but also guides product evolution. Feedback loops with AI systems allow for constant adaptation and improvement. The product manager's role shifts from creator to facilitator, ensuring that the AI-driven personalization mechanisms evolve with user needs.

Ethical Considerations

The age of hyper-personalization also brings to the forefront ethical considerations. Product managers must navigate the fine line between personalization and invasion of privacy. Respecting user data and privacy is paramount, and transparency in AI-driven personalization practices is a fundamental expectation.

AI Integration Expertise

Product managers of the future are expected to be proficient in AI integration. They collaborate closely with data scientists and AI engineers to ensure that AI models align with the product's goals and user expectations.

In short, AI-powered personalization is the future of product management. It's not just a trend but a paradigm shift that responds to the evolving demands of users. Product managers who master AI integration and leverage it to create hyper-personalized experiences will lead their products into an era where individual users feel understood, valued, and engaged in ways never before possible.

Ethical and Sustainable Product Development

The future of product management is not only about profits but also about purpose. Product managers are increasingly mindful of the ethical and environmental impact of their products. Sustainability and ethical considerations are woven into the fabric of product development. Products are designed to align with societal values, minimize environmental footprints, and positively impact the communities they serve.

As we set sail into the future, product management charts a course where ethical considerations and sustainability are not mere buzzwords but integral components of product development. Product managers are evolving into stewards of purpose, ensuring that their products contribute positively to the world. Here's a glimpse into the landscape of ethical and sustainable product development in the future:

Purpose-Driven Products

In the future, products transcend their traditional role as profit generators. They become vessels of purpose, designed to address societal needs and challenges. Product managers lead the charge in aligning the product's mission with values that resonate with users. Purpose-driven products not only meet functional requirements but also contribute to the greater good.

Environmental Consciousness

Sustainability is no longer an afterthought; it's a foundational principle. Product managers champion environmental consciousness by ensuring that products are designed, manufactured, and disposed of with minimal impact on the planet. Considerations such as eco-friendly materials, energy efficiency, and recyclability are seamlessly integrated into the product development process.

Circular Product Lifecycles

The linear "take, make, dispose" model gives way to circular product lifecycles. Product managers orchestrate strategies where products are designed with durability, reparability, and upgradability in mind. The end of a product's life is not the termination but a new beginning, with components recycled or repurposed to minimize waste.

Inclusive Design Practices

Ethical product development embraces inclusivity. Product managers ensure that products are designed to cater to diverse user needs, considering factors such as accessibility and cultural sensitivity. Inclusive design practices are not just a compliance requirement but a genuine commitment to ensuring that products serve a broad spectrum of users.

Supply Chain Transparency

The future demands transparency across the entire supply chain. Product managers work towards creating transparent supply chains, where the origin of materials, manufacturing processes, and ethical labor practices are visible. This transparency fosters trust among users, who increasingly value the ethical considerations of the products they choose.

Social Impact Metrics

Beyond financial metrics, social impact becomes a key measure of a product's success. Product managers define and track social impact metrics, evaluating how products contribute to community well-being, empowerment, and advancement. Positive social impact becomes a benchmark for the overall success of a product.

Ethical AI Integration

As AI becomes more prevalent in products, ethical considerations in AI are paramount. Product managers ensure that AI algorithms are unbiased, transparent, and aligned with ethical standards. They navigate the fine line between innovation and ethical responsibility, avoiding the perpetuation of biases and ensuring fair and just outcomes.

User Education and Engagement

Ethical and sustainable product development involves users in the journey. Product managers engage in user education, communicating the ethical choices made in the product's design and development. Users become partners in sustainability, making informed choices that align with their values.

Regulatory Compliance and Advocacy

Product managers are vigilant about regulatory frameworks related to ethical and sustainable practices. They not only ensure compliance but actively advocate for robust regulations that promote responsible product development industry-wide. Collaboration with regulatory bodies becomes a proactive effort to set and raise ethical standards.

Accountability and Continuous Improvement

Ethical and sustainable product development is an ongoing commitment. Product managers embrace accountability, regularly assessing the impact of products and seeking areas for improvement. Continuous learning, adaptation, and a commitment to doing better characterize the ethos of future-oriented product managers.

In essence, the future of product management is ethical, sustainable, and purpose-driven. Product managers, in their dual roles as architects and custodians, steer products toward a horizon where success is measured not only in financial terms but also in the positive imprint left on the world. In this future, ethical and sustainable product development is not a choice but a responsibility—an acknowledgment that the products we create today shape the world of tomorrow.

Global Market Expansion

The world is more connected than ever, and product managers are looking beyond local markets. They are exploring opportunities for global expansion, tailoring products to suit diverse cultural and regional preferences. The future of product management is international, where products are designed with a global audience in mind.

As product management propels itself into the future, it's doing so with a global compass in hand. The traditional boundaries of local markets are dissolving, and product managers are embarking on a journey that leads to a truly international landscape. Here's a closer look at the future of global market expansion in the realm of product management:

A Borderless Perspective

In the future, product managers don't just think outside the box; they think without borders. The approach is borderless, and products are designed with a global audience in mind from their inception. This perspective is about embracing and celebrating diversity in cultural, regional, and individual preferences.

Cultural Intelligence

Cultural sensitivity and intelligence are core competencies. Product managers invest in understanding the nuances of different cultures and how they impact user behaviours and expectations. They recognize that a one-size-fits-all approach no longer suffices in a globalized world.

Localization and Personalization

The future of product management is about offering tailored experiences. Localization is not a mere afterthought; it's a fundamental component of product design. Products are personalized to suit specific regions, languages, and cultural contexts.

Market Entry Strategies

Product managers are well-versed in diverse market entry strategies. They explore options ranging from traditional distribution channels to digital platforms, considering the unique characteristics of each market. They understand the significance of timing, adaptability, and partnerships when entering new territories.

User-Centric Globalization

Global expansion doesn't mean imposing products on users. Product managers champion a user-centric approach to globalization. They actively seek input and feedback from international users, ensuring that products evolve to meet their distinct needs and expectations.

Regulatory Agility

Navigating international regulatory landscapes is a key skill. Product managers stay informed about the diverse regulatory requirements in different regions, ensuring that products comply with local laws and standards.

Strategic Alliances and Partnerships

Collaboration takes center stage in the global market expansion. Product managers establish strategic alliances and partnerships, often with local businesses or organizations. These collaborations offer insights, support market penetration, and foster goodwill within new regions.

Multilingual Communication

Effective global expansion demands proficiency in multilingual communication. Product managers ensure that their teams can communicate and engage with users in their native languages. This linguistic flexibility is a cornerstone of successful global product management.

Global User Education

Global expansion comes with the responsibility to educate and support users worldwide. Product managers invest in resources and strategies to guide users through product adoption and provide ongoing assistance, irrespective of their location.

Market Dynamics Insight

A deep understanding of international market dynamics is a critical asset. Product managers are not only aware of market trends but also comprehend the socio-economic, political, and cultural factors that influence buying behaviours in different regions.

Ethical and Social Considerations

Global product management extends to ethical and social aspects. Product managers weigh the ethical and social implications of their products in diverse contexts, ensuring they resonate positively with local communities.

Continuous Learning and Adaptation

Global expansion is an evolving journey. Product managers are committed to continuous learning and adaptation, responding to the ever-changing dynamics of international markets with agility and foresight.

In conclusion, the future of product management is intrinsically tied to the global stage. Product managers embrace a global mindset, viewing the world as a rich tapestry of opportunities and challenges. It's a world where products are bridges that connect people from diverse backgrounds, and successful product management is not limited by borders but thrives on the diversity and richness of our interconnected world.

Continuous Learning and Adaptation

In the ever-evolving landscape of technology, product managers understand that learning is not a one-time effort but an ongoing commitment. They are dedicated to continuous learning and adaptation, ensuring that their skills remain relevant and that they can harness the latest tools and methodologies.

Product management exists at the intersection of innovation and adaptation. In the realm of technology, where change is the only constant, product managers serve as the navigators of this dynamic landscape. Here's an exploration of the central role of continuous learning and adaptation in the world of product management:

Lifelong Learning

The future of product management is grounded in the belief that learning never ends. Product managers adopt a mindset of lifelong learning. They are curious and open to new knowledge, always eager to explore emerging technologies, methodologies, and best practices.

Embracing Technological Advancements

Technology is in a state of perpetual evolution. Product managers actively keep pace with the latest technological advancements, understanding that being tech-savvy is not a one-time achievement but an ongoing journey. They delve into areas like artificial intelligence, blockchain, or the Internet of Things, staying informed about how these technologies can shape the products they manage.

Professional Development

Continuous learning is often formalized through professional development. Product managers attend workshops, courses, and industry-specific training programs. These experiences offer exposure to the latest industry trends and facilitate networking with other professionals.

User-Centered Insights

Product managers are committed to understanding their users. They continuously gather insights into user behaviours, preferences, and expectations. They harness user feedback to adapt their products, ensuring they remain relevant and user-centric.

Agile Methodologies

Product managers are champions of agility. They implement agile methodologies like Scrum and Kanban, which allow for rapid iteration and adaptation. These methodologies enable teams to respond swiftly to changing requirements and market dynamics.

Market Analysis

Continuous adaptation is rooted in deep market analysis. Product managers constantly monitor market trends, competitor movements, and shifts in user demographics. This awareness allows them to pivot when necessary, keeping products aligned with market demands.

Feedback Loops

Product managers establish robust feedback loops within their teams. They encourage open communication and learning from both successes and failures. A culture of feedback fosters continuous improvement.

Data-Driven Decision-Making

Data is the compass for adaptation. Product managers embrace data-driven decision-making. They use analytics to assess product performance and make informed choices about necessary changes.

Environmental Awareness

The future of product management extends beyond technical aspects. Product managers are environmentally conscious. They adapt products to align with sustainability goals, minimizing environmental footprints and addressing ecological concerns.

Market Expansion Strategies

Global market expansion requires continuous adaptation. Product managers remain agile in devising strategies that cater to diverse cultural and regional preferences. They learn about international markets, regulatory landscapes, and emerging opportunities.

Ethical Considerations

As products impact societies and individuals, product managers consistently examine ethical considerations. They adapt products to reflect ethical values and adhere to social norms, ensuring that products make a positive impact.

In conclusion, continuous learning and adaptation form the very essence of successful product management. In an ever-changing landscape, product managers are the pioneers of evolution, embracing change with open arms. They understand that the pursuit of excellence is an ongoing journey, where every lesson learned and every adaptation made contributes to the continued success of their products.

Inclusivity and Accessibility in Futuristic Product Management

In the not-so-distant future of product management, inclusivity and accessibility are paramount, reflecting a world where technology knows no boundaries. Product managers of this era lead the charge in creating products that are truly universal, breaking down barriers that once limited user experiences. Here's a glimpse into the future of inclusivity and accessibility in product management:

Augmented Universal Design Philosophy

Product managers are guided by augmented universal design philosophies, leveraging advanced technologies like augmented reality (AR) and virtual reality (VR). These immersive technologies enable them to conceptualize products that seamlessly adapt to individual users' unique needs and abilities.

AI-Enhanced User-Centric Accessibility

Artificial intelligence (AI) is the backbone of user-centric accessibility. Product managers employ AI-driven user profiling to create hyper-personalized product experiences, ensuring that every interaction is tailored to an individual's capabilities and preferences.

Blockchain-Powered Accessibility Standards

In the world of decentralized technologies, blockchain-based accessibility standards reign supreme. Smart contracts embedded in products automatically adjust interfaces and functionalities to meet individual accessibility requirements, ensuring unparalleled inclusivity.

Neural Inclusive Design Thinking

Product managers of the future embrace neural inclusive design thinking. They integrate neural interfaces that allow direct communication between the human brain and digital interfaces. This mind-to-product connection ensures accessibility beyond physical limitations.

Quantum-Powered Accessibility Testing

Accessibility testing reaches new heights with the advent of quantum computing. Product managers leverage quantum technology to simulate and test accessibility across infinite scenarios, guaranteeing products that are resilient to evolving accessibility demands.

Multilingual AI Localization

Global inclusivity is a given as AI-powered language translation and cultural adaptation are seamlessly integrated into products. Language is no longer a barrier as products understand and respond in real-time to users in their preferred language and cultural context.

AI-Adaptive Technology Integration

Advanced AI-driven adaptive technologies become standard. Products intuitively adjust and personalize themselves in real-time, from font sizes to navigation interfaces, making them accessible to everyone, regardless of ability or preference.

Neural Feedback Loop

The neural feedback loop becomes an integral part of the development process. Brainwave analysis allows users, including those with physical disabilities, to provide direct, real-time feedback that shapes the product's evolution.

Quantum-Enhanced Awareness Programs

Internal awareness and education transcend traditional methods. Quantum-enhanced awareness programs utilize immersive simulations and experiences to educate teams about inclusivity and accessibility, fostering a deep understanding and commitment to these principles.

Ethical AI Assessments

Ethical considerations take center stage as AI models evaluate the potential ethical implications of products. The AI, programmed with ethical guidelines, flags and addresses any potential ethical issues related to inclusivity and accessibility.

Accessible Product Markets

In the future, markets are defined by accessible products. These products are designed not only with inclusivity in mind but also to adhere to strict ethical and sustainability criteria. Accessible products are the new norm, and consumers embrace them with enthusiasm.

This future of product management is a world where technology brings people together rather than setting them apart. Inclusivity and accessibility are not just ideals but tangible elements of innovation, underscoring the commitment of product managers to create products that transcend barriers and empower every individual. In this future, the digital world knows no boundaries and the possibilities are endless.

Conclusion

Firstly, I must thank you to be the one who took this voyage with me, Yes, this book is not just a guide; it's an intellectual voyage, a journey that equips us to navigate the ever-shifting seas of innovation. So, as we embark on this odyssey together, where learning is a lifelong adventure, and mastery is the destination, In a world where change is the only constant, I urge you to view learning as a continuous journey rather than a finite destination. It's this commitment to perpetual knowledge that will equip us to make informed decisions, identify opportunities, and maintain a competitive edge in the dynamic field of product management.

I wrote this book in a way that you can choose to read any chapter in any order or start from any chapter that you feel interesting, as long as it invokes or awakens the "Calling" of a learnt Product manager in this digital age. Broadly, we divided this journey in multiple key parts..

At the heart of this book is a deep exploration of the pivotal role that product managers play. Together we unveiled the significance of holistic product strategies that align with business goals, the art of cross-functional collaboration that fuels innovation, and the delicate balance between embracing new ideas and ensuring stability.

The journey of product management is a lifelong adventure, one that is constantly evolving as the technology landscape and customer needs shift. As we conclude this book, let us reflect on the key takeaways and lessons learned, and contemplate the future of product management in a world that is rapidly changing.

At the heart of product management lies a deep understanding of the customer, their needs, and the problems they are trying to solve. Product managers must be able to conduct thorough market research, analyze data, and synthesize insights into actionable product strategies. They must also be skilled at design, development, and cross-functional collaboration.

The product management process is a rigorous one, requiring careful planning, execution, and measurement. Product managers must be able to identify and validate opportunities, define product requirements, and create roadmaps that align with business goals. They must also be able to manage teams and resources effectively, and launch products on time and within budget.

The future of product management is bright, but it will also be challenging. Emerging technologies such as artificial intelligence, machine learning, and the Internet of Things are transforming the way we develop and deliver products and services. Product managers will need to embrace these new technologies and develop the skills and knowledge to use them effectively.

In addition to technological advancements, product managers will also need to navigate the increasingly complex and globalized business landscape. They will need to be able to think strategically and develop innovative solutions to complex problems. They will also need to be able to build and maintain strong relationships with customers, partners, and stakeholders.

The journey of product management is not for the faint of heart. It is a challenging but rewarding field, one that offers the opportunity to make a real impact on the world. If you are passionate about technology and innovation, and you have a strong desire to help people, then product management may be the right career for you.

Embrace change, be lifelong learners, and dare to challenge the status quo. The future of product management is yours to create.

***

About the Author

Rajesh is a technologist, author and key note speaker with over three decades of accomplished experience in Information Technology (IT) domain, A diversified background in in the areas of IT infrastructure, Cloud computing, emerging technologies such as AI/ML and Data Engineering and Open source systems and is a certified ISO27K lead auditor and Project management professional.

On personal front he has authored several blogs, articles and published technology books, poetry books in Marathi, Hindi and English, besides he is a social activist, foodie, photographer and loves long drives and farming. He is based out of Bangalore, India

rajesh_dangi@yahoo.com

Twitter: @rajesh_dangi